I0147833

Talk to Your Boys

16 CONVERSATIONS TO HELP TWEENS AND TEENS GROW INTO CONFIDENT, CARING YOUNG MEN

Joanna Schroeder
Christopher Pepper

Workman Publishing
New York

Copyright © 2025 by Joanna Schroeder and Christopher Pepper

Hachette Book Group supports the right to free expression and the value of copyright. The purpose of copyright is to encourage writers and artists to produce the creative works that enrich our culture.

The scanning, uploading, and distribution of this book without permission is a theft of the authors' intellectual property. If you would like permission to use material from the book (other than for review purposes), please contact permissions@hbgusa.com. Thank you for your support of the authors' rights.

Workman
Workman Publishing
Hachette Book Group, Inc.
1290 Avenue of the Americas
New York, NY 10104
workman.com

Workman is an imprint of Workman Publishing, a division of Hachette Book Group, Inc. The Workman name and logo are registered trademarks of Hachette Book Group, Inc.

Design by Reagan Ruff
Jacket design by Becky Terhune

The publisher is not responsible for websites (or their content) that are not owned by the publisher.

Workman books may be purchased in bulk for business, educational, or promotional use. For information, please contact your local bookseller or the Hachette Book Group Special Markets Department at special.markets@hbgusa.com.

Library of Congress Cataloging-in-Publication Data is available.

ISBN 978-1-5235-2731-1 (hardcover)
ISBN 978-1-5235-2733-5 (ebook)

First Edition August 2025

Printed in the USA (LSC-C) on responsibly sourced paper.

Cover © 2025 Hachette Book Group, Inc.

10 9 8 7 6 5 4 3 2

To all the family members, friends, acquaintances, and strangers who have reached out to us for help with the boys in your lives. Your questions (and our own!) are the foundation of this book.

—

Thank you to all the experts who helped us address those questions—and especially to all the boys who shared your personal perspectives and experiences with us.

CONTENTS

"I keep a lot of feelings to myself because I don't really know how to talk about it. I don't really even know how to express it besides destroying stuff. I worry that one day I'll fully lose it and do something I'll really regret. My dad goes by the idea that 'men don't cry,' and that's heavily affected me. I wish adults would support their children through hard times and help them express their feelings."

—Kamran, age 18

INTRODUCTION

O ur society's expectations about gender are big, and they start early.

As soon as parents say they are expecting a boy, the advice starts rolling in. Well-meaning relatives and friends will often tell new parents of boys how lucky they are not to be raising a girl. "Boys are so much easier!" they say. Girls are so much more "moody and emotional." The overall message seems to be that while boys may be more active or messy than girls, they are simpler creatures that don't require as much intense attention from parents. And for the boys who do act out and exhibit reckless or careless behavior? Well, we have a ready-made phrase for it: "Boys will be boys!"

Here's the reality: This laissez-faire approach to raising boys isn't working. An increasing number of boys say they feel lonely and isolated. They are underperforming in school and opting out of college, overdosing on drugs, falling under the spell of extremism, and engaging in lethal violence and self-harm—including mass shootings and suicide. According to research by Equimundo, at least 72% of young men in the US say they've been told "a 'real man' behaves 'a certain way,'" which involves being heterosexual, tough, and a risk-taker. In a study published in *Preventive Medicine*, Equimundo and researchers at UPMC Children's Hospital of Pittsburgh found that young men who embrace rigid masculine norms are five times more likely to bully (verbally, online, or physically) or sexually harass others, and twice as likely to experience depression or suicidal ideation.

When we don't recognize the complexity of boys' emotions and relationships, we don't acknowledge their full humanity. This harms them and the people around them. We believe that something must change, and that change starts with us—their parents, caregivers, educators, and mentors. We invite you to join us and the many adults around the world who are working to consciously raise more caring, connected, emotionally reflective boys. This book is a guide for how to get started.

In this book, we focus on the tween and teen years because, in our experience, that's when a lot of boys need connection and guidance the most. Boys this age should be having deep, ongoing discussions about topics like consent, substance use, and how to manage stress and feelings of depression or anxiety, but adults sometimes put off having these talks because they worry it will be awkward, or they don't know exactly what to say.

Research shows that people are happier when they are strongly connected to others, can ask for support when they need it, and can talk openly about their feelings. But learning where, when, and how to open up can feel like a monumental task to a preteen or teenage boy. They may have had bad experiences with friends or crushes who've betrayed their trust, making them fear opening up again. They may feel judged, talked down to, or ignored by their parents and teachers, causing them to keep their deepest feelings and questions to themselves.

Our advice: Lean into the awkwardness and use the conversation guides and tips we provide to start talking to your boys. You don't need to be perfect, but you do need to get started.

Conversation is the key. Not only does it help us connect with our teens, it helps their maturity process. Mature thinking happens when kids utilize the "higher" portions of their brains, exercising logic, empathy, and rationality. As Frances E. Jensen, MD, writes in her book *The Teenage Brain*, "The brain is programmed to pay special attention to the acquisition of novel information, which is what learning really is. The more activity or excitation between a specific set of neurons, the stronger the synapse."

The more kids practice using these portions of their brains, the more reflexive their thoughtfulness becomes, making them less susceptible to the impulsivity, irrationality, and self-centeredness that are common among teens. When our boys practice using empathy, compassion, and introspection, we help them flex their thoughtfulness "muscles"—and thoughtful boys are much more likely to become thoughtful men.

How We Started Doing This Work

Before Joanna became a parent, she believed she could throw all gender-related expectations out the window and start with a clean slate. Then she had a son. Two years later she had another, and soon she started witnessing all the ways society enforces unhealthy gender expectations upon boys and men. Now, as a mom of two teenage sons and a young daughter, she has insight into how teen boys' unique needs can be easily overlooked.

When Joanna started writing about raising boys she saw how hungry parents were for this information. She knew this needed to be a fundamental part of her professional mission as a writer and media critic.

Over time, Joanna has become internationally known as an expert on raising boys. Countless parents read and shared her viral *New York Times* essay "Racists Are Recruiting. Watch Your White Sons," and her work has been featured in numerous media outlets, including CNN, NBC, and *The Washington Post*.

For Christopher, these are issues that come up both at work and at home.

As an educator, he's taught thousands of students in middle school and high school health classes about gender roles, and trained teachers about how to gracefully handle sensitive topics. He's also the father of two boys and was a foster parent for another boy for more than a year. He tries to follow and support the interests of his boys and thinks a lot about how to guide them toward becoming supportive, healthy men. Raising boys has also caused him to reflect on his own upbringing and the lessons he learned—and tried to unlearn—about what it means to be a man today.

In addition to raising boys at home, Christopher helps coordinate Young Men's Health Groups in San Francisco's public schools. In these weekly groups, boys find a safe place to talk about navigating gender roles, dating, sexuality, and the expectations of men in the world. He's found that boys really want a chance to connect and talk about their feelings. They are working things out every day, and having a caring group of peers listen really helps.

Christopher's innovative work has been featured in the *New York Times*, *Vox*, and *USA Today* and on CNN and National Public Radio. He regularly speaks to educators and parents about how to better support the boys in their lives.

How to Use This Book

This book is designed to be read in any order that interests you—but we ask that you start with chapter 1, which focuses on communication. This chapter is designed to build a foundation for communicating with our growing kids. It has tools, sample scripts, and questions, as well as advice from some of the world's most noteworthy communication experts and therapists. Once you've read chapter 1, you can jump around to whatever topic will help you most in the moment. In many chapters, we offer "Check in with Yourself" prompts to encourage you to reflect on some of these big issues. Knowing where you stand—your values, your concerns, your own history and how it may color your opinions—means you can approach these conversations with more clarity and confidence.

Not Just About Boys, Not Just for Parents

We know that many of the concerns we address in this book are not unique to boys. Parents may find the suggestions provided here useful regardless of their child's gender. This book is also not just for parents—it's for caregivers of all types. We sometimes use terms like "your son" or refer to readers as parents, but we understand that there are many kinds of caregivers and many kinds of families trying to raise boys well.

It's important to note that whenever we talk about trends we've observed among teen boys, that *does not* mean girls aren't experiencing these things or that *all boys* do. As parents and as professionals in our respective fields, we want to make clear that in writing about boys, we do not intend to minimize the experiences of any other kids. Ultimately, we want more connection and opportunities for all young people.

We write this book because we believe that raising healthy and empathetic boys will help make the world a better place for everyone.

Parenting, when done consciously and with compassion, is a form of activism. Raising kids who will do less harm than the generations before them, who will stand up for what's right and make the world a better place, is well worth the time, energy, and passion we have poured into this book. Our boys are worth the effort.

Meet Our Boys' Panel

In every chapter, you will find quotes from real boys from our boys' panel. They provide us with funny, profound, and, at times, brutally honest insights into their lives and how they believe adults can do better when communicating with tweens and teens.

The eighty-five boys on our panel—ranging in age from ten to twenty-two—come from a variety of racial, ethnic, and religious backgrounds, and live in several different parts of the US and Canada. To protect their confidentiality, the boys are referenced here only by first name, and some of them chose to use pseudonyms.

Their responses to our questions were often humorous, irreverent, and tender, but what moved us most was how thoughtful they were. They dug deep, sharing what scares them, what they wish their parents knew about them, their heartbreaks, their accomplishments, their insider view on boyhood, and what they think that we, as the adults in their lives, are doing right and doing wrong in raising them.

We hope you enjoy reading these little "We Asked Boys" boxes as much as we enjoyed collecting them to share with all of you. Our kids are a gift, one that often goes underappreciated during the adolescent years.

"My father and I have an ongoing joke where he will say in a mock-serious tone, 'It's time for another one of those father-son talks.' He will then sit me down and preface whatever it is we're about to discuss by saying, 'There comes a time in a man's life when . . .' and then he proceeds to drop the bomb, usually something minor like, 'he needs to plan his homework schedule for the next week.' This format is used for anything that I'm not a fan of discussing, like executive functioning–related things. I really enjoy the format because the theatrics of it make me more engaged in the conversation."

—Nat, age 17

Chapter 1

COMMUNICATION

Communicating effectively is the single most important skill we need when parenting tweens and teens. So, this is where our book starts. It's also a section you can return to any time you don't know how to address a topic or start a conversation.

Every kid can benefit from learning how to communicate effectively, but it is especially important for boys, who are often expected to keep their feelings quiet. This silence can have devastating consequences for their mental health.

It's typical for adolescents to become less talkative as they get older. For parents, this change can feel shocking—the little kid who never stopped chattering is suddenly the big kid who pulls his hoodie up and grunts out one-word answers.

"If boy puberty hired a marketing firm to design a logo, it would be an image of a closed door; if it were animated, the door would be slamming." This is how pediatrician Cara Natterson, MD, opens her book *Decoding Boys*. According to Natterson, the closed door isn't necessarily the problem. The problem is when we stop trying to open it. "We can't decode our boys if we don't talk to them," she writes, "even though that's precisely what many of us tend to do: *not* talk to them."

Parents have a choice: we can kick the door down and demand that our boy talk like he used to, or we can pause, recognize that he's changing, and find a new way to communicate.

Terrence Real, therapist and author of the groundbreaking book about male mental health *I Don't Want to Talk About It*, told it to us straight: "Don't accept the cultural narrative that adolescent boys just don't talk. It's bullshit."

Real, a father of two grown sons, insists that boys do *not* have to "turn monosyllabic," nor do they have to separate from us emotionally in order to grow up: "That's not psychology. That is patriarchy."

"If you want them to talk," he insists, "start by listening to them. Ask them for advice. Learn a few things from them. Stop guiding them and just *be* with them a little bit."

We asked boys:

What do you wish you could talk to your parents about?

"Mental health and emotional struggles."
—Cormac, age 16

"Everything. I see people who are almost like best friends with their parents and it's really cool to see . . . those people are very lucky. But oftentimes when I try to be silly or when I approach my mom with a subject, I notice a lot of unhealthy communication from her."
—Colin, age 17

"Social life. My girlfriend can talk to her mom about almost anything, but I don't feel like I could do that because they aren't there like that. Or they just don't understand as well."
—Isaiah, age 17

"Just about life and how it's going."
—Anees, age 18

How to Talk to Your Boys

"Forcing communication will just harden your child," fifteen-year-old Nadav told us. "Teenagers are like that stuff you make in science class called Oobleck; the harder you push, the more they resist. As the parent, you just need to be gentle enough so that they stay soft and can actually have valuable communication."

So what does it mean to be gentle enough? It starts with learning the signs that a boy is open to talk—and the signs that he's not. Too often, we say, "Sit down, son, let's chat" in moments that are convenient for us. We don't stop to consider if *he's* ready to talk.

It can be hard to tell sometimes. You poke your head into your teen's room after school and he's lying across his bed looking at his phone. His backpack is on the ground and his feet hang off the end of his bed, shoes on. To you, this looks like a kid with nothing to do. To him, a whole other scenario may be playing out. Here's what may be happening when you think he's doing nothing:

→ He's exhausted from school and zoning out to his phone, which helps him recharge.

→ His day was emotionally taxing and he's overwhelmed, so he's watching a show or video to release stress.

→ He's about to do homework and he's scanning his calendar or classroom app to see what work is ahead of him.

→ He's catching up on social media communication, so none of his friends think he's ignoring them.

→ He's reading a long message from a friend who is sharing something heavy or important.

It may not look like much, but this "doing nothing" is likely a meaningful part of his day. An interruption from you might feel like an invasion, and before you know it he's throwing up walls. So what to do instead?

Don't Interrupt, Inquire

Start by inquiring respectfully:

→ "Do you have a few minutes to talk, or should I come back later?"

→ "Are you in the middle of something or can I come in for a few?"

→ "I need to talk to you before I go to bed at nine, do you have a few minutes before then?"

When we *inquire* instead of *assume*, we send a simple but profound message rooted in one thing—respect. When we inquire instead of interrupt we tell them:

→ "I understand you've got a lot going on."

→ "I respect your time and energy levels."

→ "I recognize you're not just an extension of me. You are your own person with a complex life, schedule, and set of emotions."

Set the Tone

It's also key to let them know the tone of the conversation so they can gauge their own ability to handle it in the moment. Add an appropriate qualifier such as:

→ "It's no big deal, it's just about weekend plans."

→ "You're not in trouble, but it's definitely important."

→ "This is serious, and it's important we take some time to talk about it when we can both listen and communicate well."

It's not fair to let them sit there wondering what's wrong when there's nothing to worry about. Their concern that something major is coming may prompt them to ignore that they feel too tired or emotionally overwhelmed to show up for the conversation the best way possible. Giving them some agency over when these conversations happen also models communication skills and teaches them to respect other people's time and energy.

Take Them Seriously

Boys can tell if you are actually interested in what they have to say, or if you are just angling for time before you deliver a lecture. If they know you're going to listen—and listen with respect—they are a lot more likely to keep the communication lines open.

→ Put your phone away so you can give him your full attention.

→ Avoid making proclamations or getting argumentative.

→ Take him seriously. Let him know that you value what he is saying and believe him.

→ Show him that you're listening (nod, repeat what you hear, ask clarifying questions).

→ Be aware of your actions and facial expressions.

→ Stay open-minded.

→ Ask follow-up questions. You can use phrases like "Would you be willing to tell me more about that?" or "What did you do next?"

→ Don't rush in to fill silences. Try counting to ten after asking a question.

Get Curious, Not Furious

How do we talk to our boys when they have disappointed us? When they've broken a rule or failed to meet our expectations? Instead of punishments or formal consequences, clinical psychologist Ross Greene, PhD, author of the bestselling book *The Explosive Child* and creator of the Collaborative & Proactive Solutions model, encourages parents to start with curiosity. If a child isn't doing well, Greene insists that something must be getting in their way. Here are some examples of what it sounds like to approach your kid with curiosity rather than frustration:

→ "I've noticed that you haven't been putting your dishes away after breakfast . . . what's up?"

→ "I've noticed that you've been playing video games longer than the time we agreed on . . . what's up?"

Then you listen with *genuine empathy* to hear what's making it hard for your kid to meet a given expectation (we know this might be difficult, especially if you're angry!). Only then do you explain to them why you are concerned, using a phrase like "The thing is [insert your concern] . . ." or "My concern is [insert your concern] . . ."

After you and your kid have talked and heard each other out you can move toward generating realistic and mutually satisfactory solutions.

Greene recommends restating the concerns using a sentence frame that begins with "I wonder if there is a way . . ." The problem-solving should be a collaboration. The goal is to find a solution that truly addresses the concerns of both parties, and that both parties can actually perform.

We asked boys:

What could your parents do differently that would make you more likely to talk openly with them?

"If they weren't super critical of me and telling everyone my business, I would probably be more open to them."
—Kamran, age 18

"It would be good if maybe they were more open about their struggles and hardships at my age. Without that, there is kind of a 'family myth'—as my therapist likes to call it—about how my parents made it to where they are. If they opened up about their struggles it might make it easier for me to open up."
—James, age 21

"Tell me that I can talk to them about anything . . . there's this sort of gap between us because I don't talk about my social life or feelings with them."
—Isaiah, age 17

"Oftentimes my mother will approach me in a way that might not make me want to open up about things, but on occasion she'll approach me with an open mind and understanding, which I do appreciate. I think being approached with compassion and an open mind works well for not only me, but most teenagers."
—Colin, age 17

"Just hang out with their kids like they're best friends, because the more you hang out with anyone the more they will talk."
—Anees, age 18

Try Reflective Listening

In 1980, Harville Hendrix, PhD, and Helen LaKelly Hunt, PhD, developed the Imago Dialog system as part of their unique couples therapy model. They realized that, when people are upset, hurt, frustrated, or angry, communication often becomes challenging.

Imago is a system for making sure both people are heard accurately and that their feelings and experiences are validated. Over the last forty-plus years, Imago Dialog has been used in all sorts of settings, and while the clinical format is likely too formal for daily interactions with teens, it can be simplified.

This is an example Dr. Hendrix shared with us. He noted that he still relies upon this format when talking with some of his own grown kids. You may find it helpful when conversations get tense. There are four key steps for using reflective listening with teens:

1. Pause before responding.
2. Reflect back what we believe we heard.
3. Ask if that is correct. If not, ask them to clarify.
4. Repeat if necessary.

Yes, it's that simple. But you'll notice that when the pressure starts to rise or a conversation gets heated, it won't always come naturally. That's why it's good to practice when everything is smooth sailing.

Here's an example of how reflective listening works:

You: Hey, could you please load and start the dishwasher before you head back to your room?

Him (grumpy): Why? My sister never has to do anything, and I'm the one with the huge project due on Monday. You guys treat me like I'm your servant sometimes.

If you're like many parents, your first reaction might be to think, "This kid has it so easy! What is he complaining about?" Instead of saying that, pause and see if you can figure out what the big issue is. What's he really trying to say?

You: So, if I have this correct, you're feeling stressed out and like we're asking too much of you. Does that feel right?

Him: No, it's not that it is a super stressful chore—it's just the timing that is really stressing me out—you are asking me to load the dishwasher on top of everything I am dealing with right now.

Again, if you can resist defensiveness—even when it feels justified—and continue to try to understand and affirm, you'll likely end up with better results.

You: Ah, OK. So, what I think I'm hearing is that you feel like I'm heaping a bunch of extra stuff on top of you and you don't know if you can handle it all. Is that more accurate?

If you're able to ask these questions with softness in your voice and hear him out, it's likely he'll start to feel safe opening up and you'll get to the root of what's bothering him.

Him: Yeah, geometry has been really hard. I feel so stupid in that class.

You: Now that's a problem I think we can work through. I know it can be hard to talk about this stuff, especially when we're stressed, but I really appreciate that you explained it. Let's see what we can figure out, because feeling stupid in class is not fun at all.

What felt like a kid being lazy might turn out to be a kid feeling badly about himself, wondering if he's stupid, and feeling helpless—and those are problems you two can face together.

As grown-up as he may seem on the outside sometimes, he is still a kid and will likely feel reassured when you offer him a hug, tell him he's not stupid, and suggest that you work together to come up with some solutions. Of course, after this talk, the dishwasher will still need to get loaded. Use your best judgment about when to force the issue, or consider doing it together.

We asked boys:

What advice would you give to a parent who wants their teen son to talk to them more?

"Reveal more about yourself to make your son feel like they can connect more."

—Sam, age 15

"Let them know you're there and they can tell you anything. Tell them they won't get in trouble for whatever they tell you because the thing kids fear the most is opening up to their parents too much and getting in trouble."

—Isaiah, age 17

"Check on them but don't put pressure on them. Allow them to know that you are open to discuss anything when they want, not just when you want. Listen and ask if they want advice instead of just assuming they want it."

—James, age 21

"Just have a friendly dynamic with your kid, rather than being only an authority figure. There's a perfect balance of both, which can take some trial and error to find, but ends up strengthening your bond with your kid."

—Rahul, age 15

Talk Shoulder to Shoulder, Not Eye to Eye

Stan Tatkin, PsyD, a psychologist who developed a therapy model that considers not only our psychology but also our human biological tendencies, insists that teenage boys are like "high-octane cats" who are sensitive to feeling trapped. "If you're smart, you don't lecture them, you say what's necessary and get out of Dodge," he told us with a laugh.

Even better, insists Dr. Tatkin, do something with your teen that is rhythmic and does not require eye contact. "If you and I start a round of ping-pong or play catch, we have to look at each other to see where the other person is going to hit or throw the ball," he explained. "That keeps us in the moment. We're not staring at the other, we're glancing. We get into a rhythm that relaxes our bodies and shears off excess adrenaline that would ordinarily cause more looking up."

When we move in a fluid motion, we prevent executive functioning parts of our brains—which normally constrict and inhibit open communication—from taking over. "As long as there's striated muscle engagement—those are the trunk muscles and limbs—as long as there's movement there, there's fluidity and a constant regulation of adrenal uptake."

Other ideas for talking while moving might include hiking, walking, strumming guitars, drumming together, or putting up a tent or similar project.

A lot of people—adults included—feel intimidated by the intimacy of face-to-face conversations. They find that sitting side-by-side during a car ride is a good venue to try having these talks.

Just remember that this isn't a hard-and-fast rule. If your son doesn't respond well to talking in the car, it may be because he feels trapped or struggles to have conversations without clear eye contact. The adult and/or the child may find it challenging to understand each other without the context cues of body language.

If he seems to withdraw more or become angry when you introduce topics or ideas in the car, it's OK to back off. With less pressure, some kids will eventually seize the opportunity to open up on their own terms.

Signs Your Kids Are Ready to Talk

On an episode of Neal Brennan's *Blocks* podcast, comedian and writer Jerry Seinfeld, father of two grown sons and a daughter, said:

"People always talk about 'quality time.' I'm into 'garbage time.' You want to have 'garbage time' with your kids, when nothing's happening. It's 11:30 p.m. and one of them says, 'Do you want to have cereal?' . . . It's just garbage time. You're just sitting there—you're not even talking. It's nothing . . . but it's everything."

Garbage time can just be sitting around. Or it could be an unspoken request for communication. Here are some of the signs that your kid wants to talk and doesn't necessarily know how to ask for your time:

→ Lingering in a doorway or in the periphery of a room

→ Putting down his phone and watching you or the other people in the room

→ Staying out on the couch or hanging at the dinner table longer than he usually does

→ Coming into your room at night or your office during the day (or wherever you're busy doing other things) and just hanging out

→ Sending a text asking what you're up to

These signs could also mean he simply doesn't want to be alone—but that's an important emotional need as well. Staying present can have a powerful impact.

So hang out! Put down your laptop or look up from your knitting. Smile. Turn your attention to him and ask him questions about his day. Keep the tone light and inviting. It almost doesn't matter what you say, what matters is showing him that you're happy he's around. This demonstrates how important they are to us and allows us to seize a rare moment when they're ready to engage.

Researchers (and married couple) John and Julie Gottman have studied the lives of married couples for decades. Their research looks into the power of noticing when your partner is attempting to create connection. They call these attempts "bids" and suggest people work toward understanding what their loved one's bids look like. For teens, a bid for connection could look like:

→ Sharing something funny from a video he saw

→ Telling you what he did in his video game

→ Making a joke, even if it's nonsensical to you

→ Touching your shoulder or arm or playfully poking you

→ Asking a question, even if it seems unimportant

→ Playing you a song they like

→ Lingering on the couch or in a room with you, even when saying nothing

Bids can also appear negative:

→ Sighing loudly when you are nearby

→ Complaining

→ Mildly misbehaving, like slipping swear words into language or saying things they know will annoy you

Bids don't always look like big, important moments. In fact, they're often small and seemingly meaningless, like your boy asking where the big spoons are.

You don't have to get up and find the spoon for him to respond to his bid. When he asks about the spoon, you can say, "They're in the kitchen tools drawer" and then ask what he's making. Remember, it's less about what you say than the fact that you're open to the bid and validating his desire to connect—even if it's over something that seems silly.

How to Keep Your Cool When Your Boy Is Being Unkind

Attempts at connecting with our boys are often thwarted by sheer adolescent rudeness. The instinct to meet fire with fire is understandable, but there's something to be said for taking a breath and approaching our prickly teen with patience, using some of the skills from this chapter.

Here's an example . . .

Seemingly out of nowhere, your kid yells to you from the kitchen:

Him: I HATE when you buy this cheap pizza, Dad! It's disgusting. You don't even care, though, because you're so [expletive] cheap!

Affirm the emotion, model emotional control, and set a boundary.

You: I hear that you're really upset about the pizza, and I want to understand. But the way you just spoke to me was hurtful and unnecessarily loud. Give me a few minutes, I'm going to take a breath so I don't overreact, and then I want to talk about it.

Return within a few moments and restart the conversation.

You: OK, son, it seems like you're really upset about the pizza . . . what's up?

Him: I just hate this pizza, Dad, and I've told you that. I'm starving, I just finished practice, and this pizza is not what I wanted.

Reflect back what you're hearing.

You: Ah, OK. If I'm understanding, you feel like I ignored the fact that you don't like that pizza and bought it anyway. Is that right?

Him: Yeah, like, I've said it, but it feels like you're not listening. It made me really mad.

Reflect and affirm the emotion.

You: I can imagine it feels bad to think I don't care enough to listen.

Him: Yeah. And I get so hungry, I feel like I can't get enough to eat lately.

Reflect again, apologize, affirm.

You: I hear you. I think I forgot that you didn't like it, or maybe I just didn't take it seriously. I'm sorry. So, what can we do to make sure you get enough food throughout the day, especially before practice?

Him: I don't know.

Ask if he's ready to engage on this before diving in:

You: Do you want to think of some ideas now, or maybe later, after you've eaten? We can also just go to the grocery store after dinner and see what looks good.

Him: Yeah, let's do that. I'm tired and won't be able to think about much until I've eaten.

Renew your boundary and end on a positive note.

You: OK, great. Let me know when. Also, next time, if we can avoid yelling, let's try to. But I know you were upset, and I know how hard you're working in school and how much energy it takes to get through practice after a full day.

When Your Kid Seems to Be Struggling

Although it's common and even developmentally appropriate for an adolescent to retreat and want more time alone, you want to ensure that they don't retreat to their room and never come out. It's key to keep knocking on your son's closed door, both literally and metaphorically, to stay connected. A few helpful phrases:

→ Just a reminder that if you're ever having a tough time, there's no problem too big for us to work on together.

→ I know life is chaotic but I want you to know that I'm never too busy to have a conversation with you.

→ Remember that I love you, and nothing you tell me will ever change that.

→ I know parents can be extremely annoying when you're a teenager, but if you ever want to talk or hang out, I'm here and I always value our conversations.

Little phrases peppered throughout our kids' lives, shared with a smile, can reinforce that we are a safe place to turn to when times get tough.

Dr. John Duffy, a psychologist, father of a grown son, and author of the book *Rescuing Our Sons*, urges parents to trust their own internal wisdom to know when it's time to reach out for help. "Some degree of distance is fully expected and developmentally normal," he told us. But too often "parents dismiss this distance as normal instead of facing the problem head-on. My bias is in favor of professional help when a parent thinks [their son's distance] may potentially be an issue." Dr. Duffy suggests we watch out for the following signs:

→ You can sense that your depth of communication with your child has diminished, especially over a short period of time

→ You feel as if you are losing traction as a parent—he is listening to you less, talking with you less, and sharing with you less

"Therapy is rarely a mistake," Duffy suggests, "even if, in retrospect, it seems like an overreaction."

Staying Connected

Too many of us—including the humble authors of this very book—are sometimes so caught up in our phones, work, or other distractions that we barely notice the little things our kids do throughout the day. But noticing these little things can add up to something powerful.

In their research with married couples, the Gottmans found that couples who have about five positive interactions to one negative interaction were much happier and more likely to last. We think this can extend to the parent/child relationship.

To maintain a healthy bond with our kids, it helps to be sure that we are having more positive than negative interactions. And they can be small! Pausing for a moment and catching your son's eye and smiling—even if he doesn't smile back—is a positive interaction. Tossing in an authentic compliment ("I appreciate how patient you were with your brother this morning") adds yet another.

The goal isn't to meticulously track your interactions, but rather to simply be aware of the overall tone of your interactions and to strive for a balance. It may not be possible to have a positive ratio every day. That's OK. Just keep in mind that your kid may need some extra effort at connection and affirmation in the days to come. Here's a short list of what a positive ratio day with your teen might look like:

→ Saying "good morning" to your son with a smile +1

→ Asking if he needs anything before you leave for work/he leaves for school +1

→ Saying "Love you!" while looking at him as you leave +1

→ Texting your concern over his mounting tardies –1

→ Thanking him for putting his backpack in his room (rather than the hallway) when he got home +1

→ Telling him "no" when he asks if he can go see a concert in the city on a school night –1

→ Giving his shoulder a little squeeze as you pass in the hallway +1

→ Asking if he wants to share some chips +1

→ Laughing at his little joke +1

→ Cutting up an apple and putting it next to his keyboard while he does homework +1

→ Noting how sweet he is with the dog, when he stops to pet her +1

→ Telling him "I know you're working hard lately. I'm proud of you" before you go to bed +1

Our Teens Still Need Us

Teens may talk to their friends more, but they need their trusted adults the most. Eli Harwood, therapist and author of *Raising Securely Attached Kids*, explains why:

"When kids are little, their attachment drive is going to be towards us because they rely on us for survival, protection, belonging, and identity. But when they're getting into adolescence, the instinct becomes to learn how to create bonds outside of our core family."

Harwood told us that teens will naturally start to turn toward friends and romantic partners for support and to feel connected. This can feel like a big change to parents and it's normal if it hurts a little at first. This transfer of attachment is part of "individuation," where kids go out into the world and learn to make their own connections and social structures. It's a gradual process that often feels sudden to parents.

The good news, according to Harwood, is that this separation is sort of like our kid saying, "Mom, Dad, I've got this!"

But they still need you.

"If they're just having a bad day, we would expect they're more interested in talking to their pals about it because they can understand and relate more," Harwood explains. "But when something really awful happens to a teen with a secure attachment to their caregiver, their impulse will still be to seek their caregiver in that moment."

"We really want to be accepting of the complex emotional state that our teens are living in so that we can remain in sync with them," says Harwood.

Adolescence can be a grumpy, prickly time for some kids, which can be contagious. When our teens snap at us, it can be easy to snap back. Or to make ourselves scarce, lest we poke the bear. But our kids still need to see joy in our faces when we greet them.

Harwood shares a fun analogy for parents to help us remember to show our love.

We asked boys:

What should parents know about how teens communicate with one another?

"I think that parents need to understand that being online is not inherently bad just by virtue of it being online, and that there are many positive social interactions to be had between friends if they would just let it happen."

—Nadav, age 15

"We usually talk in a more disrespectful manner to people who we're closer friends with."

—Rahul, age 15

"Lots of it is on text and calling. A specific thing I think that's important for parents to realize is that while we're in school our friends are almost the biggest thing in our life because we're at school five days a week for seven hours and so we need to be able to communicate with our friends."

—Isaiah, age 17

"It's easier to have deep talks about life with someone who is the same age [rather] than your parents."

—Anees, age 18

She says that when greeting younger kids, we can show the same level of delight we do when we see the family dog. We can even *be* the golden retriever, all waggy and excited to see our kids, and they will probably love it.

But when it comes to teenagers who are more reserved, Harwood suggests showing your interest the way you might with a family cat. You enter the room calmly, smile and make eye contact, and keep your voice a little calmer and reserved. You make it clear you're happy to see them, without introducing a wild new level of energy to the room.

Try both tactics and see what your kid reacts best to, or adapt depending on his mood. What's most important is showing that you are delighted by his presence and interested in his life.

REMEMBER THIS:

❶ Teenagers are biologically hardwired to pull away—but we shouldn't allow them to disappear completely. They will connect more with their friends than you, but they still need you.

❷ Meet your teens where they are, and find ways to engage that recognize who they are and what they're into.

❸ Make sure you're someone your teen knows he can trust to help him handle and manage his big emotions and that you don't expect perfection from him.

❹ Try to pay attention and recognize when your teen is making a bid for connection with you.

❺ Strive to have a ratio of five positive interactions to every one negative interaction with your teen.

"Masculinity presents an impossible dichotomy: understanding and processing emotions while also being unable to feel and experience them. You're expected to know how to handle emotions in a way that doesn't involve talking about them or learning about them or showing them or experiencing them. It's very tiring."

—Nadav, age 15

Chapter 2

Talk to Your Boys About

MASCULINITY

Boys get *a lot* of messages about masculinity and how to be men. Unfortunately, they often sound like this:

"You act like a girl."   "You're a little bitch."
"Don't be a pussy."   "Real men don't ____."
"Take it like a man."   "Man up."
"Grow some balls."   "Never let them see you cry."

Masculinity is often defined by dominance, stoicism, physical strength, and the ability to provide. It has, perhaps, been even more defined by what it is not: soft, sensitive, emotional, feminine, or "queer" in any way. For many men and boys, there is little room to express fear, anxiety, depression, or even tenderness.

This construct can be very limiting. Without an outlet for their more complicated emotions, men often deal with stress by drinking or using drugs, often with deadly consequences. According to the CDC, men die of overdoses two to three times more often than women. They may also try to cope with stress by dishing out abuse or violence. Some of that violence is self-inflicted: according to the American Foundation for Suicide Prevention, the rate of death by suicide is almost four times higher for men than it is for women.

In his health education classes, Christopher often uses an activity called "Act Like a Man" to help his students think critically about gender roles and expectations and introduces a concept called "The Man Box." He draws a box on the board and writes the word "Man" on top. He then asks students if they have ever heard someone say "Be a man!" or "Act like a man," and prompts them to list stereotypes they've heard at home, at school, and in the media of what it means to be a man. To solicit more ideas, Christopher will ask questions like:

→ How are "real men" supposed to act?

→ How are "real men" supposed to express their feelings?

→ How are "real men" supposed to act/behave sexually?

→ How are "real men" supposed to act differently than women?

→ What feelings are "real men" allowed to express?

→ Do you think people ever hide parts of themselves to better fit into this box?

→ What do you think are some of the emotional consequences when a man hides parts of himself to fit inside the box?

Once students have shared their ideas, Christopher will ask, "What might a boy or man be called if they do not fit these stereotypes?" Students usually have no trouble coming up with a list of words and terms that get thrown at boys who don't fit neatly into a gender box.

This activity is inspired by exercises developed in the 1980s by Paul Kivel and his colleagues at the Oakland Men's Project. It's designed to help boys and young men understand the ways that traditional norms of masculinity constrict how they are allowed to act and express themselves. It is, essentially, a list of features and characteristics that make a man or boy acceptable in the eyes of mainstream society.

Boys learn early that if they stray too far from "acceptable" behavior, their masculinity may be called into question—sometimes with gentle teasing, sometimes with verbal slurs, sometimes with fists.

Research by Judy Y. Chu, EdD, shows that boys at four and five years old are highly relational and emotionally perceptive. In her book *When Boys Become Boys*, she writes: "The boys in my study demonstrated a remarkable ability to be astute observers of their own and other people's emotions, sensitive to the dynamics and innuendos within their relationships, and keenly attuned to norms and patterns within their social interactions and cultural contexts."

Chu noticed a profound shift starting in prekindergarten, when the same boys started to focus more on impressing others than engaging with them, withholding their personal insights and being less direct and authentic with others to preserve their place in their social group. Essentially, they started to assume the traditional cultural code on what it means to "be a man."

Chu doesn't think it has to be this way. She writes that the antidote to this change is to foster a culture of relationships that provide different values and information on other ways of being.

We asked boys:

What's something you might enjoy doing but that isn't traditionally thought of as a "boy thing"?

"Talking to girls just as friends."

—Roberto, age 14

"I like all colors, even the ones labeled 'girl colors,' like pink."

—Carson, age 14

"I like writing. Boys get stereotyped way too often as being dumb and strong."

—Ted, age 12

"Singing, reading, sewing, going to therapy."

—Nadav, age 15

"Well, I do running events for sports and while I run, I like to wear tank tops. Although I'm completely straight, people consider this weird and feminine and my parents usually try to stop me from doing this."

—Manoj, age 14

"Through developing trusting and respectful relationships with the boys in our lives, we can help boys to value and acknowledge their relational capabilities, which they may otherwise learn to discount or overlook," she writes. "We can also offer and model for them definitions of maturity, masculinity, health and success that will enable them to remain grounded in their self-knowledge (e.g., as they encounter societal pressures to conform to group and cultural norms), and to form relationships that will sustain rather than constrain them."

So, how do we help our boys break patterns that only end up hurting themselves and others? It starts with helping them understand how traditional masculinity is enforced and identifying the ways those efforts may limit or harm our kids.

CHECK IN WITH YOURSELF

It's important to get clear about your own ideas about gender and masculinity before you start talking to your kids about it. Here are some questions you might want to think about:

> Do you think that men and women are equal, and should have equal opportunities in the world? What about transgender, nonbinary, and gender nonconforming people?

> Do you think people of different genders can be platonic friends?

> How do you feel about people who push against gender expectations, like boys who wear nail polish or girls who want to play football?

> Do you support programs that encourage girls to pursue careers in fields that women had limited access to in the past, like science and engineering?

> Do you support programs that encourage boys to pursue careers in fields where men are underrepresented, like teaching, mental health care, and nursing?

How to Talk to Boys About Masculinity

You want to be able to talk about masculinity without being too serious or pushy. Pay attention to what your boys are watching, playing, and laughing about and use those interests as a starting point for conversations around masculinity. Some examples:

→ You see a dad out and about with young children, without a mom or partner around.

  Try saying: "Back when I was your age, a dad out with young kids alone would've been considered unusual. People would probably ask if it's 'Daddy Babysitting Day,' as if a dad can babysit his own kids!"

  Ask: "Isn't it weird to think that, for so many years, people thought dads couldn't take good care of their own little kids?"

→ You see a man wearing a "feminine" color or clothing item on TV or out in the world.

  Try saying: "I love that some guys feel comfortable wearing whatever works for them and don't always have to follow those stuffy old rules from the past."

  Ask: "What do you think?"

→ You see a man crying on TV or even in person, during an emotional moment.

  Try saying: "It was very rare for men to publicly cry when I was your age. But holding in emotions is bad for people, and so I'm glad more people understand the power of vulnerability these days—especially from men."

  Ask: "What do you think when you see a guy crying? Would you ever feel like you could cry in public or in front of your friends?"

→ You interact with a man working in what might be considered a "female" career, like a nurse or a kindergarten teacher.

  Try saying: "One of the coolest things I've seen happen in my lifetime is the way so many careers have opened up to people regardless of gender. There are so many women CEOs now compared to a generation or two ago—and there are also more men taking up nursing."

Ask: "I wonder what sort of benefits there are to having men in caring professions like this?" or "Can you imagine yourself going into a caring profession someday?"

Don't try to address everything in a single talk—the goal should be to start talking about these topics and keep the lines of communication open. It often can be more effective to have sixty one-minute talks than to have one sixty-minute talk.

We also need to help our boys have empathy for others who may experience the expectations and "rules" of being a guy differently. For instance, your child may be naturally athletic and fit in well with standard jock culture—and that's great if it works for him. But he may have friends who are teased or dismissed because they aren't tall, muscular, athletic, or who have different interests.

We want our boys to be awake to the ways in which they—and the boys around them—are hurt by our limited notions of what it means to be a man. To do this, we need to have simple, low-key conversations with our boys on a regular basis about issues surrounding masculinity.

The Power of Boys' Groups

Contrary to stereotypes, middle school and high school boys are very interested in talking about masculinity and what it's like to be a boy today. Christopher has seen this firsthand as the coordinator of the Young Men's Health Project in San Francisco public schools. In these groups, young men have a positive space to reflect on their lives and practice supporting one another. They are given time and permission to be emotionally vulnerable.

With a skilled facilitator, they will open up, be real with one another, and make deep social connections. After seeing how well they worked in San Francisco schools, Christopher started encouraging other schools to start similar groups, and now regularly proclaims that he believes every middle school and high school that has boys should have a boys' group.

Groups like Next Gen Men, Equimundo, and A Call to Men provide excellent resources for anyone thinking about starting groups like this.

In addition, programs like Coaching Boys Into Men and TeamsOfMen work with coaches of boys' sports teams to help them incorporate messages of support, ethics, respect, consent, violence prevention, and healthy masculinity.

One of the leaders in this type of work with young men is Ashanti Branch, the founder of the Ever Forward Club in Oakland, California. In the early 2000s, he started teaching ninth grade math and quickly noticed a lot of the boys in his classes were struggling with academics and motivation, and didn't feel much connection to school.

He decided to ask some of the boys to come by at lunch for the first meeting of the Ever Forward Club.

"I told them: I'll buy you lunch once a week. In exchange, you're going to teach me how to be a better teacher," Branch explains.

In the twenty years since that first lunch meeting, the Ever Forward Club has become an official nonprofit organization, and running it is now Branch's full-time job. Unlike many programs focused mostly on tutoring or academic support, the Ever Forward Club puts a big emphasis on "heart work"—providing emotional tools to help boys feel safe, seen, and heard. And it is very successful: every member of the club has graduated from high school, and 93% of them have gone on to attend college or a trade school or join the military.

In workshops, the club uses a simple mask-making activity to bring participants together and change how they see one another.

Here's how it works: everyone gets a plain piece of paper (or a paper with a mask outlined on both sides of the paper), and these prompts:

→ On the front of the mask: What are the qualities and characteristics that you gladly let others see? Add at least one drawing and six words.

→ On the back of the mask: What are the qualities and characteristics that you don't let others see? Add at least six words.

Once people are done, they are asked to share their masks in small groups, and then process the experience using questions like this:

→ How did it feel to share your mask?

→ How did it feel to listen to someone else's mask?

→ Did you notice any similarities between your mask and the rest of the group?

→ How did this activity change the way you think about the other people in the room?

→ What do we protect by only showing the front of our masks? What does it cost us?

→ What is the importance of friendships where you can just be yourself?

→ Is there anything you are thinking about doing differently as a result of this experience?

By encouraging vulnerability and sharing, this activity helps young people and communities gain a deeper understanding of how much they have in common. The Ever Forward Club shares this activity publicly as part of what they call the "Million Mask Movement," and maintains a gallery of masks people have made from around the world at MillionMask.org.

Boys' groups that focus on communication and emotional expression can be powerful engines for growth and change. We encourage you to advocate for them in your community or at your local school.

Ashamed of Being a Boy?

Decades of effort from feminists to shift cultural norms around what girls are allowed to do has produced a remarkable amount of social change in the way society sees and talks about girls (although there is still much more to do). But it's possible that an unintentional consequence of this change has been an obscuring of positive messages aimed at boys. In recent years, we've seen a trend where powerful men are being held accountable for abuse and assault more often. This calling out of "toxic masculinity" has not gone unnoticed by boys. The irony is that despite all of the noise and the very real advancements that girls and women have made, the patriarchy is still alive and well. But for many boys and young men who are trying to find their place in the world, it can feel like there is a lack of positive messages that point a path to a healthy fulfilling future. This can lead to a sense of confusion or shame

Why We Don't Love the Phrase "Toxic Masculinity"

The phrase "toxic masculinity" has been used much more widely in recent years, particularly following the rise of the #MeToo movement. The term refers to a set of attitudes and ways of behaving by men that have a negative effect on those around them. While it is not meant to be an indictment of all masculinity, its overuse and misuse means that when many boys and young men hear it, they often feel like they (or boys and men in general) are being told they are toxic. If people are arguing about terminology, it can make it difficult for them to fully engage with ideas. We've found that we can make more progress in actually discussing masculinity with boys and men if we use more specific examples, rather than leaning on this sometimes-controversial term.

around being a man—and at its most extreme, a dangerous sense of alienation and anger toward women.

This doesn't mean we stop sending positive messages to girls—it means we make sure boys can see clear paths to their own healthy, fulfilling futures.

What should we say when our kids ask if all men are bad, or express frustration that others are angry at men? Here are a few ideas:

→ "Sometimes people say things like this from a place of hurt or frustration. If something is going on in the news, or even in someone's life, they might feel overwhelmed with feelings of fear or anger. I think we can understand why they feel that way and still look for examples of great men who want everyone to be safe and treated equally."

→ "Why do you think someone might say that? Do you think they mean that every man or boy is bad? In my opinion, they might be influenced by someone who has experienced a lot of hurt or they may have been hurt themselves, and we can be understanding of that without adding to it."

→ "I'll tell you the truth. Sometimes I get frustrated with the system that has allowed so many people to be hurt. When we're in that hurt or scared frame of mind, we tend to react in a more extreme way, and I suspect that's where this person is coming from. But then I remember all the men and boys I know who are good and want the world to be a better place."

If a boy says something like *Girls have it so much better!* or *Why would I care about girls? Nobody cares about boys!* try an appeal to an interest in fairness, moving them away from thinking about boys and girls being in competition.

Try saying:

→ "You can root for girls to have lots of opportunities and encouragement without being 'against boys.'" Follow up with statements such as:

→ "Gender equity is beneficial to all of us, and the world is better when everyone has great opportunities."

→ "You can be involved in the movement to break down barriers and give everyone a fair chance."

Keep the Conversation Going

One good way to get the conversation going is to ask questions—and keep an open mind as you listen to the answers. Here are some great discussion questions to bring up with boys:

→ Who is a man you respect or look up to? What do you admire about them?

→ What's something boys might get teased about but girls probably wouldn't? What's something girls might get teased about but boys probably wouldn't?

→ Have you heard people use phrases like "you throw like a girl" as an insult? Why do you think people use this word to insult boys?

→ What does it mean when some boys call another boy "gay" or say that something is "gay"?

What's the hardest part of being a boy today?

"Trying to look tough and be masculine. Not being too 'girly' or liking 'weird' things, like certain TV shows or video games."
—Xavier, age 15

"Staying strict to the norms about how boys are supposed to be."
—Manoj, age 14

"Being expected to provide absolutely everything, and being blamed for stuff without being able to fight back."
—Roberto, age 14

"The inability to share feelings and emotions with peers and trusted adults."
—Nadav, age 15

"Being held to a standard of being strong and not affectionate."
—Carson, age 14

→ What do you think about phrases like "be a man" or "man up"?

→ If you were raising a son, what lessons or messages would you want to teach him?

"Masculinity comes with a set of perks and pitfalls that are often tangled up with race, age, body type, and other aspects of diversity," according to psychologist and author Dr. Donald E. Grant Jr. "These intersections push young men into rigid templates of who they should be," he told us, "while society practically hands out gold stars for avoiding anything that resembles introspection."

As parents, we can encourage our boys to resist the confines of this rigid template of masculinity in a wide variety of ways. Dr. Grant suggests practices like mindfulness, meditation, and yoga.

He recognizes that for many young men, "those sound about as appealing as voluntarily giving up the remote during a game," but encourages us to reframe these practices as ways to grow a different type of strength.

"By teaching boys and young men how to flex their critical thinking and emotional intelligence muscles, we disrupt that cycle," he explains. "We push them to try on new identities, see what fits, and figure out what feels genuine in the moment. It's a bit like a mental spring cleaning—keeping what resonates, tossing what doesn't, and coming out with a version of themselves that's actually their own."

We want to create a world where boys are comfortable accessing and expressing a full range of emotions, where creating community and helping others is seen as a sign of strength. It's a change that benefits boys, for sure, but also their friends, their families, their future partners and children, and the world at large. Thankfully, things are changing, and boys are looking for guidance about how to be "real men" while also being their authentic selves.

These are complicated issues and can be a lot to take on. You may want to look for emotional or practical support for yourself, and you may want to look for positive support programs that your boys can join.

When to Reach Out for Help

There are a few common signs that a boy may be struggling with more serious issues. These include:

→ Avoiding personal responsibility and blaming girls/women for his problems

→ Behaving in a controlling, manipulative, or abusive way toward girls or women

→ Frequently dismissing girls/women as "crazy"

→ Joking about gender-based abuse or violence

→ Identifying as an "incel" or echoing sentiments from online extremists

REMEMBER THIS:

❶ Gender roles affect everyone—including boys. Boys often feel pressure to conform to a narrow set of rules about what it means to be a "real man."

❷ The term "toxic masculinity" may do more harm than good, because it can get in the way of productive conversations.

❸ Consider working with your local school to start a boys' group— it can be a powerful tool for encouraging critical thinking and emotional development.

❹ Get curious, not furious: ask questions and really listen to the answers.

❺ It's OK to reach out for help—you deserve empathy, support, and encouragement.

"When I'm going through episodes of extreme sadness, I often reach a point when I just feel hopeless and numb. I am aware of how unhelpful it is to spiral into that state, and it just leads to me berating myself in my head for not trying harder to improve, or being strong enough to handle my emotions without shutting down."

—Ty, age 18

Chapter 3

Talk to Your Boys About

EMOTIONS AND MENTAL HEALTH

We are experiencing a youth mental health crisis. In 2021, US Surgeon General Vivek H. Murthy issued "Protecting Youth Mental Health," a fifty-three-page advisory that described the challenges young people face as "uniquely hard to navigate." Per the report, between 2009 and 2019, the number of high school students reporting persistent feelings of sadness and hopelessness increased 40%; between 2007 and 2018, suicide rates among preteens, teens, and young adults rose by 57%. And these numbers are all from before a global pandemic disrupted lives and took a toll on our mental health.

The youth mental health crisis isn't happening solely to boys, but boys and young men face unique challenges around expressing emotion and reaching out for help.

It's imperative that we teach our boys that emotions are healthy—even the ones that can feel uncomfortable—and that recognizing and getting comfortable with our emotions is an important skill. We need to remind them that asking for help, support, a hug, or simply talking about how they're feeling, is a sign of strength. While we may think these messages are obvious, they may be far from obvious to our boys. As experts and researchers have noted, most boys learn to force themselves not to cry in elementary school.

This is an issue clinical psychologist Dr. Lisa Damour discussed on *The Rich Roll Podcast* in 2023:

"Boys are socialized to not talk about emotions as much as girls are, and we know that comes at a cost to them," Damour says. "For a lot of boys, especially around middle school as they are starting to consolidate a sense of masculinity, a lot of them decide that talking about feelings is a 'girl thing' to do."

She suggests that one of the most effective ways to combat this stereotype is for the men in boys' lives—dads, teachers, coaches—to talk more openly about their emotions and to prompt boys to have real conversations about their feelings.

It is equally important that we make our homes and families safe places for our boys to feel any and every emotion, and to ask for help or support when they need it—judgment-free. That means making sure that you and other trusted adults are willing to listen and be compassionate, and not tolerating teasing, mocking, or any form of cruelty from siblings or other people in the home when a boy is expressing his emotions or asking for help.

CHECK IN WITH YOURSELF

By talking openly about mental health, you'll be reducing the stigma and letting your kids know that you are a safe person to come to for help when they need it. As you get ready, it's smart to do a little self-reflection. Here are some questions to get you started:

> How do you feel about boys or men going to therapy?

> Are you ever judgmental when men seek help rather than handling problems themselves?

> What do you think about people who talk openly about going to therapy or taking medication to help with mental health issues?

> Do you think boys could probably overcome issues like anxiety or depression if they just worked a little harder?

> How do you feel when you hear boys addressing other boys with phrases like "boys don't cry" or "man up"?

> If you go to therapy, take medication, or do any proactive work to help maintain positive mental health, how do you feel about talking with the boys in your life about your efforts to stay healthy?

Lost in the "Man Box"

Before GPS became standard on smartphones, the joke was that men who got lost would never stop to ask for directions. People said men would drive until they were out of gas before they'd ask for help. Nowadays, there's rarely a reason to ask for directions—but there are still plenty of reasons to ask for help.

A 2022 study conducted by UCLA professor Mark Kaplan found that the majority of men who die by suicide have no known history of mental health problems. This doesn't mean suicide comes out of nowhere, but rather that men in crisis are not seeking the support that could possibly save their lives.

What is keeping our boys and young men silent, even when they may be in danger? There are many contributing factors, but the stigma against men who struggle emotionally or seek help for emotional or mental health struggles is often considered the primary contributor to this scary statistic. They are lost in the Man Box.

We asked boys:

Why do you think many boys don't feel safe expressing their emotions?

"When expressing emotions, even from a very young age, both peers and adults will ridicule boys for not being strong enough."
—Nadav, age 15

"Because it doesn't correspond to 'masculinity.'"
—ML, age 15

"Because they are made fun of for it. And I think parents are the main reason. For example, my dad goes by the idea that men don't cry and that's heavily affected me."
—Kamran, age 18

We can help our boys notice the harmful ways in which restrictive ideas of masculinity keep boys and men from being fully in touch with their emotions. Ask your boys to imagine some scenarios:

1. One of the guys in a friend group weighs more and has a less athletic physique than his friends. For years, his friends have called him nicknames like "Big Boy" and he's laughed along, but inside he hates it because it reminds him that his body doesn't fit the ideal they all see in the media. He wants to ask them to stop, but he doesn't want them to see him as weak.

2. At one school, homophobic slurs are commonplace in the locker room and everyone seems to throw around the F-word like it's no big deal. Nobody ever speaks up against it. One of the kids knows he's gay, and even though he thinks the other kids wouldn't beat him up if they knew, he definitely feels like his school is not a safe place to come out and tell his truth.

3. One of the bigger, more successful kids on the football team was just cheated on by his girlfriend. He knows if he tells his friends, they'll be pissed at her and tell him to dump her or call her disparaging names. The problem is, he doesn't come from the type of home where he has a lot of support, and without her, he wouldn't have anyone to open up to. Who could he go to when he was scared, sad, or needing emotional support if she were no longer his girlfriend?

Now ask them to consider this: What if these boys could ask for help, open up to their friends, and be vulnerable without the fear of being mocked or losing friends?

You can normalize talking about emotional health and our feelings by simply introducing some deeper questions into everyday conversations. Here are a few examples:

SCENARIO: Your kid shares that a teacher scolded him for not completing an assignment that your kid is certain he completed and handed in.

Instead of: Skipping straight to problem-solving mode, address the feelings he may be having . . .

Try saying: "That sounds stressful, how did you feel when that happened?" (Once you've heard and validated his experience, then you can move on to helping him solve the problem, should he want your support.)

SCENARIO: Your kid shares that he's heard a rumor that the person he's had a crush on for a while is dating a jerk whom he hates.

Instead of: Dismissively saying, "Well, there will be other girls," admonishing him for not having "made a move" earlier, or suggesting he ask around to see if it's true . . .

Try saying: "Ugh! How are you feeling about that?"

"Emotional Downloads"

When our kids come to us with a lot of emotional energy, it can be overwhelming—especially when the emotions are anger, frustration, or sadness. But, as Dr. John Duffy shares in his book *Parenting the New Teen in the Age of Anxiety*, it can be an opportunity to help them learn to process feelings and manage them in healthy ways:

"How mighty and noble and warrior-like it is as a parent to stay in the game, and hang in with your child, in the face of a slammed door, or rejection, or a wretched attitude. Because when they come to you, they let their guard down. They vent. They transfer, or download, a day's worth of stress and fear and identity traffic and anxiety into the safest place they know: you."

It should be noted that just because we show up for our kids' big emotions doesn't mean we should tolerate harmful behavior or abusive language.

Instead, Duffy suggests, find a moment of quiet and share that you are available for a "calm and rational download," a discussion of whatever might be bothering them based on mutual respect. This teaches our kids how to treat others in their lives, all while showing them that we are here for them—even when their feelings are big and uncomfortable.

----- No Wrong Answers: Questions to Get You Talking ---------

Are men allowed to express "unmanly" emotions—and when?

As a guy, when would you feel like it is appropriate to cry . . .

... in public?

... in front of your friends?

... during a national tragedy?

... during a bad breakup?

... in front of your family?

... alone in your room?

... when feeling overwhelmed or anxious?

Ask:

→ What would you think if a guy cried in these situations?

→ Is that your opinion or does it come from society?

With whom can you see yourself . . .

... admitting that you are afraid?

... telling a story where you looked foolish?

... talking about a time you were emotionally hurt?

... admitting you made a big mistake?

... asking for help when you're struggling emotionally?

What can girls "get away with" emotionally that guys can't, as far as . . .

... confiding secrets and feelings?

... sharing items?

... platonically hugging or cuddling?

... talking through problems and finding solutions?

Ask:

→ Are there any ways in which you've envied what girls can share?

→ Are there any guys you know who connect more deeply than your current group of friends?

Your kid may not get super dramatic or specific when you ask about his feelings. In fact, it's likely he'll say something more along the lines of "It sucks" or "Whatever, I guess." His answer doesn't matter as much as the fact that you are asking about his feelings, and he knows he can talk to you about them should he need or want to.

Helping Your Kid Regulate His Emotions

It's completely normal to have big hard feelings, and it's also normal to sometimes feel overwhelmed by them. One of the hardest things about being a parent is accepting that we can't protect our kids from disappointment, frustration, or hurt. So, while we can't slay every dragon for them, the next best thing is to give them the tools to do it themselves.

If it seems like your child is struggling, try to approach them with curiosity. Empathy is your goal here—try understanding their feelings without leaping into problem-solving mode. Sometimes just feeling heard can be deeply healing to people. Ask open-ended questions and listen—really listen—to what they have to say.

→ "You seem like you're kind of down. Do you want to ride bikes down to the park with me?"

→ "I've noticed you've seemed less happy than usual. Do you want to play a video game with me later?"

→ "We don't need to talk about it now, but it seems like you're going through something heavy. I know when I'm feeling the weight of something big it helps to know there's someone to talk to. I'm here anytime you want to talk. You can text me, too."

It's also important that we strike a balance between taking our kids' feelings seriously but not overidentifying with them. We want to strive for what experts call co-regulation—keeping our own emotions in check while we help our kids navigate their own.

"Adolescence is a brain storm, and we need to be the calm at the eye of the storm," says therapist Eli Harwood, author of *Raising Securely Attached Kids*. When we are in an active feeling state with very big emotions, we need other people in our lives to be co-regulated with us. "We need someone who can catch what we're feeling but stay grounded," Harwood explains. "I think of co-regulation like this: Take a little sip of the feelings. Just enough of the feelings that we understand, but not a whole gulp where you go under the water with them."

One simple tool for helping your teen when he is overwhelmed or struggling is to ask him to describe a physical sensation he's experiencing. Often, men and boys find it easier to talk about their bodies than their emotions. Because our bodies and our emotions are so tied to one another, this can help us get to the root feelings.

Example: Your son comes home clearly irritated and upset. He throws down his backpack and then goes to his room and shuts the door in a huff.

Give him a few moments alone to decompress and then knock and ask if you can come in or if he'd like to come out and talk. Ask how he's feeling and simply listen.

If he struggles to express the emotion, ask: "What is your body feeling? Do you feel tightness or tension somewhere?" It may take a moment, but he may say something like "I feel like my hands are shaking," "My chest feels tight," or "I feel like my throat is burning." Reassure him that what he feels is totally normal and is likely tied to an emotion he's feeling. Ask if he'd like to:

→ Take a walk or go on a run, or do something like hit the punching bag to help all those "shaky" chemicals disperse.

→ Take some deep breaths with long exhales or do a box-breathing exercise (see box on page 50).

→ Close his eyes and listen to some soothing music until the tightness in his chest feels less intense.

→ Have a good cry or yell into a pillow, which can help relieve the burning throat feelings.

A physical outlet can help our boys settle down, and talking about physical sensations can open the door to talking about emotions.

You don't have to wait for a crisis to start talking to your boy about how to regulate their big feelings. Ideally, you can start by asking your son what things he already does that make him feel good, calm, relaxed, and safe. Listen for answers that feel like good coping skills, things like:

→ Spending time in nature   → Exercising

→ Connecting with friends   → Playing sports

→ Journaling   → Building things

→ Stretching   → Solving puzzles

→ Sharing meals   → Listening to music

→ Reading   → Making art

You can point out to your son that some of the things on this list are more than just hobbies—they are great tools for managing mental health and should be relied upon when they are feeling down or stressed.

If he says things like video games or looking at his phone, it's a chance to talk about the difference between activities that help us wind down and activities that boost our serotonin—but don't presume to know whether his screen time is bad for him. For some kids, video games are an opportunity to decompress from stressful days full of school and activities. Share your own experiences with technology and how you know when you've crossed from relaxing to avoiding important feelings and emotions.

In an interview with *The Washington Post*, psychologist Michael C. Reichert, PhD, encouraged parents to spend dedicated time with their boys, doing what they like, without lecturing, scolding, or coercing: "Find a way through all the insecurities, doubts and worries you have and locate the place in your heart where you can be delighted with your son."

Delight is "like sunlight to a young man," Reichert says. "The more you beam it toward him, the more he's going to feel safe and the more likely he'll be to open up to you. . . . Parents have an enormous power to validate their son's existence."

The human brain isn't fully developed until people are well into their twenties, which means that the area of your teen's brain that regulates emotions—the prefrontal cortex and the areas below the cortex—are still being formed. In other words, teens are wired to feel deeply and have big emotional reactions, often in ways that may not make sense to adults.

In his book *Brainstorm: The Power and Purpose of the Teenage Brain*, Dr. Daniel Siegel writes about a brain study in which teens were shown images of people whose faces reflected neutral emotional states. Researchers found that "a major area of the limbic region, the amygdala [where emotions are processed], becomes activated [in teens]." By comparison, when adults were shown the same images, scans showed activity in their "reasoning prefrontal cortex."

Box Breathing

Breathing techniques can help us feel grounded. Here is a simple but effective one.

1. Sit quietly and close your eyes.

2. Inhale slowly for four seconds, letting your lungs fill with air.

3. Hold that breath for another four seconds.

4. Exhale slowly for four seconds.

5. Hold your breath again for four seconds.

6. Repeat four times, or until you start to feel more relaxed and in control.

The study showed that teens may feel an "inner sense of conviction that even another person's neutral response is filled with hostility, and he cannot be trusted."

This is good information to have when we may feel baffled by our teens' big feelings. It also could be good information for our kids—reassurance that their feelings aren't character faults. Ideally, they may learn to recognize any irrationality and talk themselves into a less reactive state. In the meantime, we can help them regulate.

How to Deal with an Angry Teen

Jason Mechanick, PsyD, is a psychologist who has worked with teens and their families for more than twenty years. We asked him how he helps families deal with teenage anger.

When working with young people, he emphasizes that learning how to communicate and react to our emotions is one of the major differences between being an adolescent and being an adult. "I encourage kids to be aware of, and own, their emotions, not hide from them," he explains. "The biggest point that I try to make is that all emotions are natural and welcome. The key is how we handle the emotions when we have them."

Our boys can't learn to control their expression of anger until they learn to first recognize the feeling in themselves and make friends with it—or at the very least, learn not to run from it by being reactive or shutting down.

We know firsthand how much patience and self-control it takes to not meet our boys' anger with anger of our own. But if we can stay calm, their outbursts are an opportunity for us to teach them how to acknowledge their anger and express it in a healthy way.

Instead of saying: "You are out of control—this is too big of a reaction just because a restaurant was closed. Stop right now or I'm going to take away your car keys for the weekend."

We asked boys:

What do you wish adults understood about emotions and mental health?

"Sometimes kids are just sad, and it's fine to let them solve things on their own."

—Sam, age 15

"Mental health is like a boomerang: it goes away and comes back, and if you don't pay attention to it, you will be feeling the repercussions of it."

—ML, age 15

"You can't expect someone to just 'soldier through' emotions, and you need to be able to recognize signs of mental health–related issues so you can try to be aware that you are not worsening the situation by addressing the issue in a tone-deaf or unexpectedly harmful way."

—Ty, age 18

"Guys my age feel like they're held up to a standard where showing emotion makes them look less masculine."

—Carson, age 14

Try saying: "I hear how pissed you are, and I totally get it. It's so disappointing and you had your heart set on birria tacos and I know you're starving. I'm really sorry that happened."

Does the second response feel weak to you? Like you're just rolling over? We understand. But let us ask you this: Have you ever felt calmer when someone commanded you to calm down? Have you ever felt more connected with someone scolding you and telling you that you're over-reacting? Our guess is no.

Validating your kid's anger or big feelings allows him to feel safe with you. Once he lets you in, you can tone down the conversation together. Try following up your validation by saying: "I get all of it, Bud, but I'm doing the best I can here, and your raised voice is causing me to feel super stressed out. Let's talk about this after dinner when I have some time to really focus."

Shouting back and meeting their anger with your own can be counterproductive. Even if your shouting leads to him quieting down,

A Message to Men Raising Boys, from Therapist Terrence Real

We asked Terrence Real, famed marriage and family therapist, dad of two grown sons, and author of the pioneering book on men's mental health *I Don't Want to Talk About It*, how dads can break unhealthy patterns of silence and stoicism.

"Our kids don't need strong fathers, they need connected, big-hearted fathers," Real told us. "And that's very different from your father and the way you were raised. Be a pioneer, change the legacy. You do that by opening your heart."

"And how exactly do we do that?" Christopher asked.

"Do your work, get into therapy. Do your own trauma work. Go away for a weekend. Do a men's group. Do something to open yourself up and let them see it. The best gift you can give your children is your own recovery. Break the legacy by doing the work."

Eli explains, he may not be calm—he may be pushing down his feelings or even disassociating. "It doesn't mean he's self-soothing. It most likely means he's learned there's no safe place for him to feel his feelings with you."

In a speech delivered to a live audience and shared on social media, clinical psychologist Dr. Becky Kennedy notes that one of the cruelest things we do to our kids is expecting them to behave in ways that aren't developmentally possible for them.

In the same way that it is unreasonable to expect a three-year-old to sit at family dinner for an hour without anything to distract them, it's also unreasonable to expect an adolescent to never take a sharp tone, convey grumpiness, or act irrationally.

Expecting them to be "perfect" prevents us from guiding them through bad moments so they know how to handle them in the future. Of course, it can be irritating when our kids are rude or reactive, but as parents, it's our job to make room for any feelings they're having to be OK.

Dr. Becky suggests imagining that you're sitting on a "feelings bench" with them.

"All they actually need is for us to sit with them," she says. "Because as soon as you sit with them, what you're really saying is 'I still like you when you feel this way. This feeling that's overwhelming to you isn't overwhelming to me. I'm not trying to convince you [that] you should feel a different way. I'm not trying to convince you [that] you don't actually feel the extent of the feeling. I see you and I'm willing to sit with you in it.'" Your kid may feel he can't tolerate this feeling alone, but he can learn to tolerate it and move through it if he has an ally by his side.

In other words, demanding that our kids always remain calm, cool, and collected teaches them that we can't tolerate their big feelings. And if we can't tolerate their big feelings, how will they ever learn to tolerate them? Who will teach them the right way to handle them, if not us?

Of course, that doesn't mean you should allow your child to scream and yell at you or to threaten you. You always have the right to take a break from a conversation and draw a line at what is tolerable. Just remember that when you do this, you should separate the behavior from the feeling.

Finally, if your teen doesn't recognize that they are shouting or otherwise behaving inappropriately, Dr. Mechanick suggests recording your dialogue with him to show him how it sounds. Be careful not to use this as a threat, but rather a tool to help the two of you communicate better in the future. You might even learn something about your own tone or volume in the process!

Guilt and Shame: Toxic BFFs

Brené Brown—professor, social researcher, and author of books such as *Dare to Lead*—said in a TED talk, "If you put shame in a petri dish, it needs three ingredients to grow exponentially: secrecy, silence, and judgment. If you put the same amount of shame in the petri dish and douse it with empathy, it can't survive."

Let's clarify the difference between guilt and shame. In her talk, Brown explained, "The thing to understand about shame is, it's not guilt. Shame is a focus on self, guilt is a focus on behavior. Shame is 'I am bad.' Guilt is 'I did something bad.'"

Researchers from the Institute of Cognitive Sciences and Technologies in Rome, Italy, posit that "Shame implies perceived lack of power to meet the standards of one's ideal self, whereas guilt implies perceived power and willingness to be harmful, that is, to violate the standards of one's moral self."

Regardless of how we define it, feeling guilty is a part of life. We all make mistakes, say things we later regret, and make decisions we wish we could undo. Shame, on the other hand, can easily immobilize us rather than empower us to make better decisions.

Instead of learning from shame and moving on, we tend to relive it over and over again, spiraling from the sense that we are irrevocably bad, or that our mistake or error is a reflection of our character. The worst part of this feeling is that it can disempower us from wanting to grow and change. After all, why would we work toward becoming better people and learning from mistakes if we believe our mistakes reflect how bad or broken we are, fundamentally?

Shame is often so painful, we don't want to look at it, so we shove it down. And, as Brown says, shame grows and multiplies when it's pushed underground. If not properly addressed, shame can also turn into anger at others and/or further retreat from one's own moral and ethical standards. That's why we need to prepare our boys to handle guilt and shame

We asked boys:

Do you ever have emotions or feelings you wish you could talk to other guys about?

"I wish I could talk to them. I had a breakup a while ago and I felt really stuck. I didn't cry when she broke up with me, so I felt like I was a bad person or that I really didn't love her. It ate at me for a while."

—Kamran, age 18

"I figure out that kind of stuff on my own. I know what my friends would say, so I imagine that and use that to help me."

—Octavian, age 11

"I definitely would prefer to be able to share my feelings with my peers, but I just feel like everybody is struggling in their own way and it's not my decision to burden someone with my emotions while they're still working on themselves."

—Ty, age 18

productively, so it doesn't make them feel hopeless.

An article from the Gottman Institute called "How to Deal with Shame" explains that "the less you talk about [your feelings of shame] with someone safe, the more control it has over your life and psychological well-being.

"The fear behind shame," it explains, "is usually the belief that sharing your story and being who you are will make people think less of you. It fights against the human need for acceptance."

The trick, it says, is to practice talking about your feelings with people you trust: "You need to tell your story to safe people who will listen and not judge. Such safety is necessary to feel vulnerable. Talking to a therapist with whom you connect can start this process of feeling internal safety."

As parents, it is our job to make clear to our children that we can be those safe people. That we will listen and not judge, that we will help them find solutions, and that we will love them even when they don't feel worthy of love. In addition, we should not use shame as a way to control our kids' behavior—it simply doesn't work.

Ways Your Teen Can Manage His Anger Productively

Not everyone processes anger the same way. For some, an "angry" activity, like punching a pillow, may release the feeling and allow them to feel regulated once again. For others, these types of behaviors may actually make anger worse—or at least not help. For those kids, one of the more traditionally soothing activities may be better. Here are some ideas to try with your boy.

→ Going for a run

→ Punching a pillow

→ Listening to a guided meditation track or other centering sound, like binaural beats or soothing music

→ Going to the gym to lift weights or hit a kickboxing bag

→ Playing a video game

→ Writing in a journal

→ Listening to music

→ Playing an instrument

→ Kicking a soccer ball into a goal or shooting hoops

→ Watching an emotional movie or show that can help him feel less alone

Teen "Therapists"

It is common for teen boys, whose friendships may be less emotionally intimate than girls', to rely heavily upon romantic partners or friends who are girls to provide emotional support.

Boys may fear the judgment of their parents or worry that their parents will minimize their problems, or they may simply not know how to express their feelings to anyone other than a romantic partner. This can become an unhealthy dynamic, as it's hard on anybody to have to serve as someone's fill-in therapist—especially when they are so young and relatively inexperienced.

In addition, many teen girls (and women of all ages) report that the pressure to be 100% of a boyfriend's or male partner's emotional support system can make their partner act desperate to keep them close. This desperation can feel cloying, constricting, or even abusive depending on the severity of the behavior.

The mother of one teen girl, whom we will call Ziva, told us about a relationship Ziva had with a boy in ninth and tenth grades. It started out great. The boy was kind, respectful, and seemed pleasant and upbeat. Ziva's parents knew his parents socially, and the two families often spent time together.

The tone of Ziva's relationship shifted dramatically as the boy became more and more emotionally dependent upon her. This included phone calls at all hours of the night, including times when he was in the middle of an anxiety attack. At first, Ziva appreciated the opportunity to be emotionally intimate with a partner, but after a few months she grew afraid of what he would do if they ever broke up. She confided in her mom, who advised her on a few boundaries to set. When she set them, the boy became desperate and threatened to harm himself, saying he had nobody else to talk to about his feelings.

Ziva's mom was shocked at this turn of events, as the boy and his parents seemed to have a great relationship. Out of an abundance of caution, she called the boy's mom and shared her concerns for his safety. His mother had no idea her son was struggling.

If your kid is turning to other kids for help (or is helping others), you likely won't know he's doing it—so this is a topic worth raising yourself.

Try saying:

→ "If you're really struggling, please know you can come to me with anything—and I mean anything—and we will work on it together."

→ "Friends can be an incredible source of support, and I hope you have some friends you can trust. Just remember that our friends aren't trained for major emergencies, so there are times going to an adult is a better choice. Your mom and I are always here to listen without judgment and help you sort out problems or questions."

→ "I love that you have such great friendships and that you support one another, but please remember that serious issues should be handled by parents or professionals, and you can come to me if you feel in over your head supporting someone and we'll find a solution together."

Also share some specific situations that require adult attention:

→ Suicidal ideation, especially if they appear to be making plans

→ Serious mental health crises, including eating disorders that appear to be getting worse

→ The use of drugs that can kill, like street-obtained pills or drugs that are injected; drinking to the point of blacking out, driving under the influence

→ Suicide-adjacent risk-taking, like driving at very high speeds, hitchhiking, starting fights with dangerous people, or other extreme behavior that indicates reckless disregard for his or another's safety

→ Ask your son: What would you add? Can you think of any other scenarios that would require adult intervention?

Signs That Your Boy Is Struggling

"Teenage boys are just as easily hurt as girls," William Meleney, a therapist with thirty-five years of experience, including supervising a program serving boys on juvenile probation, told us. The difference, he says, is that boys may not cry the same way girls typically do—or in the same situations. But that doesn't mean they won't—or shouldn't—shed tears, they just may do so in private or while expressing anger.

Depression may look like "super-contained anger with sarcasm and eye-rolling," Meleney advises. "They may hate everything or think that everything they used to like is now 'stupid.'"

Ultimately, Meleney wants those of us raising boys to be careful not to bring a gendered bias to what depression is "supposed to" look like, or we could miss crucial warning signs that our boys are struggling.

We asked boys:

Have you ever kept a feeling to yourself? Why?

"I keep a lot of feelings to myself because I don't really know how to talk about it. And I don't really even know how to express it besides destroying stuff."

—Kamran, age 18

"Sometimes feelings are personal, so obviously I keep them to myself. Additionally, I fear what other people, those around me, will think about my actions/beliefs/thoughts and judge me or think less of me because of them."

—Nadav, age 15

"When you allow yourself to express emotions, especially emotions that are more commonly perceived as negative, you are forced to confront them in a more real and scary way than if you were to try and bottle them up."

—Ty, age 18

"I have kept many emotions secret because I thought it wasn't right for a boy to show them."

—ML, age 15

"Parents need to know that being male is the biggest risk factor for suicide. The chances of your son taking his life by suicide are about four times higher than your daughter's," Richard V. Reeves, president of the American Institute for Boys and Men, told *The Washington Post*. "I have been quite shocked by people's lack of awareness of this problem." Data from the Centers for Disease Control and Prevention underscore just how big of a concern this is:

→ Suicide is consistently the first or second leading cause of death for boys and men ages 15 to 34.

→ In 2021, suicide was the second leading cause of death for kids ages ten to fourteen.

→ While teen girls attempt suicide more than teen boys, boys are more likely to die by suicide.

→ More than half of all deaths by suicide involve firearms.

Given the emotional ups and downs of adolescent life, and that out-sized emotions are developmentally appropriate in teens, it can be hard to know when your child is truly suffering. So what should parents look for? For this advice, we turned to psychologist Patricia A. O'Gorman, PhD. She has decades of experience helping adolescents with a multitude of mental health challenges, including addiction and suicidal feelings.

Before we list these warning signs, please note that one sign, one time, may not be a cause for concern. Look for emerging patterns, or clusters of signs. The Child Mind Institute recommends watching for the "Three Ds": Distress, Duration, and Disruption. Here are some questions to consider:

→ Distress: How hard is your child struggling?

→ Duration: How long has this been going on?

→ Disruption: How much are their symptoms getting in the way of what the child needs or wants to do?

In general, Dr. O'Gorman says to keep an eye out for these signs in your kids:

→ Rapid change in dress, hygiene, and self-care: not bathing regularly, not changing his clothes

→ Changes in how they eat, such as eating markedly more or less

→ Increased sexual interest or activity that is more intense than before

→ Suddenly canceling plans for activities and events they had been looking forward to attending

→ Changes in how they care for their room and what is in it

Emotional changes:

→ Expressing a lot of worry about a friend who may be going through a hard time

→ No longer making eye contact

→ Withdrawing from physical touch

→ Inability to follow a conversation

→ Bouts of crying or sudden flashes of anger

→ Major fluctuations in mood (like going from being chatty to withdrawn) or newly erratic behaviors

→ Racing thoughts or new worries that he cannot get out of his head

→ Repeatedly becoming upset, hitting himself, and/or running from the room

→ Expressing that he feels very pressured about his schedule and that he has no time for himself

Social changes:

→ Changes in how they socialize during family activities such as meals

→ Changes in communication, going from his usual level of interaction with siblings and family members to withdrawing and being markedly less available

→ Withdrawing from their pet or changing how they care for their pet

→ Suddenly uninterested in many of the activities that they once loved

→ Withdrawing from his friends, breaking up with his love interest

→ Withdrawing from his community

→ Developing a new set of friends and acquaintances who are markedly different from his previous friends

Signs of drug or alcohol use:

→ New smells on his hair or clothing, or coming from his room

→ Hidden pills or drug paraphernalia; missing alcohol or medications from the family's cabinets

→ Random "friends" showing up at the door and not staying long

→ Signs of academic struggle and inability to concentrate on schoolwork

→ Missing project deadlines or skipping school

→ Having social problems in school—anger, fighting with peers or with school personnel

→ Wanting to drop out of school or suddenly not wanting to go to college

Indications of self-harm:

→ Cuts and/or burns on legs, arms, or torso; frequently burns will be the size of a cigarette

→ Unexplained bruises; missing, burned, or shaved chunks of hair; ripped out ear studs

→ Handmade tattoos

→ Loss of personal property, likely due to giving away his possessions

Trust your gut. You know your child. If you have a sense that something is concerning or has changed, pay attention to that sensation and gather more information.

Body Image and Bulking Up

It's a well-accepted fact that exercise is good for your body and your mind, so many parents are delighted when their son expresses interest in going to the gym and becoming more physically fit—and it is, overall, a great thing. What parents of boys often aren't prepared for is the potential for their son to develop body dysmorphia or to struggle with an eating or exercise disorder.

These disorders are nothing new, but researchers have identified a sharp rise in the rates at which these disorders are affecting boys and men, who often want to look bulkier and more muscular. According to a report from the National Alliance for Eating Disorders (NEDA), nearly 90% of those struggling with muscle dysmorphia are young men

Talk to Your Boys About:
Therapy as a Tool in Life's Toolbox

Therapy shouldn't be seen as a weakness, nor should it be seen as a luxury, like a Caribbean vacation or a sports car. Therapy is simply a tool, a way to hire an expert to help you with life's challenges.

Here's a helpful analogy you can use to explain therapy to your boy. Imagine your sink isn't working. Sure, you're going to try to unclog it and solve the problem, but sometimes you need to call in a plumber. After all, they're trained, experienced, and have all the necessary tools. It's the same when it comes to emotional emergencies. You're not expected to handle all your plumbing problems on your own, and we don't expect you to handle all your emotional challenges on your own, either.

between the ages of fifteen and thirty-two, a development that some refer to as "bigorexia."

"Young men and adolescents experiencing body image issues and eating disorders often attempt to increase muscle mass by excessive weightlifting and exercising, misusing supplements such as steroids, and binge eating," states the report. "It is also common among young men and teen boys to use purging and fasting to increase muscular definition. Bodybuilders and athletes of all ages and genders are also at a higher risk of struggling with bigorexia, given the environmental focus on body shape, body weight, strength, and perfectionism."

According to NEDA, eating disorders in males are increasing at a faster rate than for females, and they can be deadly. Studies suggest that the risk of mortality for males with eating disorders is six to eight times higher than the rates for men and boys without an eating disorder. For insight on how to help a boy develop a healthy gym and muscle-building habit, we turned to Josh Townshend, a bodybuilder who is a motivational coach, men's group leader, and youth mentor in New Zealand. Townshend, who has an adolescent son himself, shared how men and teenage boys often start going to the gym without fully understanding why they want to start bodybuilding.

"They want to look athletic," he told us. "They want women to select them based on that." But it's about much more. "They also want to deter other men from fighting [them]."

Ultimately, says Townshend, they want to feel safe.

According to Townshend, society pushes a singular, unhealthy ideal down their throats: "You need to make money and you need to get massive. Make money, get massive."

Townshend doesn't necessarily feel it's unhealthy for young men to strive toward "getting massive," as he puts it. "As long as you understand that once it starts affecting your life negatively, it can become a big problem."

He suggests a list of questions to ask your boy about his relationship with the gym, his body image, and his fitness goals. These questions are designed to be asked many times throughout a kid's fitness journey, not just once.

→ Why are you doing this? What's the desired outcome? What will you do and feel when you get there?

→ Is your gym work giving you a sense of purpose? If it is, is it all you're relying on? Or can you look to other things as well?

→ How much do you care about what other people think? Is your own validation enough in this situation?

→ If it's other people that you're getting your validation from, who is it and why is their opinion important?

→ Why are you working on this? Are you doing it because you had a horrific breakup? Do you want to make your ex jealous? Is it because your best friend is bigger than you?

We also want to urge parents to plan a visit to their son's health care provider to get an all-clear for weight lifting and any major changes to his diet or fitness habits.

"Ultimately," Townshend explains, "if you don't have an endgame, if you don't have a desired outcome that you're going to shoot for, then you're a rocket heading off in a direction with no real sense of where to go." And that's where things can start getting unhealthy.

In addition to asking these questions and monitoring to make sure your son is healthy, Townshend suggests setting mini-goals for his fitness and then plan a check-in. For instance, set a dead-lift weight mini-goal, or one for push-ups or pull-ups—whatever matters most to him. Here is a sample conversation Townshend shared that may help:

You: So, what is your first goal?

Him: Well, I want to dead lift 400 pounds.

You: OK. And what difference would that make to your life?

Him: Well, I'd be happy.

You: OK, so you'd be happy. And describe "happy."

Him: Well, I'd feel like I'm enough. I would feel *enough*.

You: OK, so what you want here is to feel enough. And so what we're going to do is, when you get to 225 pounds, which will probably happen in the next few weeks, let's sit down and reassess and see if you feel like reaching 400 pounds will make you feel like you're enough.

It should be noted that this isn't a "gotcha" conversation. You aren't trying to catch him being illogical. You simply want to be there to help him set a goal and adapt as need arises. You also want to be there to support him as he learns that achieving external goals rarely makes people feel like "enough." If your son does get into a "nothing will ever be enough" mindset and you are concerned, look for the following signs:

→ Does he recognize his gains and progress?

→ Is he realistic about his size, or does he still see himself as too thin (or too big)?

→ Is he restricting or "bulking" in a way that seems unhealthy or dangerous?

→ Is his fitness or gym routine interfering with school, work, friendships, partnerships, or family time?

If the answer to any of these questions is "yes," or if other things concern you, reach out to your doctor or a qualified therapist.

Home as an Emotional Safe Zone

We believe that creating a safe zone for our boys' feelings not only helps them when they face hard times, it also models for them how to support others who may be struggling. One way to build this safe zone is to listen to your boy when he opens up to you—regardless of the subject. Delight in him and make him feel seen. Help him navigate his big feelings. Give him the tools to do it himself. And be attuned to any worrisome shifts in mood.

REMEMBER THIS:

❶ Men are dying from suicide at high rates, and most of them have never reached out for mental health support.

❷ There are cultural restrictions put on boys when it comes to emotions—they feel it, and it makes life harder for them. We can help them break free from restrictions, and it starts in our own homes.

❸ We can help alleviate emotions that may spiral by helping boys learn to talk openly about their feelings and their mistakes or regrets.

❹ There are ways to help a teen talk about his feelings, even when he feels like he can't find the words. Ask him to describe the physical sensation in his body to start.

❺ Kids will turn to their friends for support, which is wonderful, but some problems need to be solved with an adult. Review with your son which issues should also be discussed with an adult or maybe a therapist.

❻ Exercise and physical fitness are great for our physical and mental health, but boys are increasingly dealing with body image dysmorphia and eating and exercise disorders. Your son should feel supported in his fitness journey, but be supervised in order to make sure his motivations and practices are healthy.

❼ Therapy is good for almost everyone, and going to a therapist is a normal and positive thing—even for men!

"I hope this doesn't come across as bragging, but my relationship with my girlfriend is very strong. The most crucial reason for this is COMMUNICATION—we're able to talk through just about anything that happens. The ability to talk things through has also been essential for consent; knowing that we're both fully enthusiastic about anything we're doing makes the experience so much better."

—Rory, age 16

Chapter 4

Talk to Your Boys About

DATING AND RELATIONSHIPS

"Boys don't want relationships in high school anyway!"

"My daughter is who I worry about when it comes to dating; boys are the easy ones."

"Teenage romances aren't a big deal; they're just 'starter relationships.'"

These are a few of the myths we've heard from parents when talking about adolescent relationships. Not only do these old-fashioned ideas fail to prepare our boys for reality, they may also send a message that their feelings don't matter and that we aren't really interested in their experiences.

When girls start dating, parents often put a lot of emphasis on making sure they feel empowered to set and maintain boundaries. In essence, we teach them how to set expectations for how they should be treated and how to be a good partner. For some reason, we rarely do this with boys, who often feel lost in their first relationships, not knowing what to do next or how to gauge romantic situations when they're ready.

Every person finds themselves ready to date or have relationships in their own time. Some kids have crushes as young as preschool and girlfriends or boyfriends in fifth grade. By middle school, they may have what they consider to be a serious relationship. Other people may not be interested in dating until high school or even later. Some never experience these feelings at all—they might end up identifying as "asexual" or "aromantic."

No matter where your kid is on this path, it's normal.

With this in mind, we caution parents against assuming their child hasn't reached the "looking for love" stage simply because they haven't heard their son mention anyone he likes. In fact, the experts and boys we spoke to say that this is the topic that boys are *least likely* to bring up on their own. Rather than braving the awkwardness, they look for information and answers from their peers, online, or in the media. So it's up to us to broach these conversations with our boys, including:

→ How to approach someone respectfully

→ How to "read the room" and assess the situation before approaching someone

→ How to make a social plan together

→ How to gracefully hear a "no"

→ How to speak up for your own wants, wishes, and desires

→ How to listen to what your friends or partners want

→ How to stay in touch without becoming obsessive or overbearing

→ How to be emotionally intimate without being overly reliant on your partner

→ How to handle feelings of jealousy or fear of rejection

→ The difference between flirting and sexual harassment

→ How to step in if you see a friend in a potentially unsafe or unhealthy relationship

→ How to deal with a breakup

We don't expect our boys to pick up a new instrument or sport and know how to play it perfectly. It takes practice and coaching. When it comes to matters of the heart, your son is going to need your guidance, care, and support.

Starting and maintaining healthy relationships is a skill that people can get better at with time and practice, and the teen years are when many people start practicing. It's important to remember that, at this age, our boys may not have the right words to describe what they're going through. By bringing it up, you are letting them know that you're comfortable with the topic, interested in how they're feeling, and available to talk.

There's a fine line between being curious and being intrusive, and with these conversations you can model for your son how to show interest in someone while also respecting their boundaries. Pay attention to your son's face, body language, and mood, and back off if he seems uncomfortable. Remember that you're not trying to have a single talk and be done with it. You're just trying to start a conversation—one you can come back to again and again.

What Not to Say: "Do you have a girlfriend yet?"

Asking specifically about girlfriends sends a message that you assume your son is heterosexual. He may even hear this and think, "They won't accept me if I'm not straight." Second, this question assumes your son is interested in having a romantic partner, and he may feel ashamed to say "no" to you. Finally, this question implies that you think he should have one by now, and if he does not, he's failed.

What to do instead:

Ask open-ended questions and offer reassurance. Say, "I bet some of the kids in your class have girlfriends and boyfriends by now. Have you had any crushes or people you've liked?" or "Have you noticed any of the students in your school coupling up? What do you notice? How do you feel about it?"

You don't have to wait for your kid to be interested in a teen love story to talk about all of this, either. Action movies, comedies, and even kids' shows offer opportunities to talk about relationship dynamics in ways that can help them be successful in dating and relationships.

CHECK IN WITH YOURSELF ━ ━ ━ ━ ━ ━ ━ ━ ━

Before you dive into these conversations, it's good to get clear about your own values around teen relationships. If you have a spouse, partner, or co-parent, it might be a good idea to talk through your own rules and values together before approaching your son.

> What are the general "rules" about dating you want to have for your boy?

> Are those rules the same for any other kids in your house? Why or why not?

> How do you expect the rules to change as your boy gets older?

> How do you want them to treat people they are dating? How do you want people they are dating to treat them?

> How do you feel about casual relationships and "hooking up"?

As you consider your values around dating and relationships, remember the messages your son may receive from friends, teachers, the media, and even you about the role men play in relationships. For instance, some boys may feel pressure to have a high "body count," aka a lot of sexual partners. If your values don't align with what is common among today's teens, it's important to counter the messages not just with your own values, but also the "why" and "how" behind them.

For instance, if you are strongly opposed to your child being sexually active during middle school or high school, you will need to have regular, shame-free conversations with your boy. Go beyond "these are our house rules," into logical, thoughtful, emotional, and spiritual reasons why you believe this is the best choice for your son. But please remember this: he may be your kid, but this is his life and he needs to be armed to make his own choices.

We also want to be sure our kids know that we will always be available should they need advice, support, or guidance. To be truly available to our kids, we need to be aware of any emotional baggage we may be carrying. Kids have a strong "BS Meter," and if they sense we're being disingenuous or hypocritical, they likely won't trust us to be open, honest and nonjudgmental.

Teen Dating in the 21st Century

In just a few generations, the notion of what it means to "date" someone has changed dramatically. When our parents were in high school, dating often meant a boy asking a girl to a dance or a movie. The boy might drive to pick up the girl, greet her parents, and then escort her to a public place for a meal or a movie. After a few dates, the couple might declare they were dating or "going steady," or they may move on and date other people. For Gen X and Millennial parents, it was probably a mix of formal dates and casual hookups.

First dates for our kids often look quite a bit different. Sometimes they're "hangouts," where two people who like each other might watch a movie and see if they have the right chemistry to kiss or touch. While this sounds a lot like the movie-watching dates we had as teens, our kids would likely not call this type of situation a date—but their hangout serves a similar purpose to our dates of yore. These hangouts are a way for kids to test out a romantic or emotional connection and see if they would like to spend more time together.

While our kids may laugh off or dismiss the idea of planning a "date," encouraging kids to put some thought into a date (or a hangout) can help prepare them to be in a healthy relationship. The planning process requires them to think about a partner's feelings and expectations in a way that actively engages their empathy skills and reminds them that there is more than one person who matters in every hookup, date, or relationship.

Going on an actual date is a great way to learn about someone you're interested in. You discover how someone reaches agreement, how they react when they disagree, how they negotiate likes/dislikes, and whether you share the same values. For instance, your teen may notice that their date is rude to the servers and hosts at a restaurant they go to together. If they just stayed home, that example of rudeness—and the conversation the couple may have about it afterward—would never have played out.

When talking to your son about hangouts or dates, especially when he's in his younger teens, ask practical questions. This can feel like an interrogation, so make sure you explain that these are just questions to get him thinking and making a plan.

→ Is it just the two of you or are other people going?

→ Where will you go? How will you get there?

→ Will there be supervision?

→ Who pays?

→ How do you expect the date to end?

A Little Bit of Thinking Ahead

Here are some more questions that can help you sort through this new phase of your family's life:

→ Do you think your son is ready for a romantic relationship or dating? If not, why?

→ Do you want to meet your son's dates before they go out? Do you want to talk to the parents of his dates to make sure you're on the same page?

→ Will you change any house rules regarding guests now that your child has friends he may be attracted to? Are they allowed to be home alone together, with no adult supervision? May they spend time in his bedroom? How about at his partner's house?

→ Is there a limit to how much time you'd like your son's partner to be at the house or how long you'd consider too much time spent at their partner's house?

→ How would you feel about public displays of affection (PDAs) both inside the house and out and about?

→ What are your family's values and expectations when it comes to sexual contact? Are they based on values that feel honest and current to who you are today, or do they carry over from your own adolescence or teen years?

→ How can you best guide your son to know his own boundaries when it comes to romantic and sexual interactions? How will you convey that it's OK for him to not be ready to have sex?

→ Are you prepared to talk about proper condom use?

→ Have you talked about consent recently—what it looks and feels like?

You may also want to explore his (and your own) gendered expectations and values. For instance:

→ Do you think the boy should always pay for a date or should kids always pay their own way? Or maybe the asker always pays?

→ Do you believe he should open doors for someone he's dating?

→ Should he go inside to meet his date's parents before they leave?

→ Does he want to do all the planning himself, or does he hope to plan together?

He may feel these are all outdated customs, but you may feel there is a lot of value in some of them. Either way, just talk about it! There are no wrong answers here.

When you do discuss his plans, respect your teen's opinions on traditional gender roles—even if they are different from yours. As long as he has a plan and makes clear that he will show respect to his date in the ways that are meaningful to them, he's probably on the right track.

Helping Your Boy Develop His Own Sexual Ethics and Values

Boys may lose sight of their own values in pursuit of more surface goals like popularity, social acceptance, or even fleeting validation. Why? Because we often think that guys who hook up with lots of partners will be celebrated as "studs" or "players." In reality, the behavior can also indicate a boy has drifted from his values due to deeper emotional challenges. The following hypothetical is a great thought experiment to get boys talking about their sexual values systems.

Imagine Matteo, a handsome, affable college student who was a star athlete in high school. On a surf trip with his dad, Armando, he confesses that he's having trouble with girls at college.

Matteo had no problem meeting or connecting with girls as a teen. He casually dated a few girls from his school and had a short-term relationship with a girl from a neighboring high school when he was in eleventh grade. But most of the time, Matteo was known as more of a "player." He was respectful and friendly with girls, and they seemed to naturally gravitate toward him. While he had a reputation for hooking up with a lot of girls, nobody seemed to hold it against him.

This pattern continued into his freshman year of college, which fit well with his lifestyle at a school known for partying. But as a sophomore, Matteo started wishing he had one girl he could count on as a partner. He tells his dad he would really like a girlfriend, but he fears he couldn't stay faithful.

"What makes you feel like you can't be faithful?" his dad asks.

"I guess I don't really know who I am if I'm not, like, hooking up with a lot of girls," he confesses with a wince. "That's how I earned respect in high school—by getting girls to like me and having a high 'body count.' Now I don't know if that was a good thing to do."

A few questions Armando could ask Matteo to learn more:

→ What about a monogamous relationship sounds appealing to you?

→ Have you changed and matured in other ways—unrelated to dating and monogamy—that show your capacity to grow?

→ What would it feel like to *not* hook up with a bunch of girls?

→ Is there something about monogamy that scares you—aside from the fact that you think you don't know how to do it?

→ Can you envision yourself being happy with just one girl?

If your son isn't dating or hooking up yet, you can still ask some questions to get him thinking about his own values regarding dating and the types of relationships he might like someday.

Questions about hookups to ask your teens:

→ What are some good reasons to hook up with someone? What are some bad reasons?

→ In what circumstances would a casual hookup not feel right?

→ Can you imagine some reasons people hook up that might be more than just "because I wanted to"? Deeper reasons?

→ How will you know that your motivations for a hookup are really true to what you want and your own values?

→ How would you know if they just want to hold your hand or hug you?

→ How will you know when they want more, to kiss or be physically closer and more intimate?

→ How will you know when they don't want to do any of that? How will you respond?

→ What if they want to and you don't want to?

Hypotheticals (i.e., questions he doesn't have to answer, but rather just consider for himself):

→ Would you be comfortable hooking up with someone you don't know well?

→ Would you be OK hooking up with someone you don't want a relationship with?

→ What might make you regret hooking up with someone?

→ Who can you trust to talk to about sex, hookups, and dating that you feel could guide you toward sexual and romantic values that feel authentic to you?

Setting Limits Is Good for Boys Who Date Boys, Too

The natural instinct of many parents is to establish a lot of rules and boundaries around sex and relationships. But for parents of gay or bisexual boys, sometimes the opposite is true. In an effort to be affirming, parents today can sometimes be too permissive with their gay sons, a mistake social worker Michael Payne urges them to avoid. "There's always a risk that a kid may get in over his head," he warned us.

"Sometimes, when trying to be super accepting, parents may not set limits or enforce rules for the kid in fear that they will appear judgmental," Payne said. "They may also be afraid of constricting their gay child by setting limits the way they would with a straight kid of the same age."

When it comes to setting limits and rules for your household, Payne feels this is an area where "parenting is parenting" and good parenting means setting limits for our kids. For instance, "if you have an instinct

about someone they're hanging out with that's not a good influence, by
all means, speak up—as long as it's not so much about the sexuality as it
is about their behaviors."

We shouldn't allow our teens to wind up in situations they aren't
developmentally ready for just to signal that we accept our child's sexuality. Instead, "talk to your gay son about the limits in the household,

We asked boys:

How do you think adults talk about relationships differently to girls than to boys?

"Adults tell girls it's a horrible thing to be dating, while it's kinda the
opposite for boys."

—Roberto, age 14

"I feel like only girls get warned about abusive partners."

—Carson, age 14

"I feel like adults talk to boys from a standpoint that they have to be
careful in what they do, and make it clear how important it is that
the person they choose to be with is really who they wanna be with."

—Jake, age 20

"Adults talk to girls and tell them to 'be careful about who you get
with because boys are scary' and for boys I feel like it's more of
'make sure they respect you and aren't just playing you.'"

—Isaiah, age 17

"The vile fact of the matter is that girls are taught to defend
themselves from the inevitability of sexual assault and rape.
By comparison, very little energy goes into teaching boys that
treating people like this is unacceptable. Girls have to be on edge,
alert, constantly wary of everyone—and while boys do as well, it's
not really to the same extent. The little education provided to us is
terribly misdirected."

—Rory, age 16

your family values as far as relationships go, and emphasize the importance of getting to know somebody in a relationship."

Payne also suggests exploring sexual scenarios your teen may find
himself in that could be uncomfortable for him or even dangerous.

"Talk about peer pressure!" he urges. "Encourage him to think
about what he's comfortable with based on what he really wants," he
says, not what he thinks he *should* want.

Ask questions like: "Have you been in a situation where you are being
pressured to do something you don't feel like doing?" Explore scenarios
so he feels prepared, setting up a fictional scenario and asking, "What
would you do in that case? How would you handle that?"

This is solid advice for parenting *any* teen, regardless of gender or
sexuality, but what makes it especially important with gay or bisexual
boys is how it shows that you are willing to have conversations about
queer sex and sexuality. Just be sure you aren't focusing too much on the
negative, and that the positive, rewarding aspects of dating and sexuality
are reflected in your conversations, too.

The Power of Emotional Vulnerability

Anti-bullying educator Jamie Utt-Schumacher, PhD, has met with over
10,000 young men, giving talks and hosting conversations, meet-ups,
and discussion groups. He believes that one of the biggest ways we fail
to prepare our boys for relationships is by ignoring the topic of emotional vulnerability.

He believes teen boys are still conditioned to resist being vulnerable. "It's terrifying to them," he explains, "because of the ways we have
socialized them to understand what it means to be a boy in our society."

"When I was younger, I felt I had to project a certain way of being
a man," Utt-Schumacher shares. He believes that teenage boys often
wall off their ability to be vulnerable. "That's what we, as a society, have
told them to do," Utt-Schumacher explains. "But they have no idea what
they're missing out on: love, passion, connection, and true partnership,
among other wonderful parts of being truly engaged human beings."

Not only have we taught them to wall off their emotional vulnerability, we also often outright mock and condemn men and boys when
they show any "softer" feelings. But when it comes to relationships and

We asked boys:

What characteristics would you look for in a partner if you were interested in a relationship?

"I want to be in a relationship with someone who is able to voice themself but can be open to other opinions, and who can communicate their opinions even in the face of fear. I want to be in a relationship with someone who can enthusiastically put in their share of effort to keep the relationship going. I want to be in a relationship with someone who is aware of how people are incredibly complex and how people can change, who can accept how I change and let themself accept their own changes."

—Nat, age 17

"Someone who is a good friend, loyal, funny, kind, and shares some of the same interests as me."

—Carson, age 14

"A great personality. Someone who's like me in a way where we can have fun together. Shorter than me. Respectful but can also joke around. (I've had a girlfriend for the last three years already.)"

—Isaiah, age 17

"Someone who's fun to talk to, sweet, kind. Someone I can be weird around that still accepts me for it. Someone that will see my flaws and challenge me to correct them instead of perpetuating them and enabling them."

—Jake, age 20

"How nice they are, how smart they are, how kind they are."

—Elie, age 11

"Great morality and integrity of character."

—Jeff, age 16

dating, that stoic nature can become almost toxic to the boy—and, by extension, to his partners.

How can a man or even a teenage boy's romantic interactions be truly healthy if he's trying to balance a hardened exterior with the emotional vulnerability that naturally arises when we feel romantic or loving feelings toward someone?

We talk a lot about raising boys to be good men, but we don't often break down what that means when it comes to relationships—and that leaves our boys modeling their romantic relationships after what they feel they are *supposed to* have, whatever that means to them. This can lead to boys feeling insecure or "all over the place" when it comes to actually building relationships.

That's why we suggest starting conversations about the man your boy wants to be when he settles into a serious relationship. Does he want to settle down early and have a traditional marriage? Does he want to have many relationships and adventures with partners before deciding to get married? Or does he see himself never getting married at all?

He very well may not be able to imagine any of it right now, and that's OK. But when talking to our boys about dating and relationships, it's good to have them thinking about the men they want to grow up to be—and how that starts now, in their adolescent years.

Building Equal Partnerships

As a marriage and family therapist, Terrence Real sees many young couples who believe they are breaking the mold of traditional relationships, but who are still stuck in unhealthy and outdated relationship patterns from the past.

"A lot of times," Real told us, "young men in these relationships will allow for emotion and be more emotionally sharing, but they'll pair that with traditional male entitlement."

In other words, "while I am a more sensitive guy, mostly what I'm sensitive to are my own feelings, not yours," he explained.

So, how do we teach our boys to be more aware of their own needs, so they can be healthy, loving, supportive partners? "You have to make it explicit," Real suggests. "It isn't just about, 'What does the world have for me?' It's also about asking, 'How can I grow by learning to truly love?'"

We want our boys to be prepared for healthy, mutually fulfilling relationships. To do that, we can help our boys practice imagining how people feel—not just partners, but also their friends, classmates, and even us, their parents and caregivers.

Therapist Brian Spitulnik explained to us that "many young men don't know what an actual equal partnership looks like or that you can have an interdependence without having a codependence." Yes, Spitulnik insists, "You *can* be an individual while sharing your life with someone."

While our boys probably won't be thinking about sharing their lives with someone just yet, it's never too early to start thinking about healthy relationship dynamics.

Ask your boys:

→ What relationships can you think of—in real life or in fiction—that seem like they're healthy and equal partnerships? Which ones can you tell are not?

→ Which one of these can you see yourself enjoying being in the most?

→ How do you think you can tell when one person in a relationship holds all or most of the power? Would you be comfortable in that situation?

→ What could you do if you felt like a relationship wasn't as equal or healthy as it could be?

→ Can a relationship be truly healthy and equal if one person won't open up emotionally, apologize, or do other things society might see as "not masculine"?

The goal is simply to get our boys thinking differently about relationships, emphasizing equality, balance, and the health of the relationship overall—which sadly is not discussed with boys often enough.

Getting Serious

When your son seems interested in getting serious with someone, ask him what he wants out of a relationship. Remind him:

→ There are no wrong answers to questions about relationships.

→ It's OK to just want to kiss or be near someone, even if he doesn't want to be their boyfriend—as long as he is being honest with the other person.

→ It's also OK if he just wants to text, call, or video chat a person he likes, even if he doesn't want to go on dates or have a physical relationship with the other person.

→ It's a good idea for him to ask his partner what they want from a relationship, too, so he can see if their expectations match.

It can be easy for a young man to fall into an expectation that being nice to someone they like means the other person will fall in love with them. While being kind should mean someone is kind in return, attention, love, and sex are never guaranteed or owed.

It might help to use an example to illustrate this, asking him to imagine someone liking him and being super kind and generous—but this isn't a person he feels romantic about or attracted to. Should he get into a relationship with them anyway? Now, extend that out to the person he likes, and help him use empathy to imagine how it doesn't—and shouldn't—work like that.

Questions to ask your son before his relationship gets serious:

→ What do you think you want from this relationship? To spend a ton of time together, have all the same friends, and hang out after school most days? Or something more casual like hanging out with a group of friends together and maybe a few one-on-one dates a month?

→ How much contact makes sense to you? Texts or social media connections on and off all day? Do you check in when you go somewhere, or does that feel controlling?

→ Do you feel like you can balance your schoolwork and activities along with this relationship? What will you do and say if it feels like it's getting to be too much?

→ What will you do if you have a fight/disagreement? Who do you talk about it with? Who do you feel can support you and give you good advice? What would feel right as far as tone/intensity of these discussions and how do you bow out when things get too intense?

→ Is there something we can do to help you when you feel overwhelmed by the relationship? Would it be helpful to know that we can set stricter rules when you feel like things are getting too intense? Would it be helpful to have a code you can text one of us, something you could say to us to get you out of a situation?

→ What are your expectations about sex and physical intimacy in this relationship and how does that fit in with our family's values and the values of your partner?

→ How will you know if your sexual desire for your partner comes from an authentic part of yourself? What outside influences may motivate you to start a physical romantic relationship? For example, what your friends are doing, fear of missing out, fear of disappointing your partner, a desire to make sure your partner's desires are being fulfilled, or maybe the notion that being physical with your partner means you love them more (confusing love and sex).

→ What will you do if and when your partner's feelings about any of these things differ from yours?

Dealing with Breakups

We've all seen plenty of movies where a woman or teen girl whose heart has been broken sits on her couch surrounded by girlfriends or next to her mom, talking and crying. It's funny—and honestly quite sad—to think that there isn't a similarly cliché image of boys and men processing their feelings in healthy ways. Instead, we get to see the brokenhearted guy angrily punching the wall or maybe doing things to their ex that border on stalking, like showing up at her work or watching her house from outside. But crying and talking about his feelings or hugging his parents? That's a scene we rarely get, even though it's common in real life.

Boys and men can also feel obliterated by a breakup and cry themselves to sleep night after night. Boys, too, can wonder why they weren't good enough or what they did wrong. Boys may deal with self-esteem issues after being dumped, just like girls. And yet, as a society, we ask them to toughen up and move on by finding a random hookup or someone new.

No wonder so many boys end up angry and depressed and not knowing where to turn.

The most important thing for parents to remember is that young love may be felt very deeply, and a person's first heartbreak often stays with them forever. As adults, we've likely experienced multiple breakups—maybe even a divorce or the end of a very long-term relationship—and it's easy to minimize the seriousness of a teen breakup. But telling your son that it was a meaningless relationship or that he shouldn't feel devastated by the end of it will only make him feel ashamed of his natural emotions or try to push them away.

First, talk to your boy about how to know when a relationship is over—before it appears to be the end. Make it clear that there are no right or wrong answers, but that it's helpful to know what your deal-breakers are or signs that you're not feeling the way you used to.

Make it clear that he doesn't have an obligation to stay in a relationship where he's not happy. When you're discussing this, make it clear that boys and men can also be victims of emotional abuse, controlling behavior, and even relationship violence, and that there's no shame in asking for help dealing with an unhealthy situation and that you will support him without judgment or blame.

If your son is considering a breakup, it's wise to discuss what he envisions for his breakup, and make sure that he understands that while he might like a "just be friends" breakup, his partner may want a "no contact" breakup. While neither of them are wrong in what they'd like, he would still need to be prepared to respect a "no contact" breakup framework.

In addition to reassuring him that what he feels is real, explaining that almost every human has been through an experience like this can be comforting, too, as long as it doesn't come across like his feelings are being minimized.

Instead of saying: "It's nothing, move on and forget about your ex."

Try saying: "I know it feels awful right now, I'm so sorry. The good news is, almost all of us have felt what you're feeling right now, and it does get better."

We asked boys:

What kind of messages have you received about dating and relationships? Where did you hear them?

"I heard that you can like whoever you want. I learned it from some Pride people who came to our school."

—Elie, age 11

"Be smart—don't date someone who would use you or not complement your life. I learned the most from my mom and my health teacher."

—Carson, age 14

"I was taught very young not to date and not to get into relationships. My mother was very firm on that fact. And through the media I got the sense that relationships are extremely important and not to be done willy-nilly."

—Jordan, age 19

"I heard this from my parents and friends that I shouldn't date early, like in middle school or high school, because it's bound to end wrong and distract me from school."

—Isaiah, age 17

"I heard on a TikTok video explaining flirting to autistic people (which I am, hey hey!) that flirting essentially consists of a back-and-forth game of raising the stakes. One person might make a suggestive statement, and the other might proceed to reply with something slightly more flirty in turn. This really helped me understand how to flirt!"

—Nat, age 17

In addition to validating his feelings, make sure you let him know that it's OK to cry. These days there are few parents who explicitly tell our sons to suck it up or that "boys don't cry." But the message is still strong out in the world, particularly among their middle school and high school peers. It can be helpful to remind them that they are always safe to cry and feel all sorts of big emotions with you and within your home.

For dads and other male adults, if you remember a bad breakup, share the story with your boy and don't sugarcoat it or make yourself seem tough. He needs to hear that he's not alone.

> **Example:** "I remember when I was in tenth grade and Jenny
> Ramirez dumped me the day after school started. I had to
> spend the whole day walking around feeling like crap knowing
> I would be made fun of if I cried at school. When I got home,
> I really let it rip and cried the whole day. When your grandma
> got done with work, she made my favorite dinner, and we
> watched TV together. The next day was way better, but it took
> a while to stop sucking so much."

This might feel vulnerable or awkward, but it's good for your boy to hear that you've been there, that he's normal, and that it's going to feel better. What to watch out for when your boy is breaking up:

→ Have a conversation with your son about how he should talk about his ex, making clear that saying degrading things about his ex won't help him feel better any sooner.

→ Feeling anger and focusing on what bugged him about his ex can be a normal part of dealing with grief, but it should be made clear that degrading language, such as "she's a bitch" or "she is a slut, anyway" is unacceptable and will only create more anger, more drama, and more negativity in his life.

→ Reinforce that dehumanizing language can become a habit and even affect how he sees and feels about other girls or potential partners in the future.

→ Keep an eye out for aggressive or controlling behavior: while being angry is a normal part of processing heartbreak, burdening another person with that anger is not healthy or "normal," and it does not help people heal.

→ Showing up at an ex's place of work, waiting outside of their house, and making threats to them or a new partner are all inappropriate reactions and may even be considered a crime.

Teen Love Is Real Love

When a friend of one of Joanna's sons asked if he could speak with her about a breakup, she knew he must've really been struggling. After all, it takes a lot for a teen to reach out to an adult for support with something so personal.

"I know I don't really know what love is," he told her, "but I really miss Kylie and feel like I still really love her."

"You absolutely know what love is," Joanna reassured him. "I'm not sure who told you that you don't, but I don't think anyone should tell you what you feel or don't feel."

The relief in this teen's voice was palpable, and her son, who was also involved in the conversation, smiled. This teenager had nearly been gaslit into believing that he couldn't take his feelings for his ex-girlfriend seriously, causing him to doubt himself, which was a very unsettling feeling for him. In order to mourn his breakup, his original feelings of love for Kylie needed to be validated.

Another topic that may arise after a breakup is the idea of reuniting. You may have heard a lot of negative things about your child's ex and have some biases against them—justified or not. Despite all of that, in most cases, it is your son and his partner's decision—not yours.

Instead, start a conversation where you ask open-ended questions and do a lot of listening. Get him thinking about what a reunion really means.

Asking open-ended, non-leading questions allows your child to give longer, more detailed answers than simple "yes" or "no" questions. While yes/no questions can be helpful when talking about our feelings, when followed up with more detailed inquiries, open-ended questions often inspire us to think about what feels right. They also create space and time to talk through answers.

Examples of open-ended, non-leading questions that might be helpful:

→ What will you do if you start feeling like you want to get back together?

→ What is a healthy exploration of that versus something that comes off as stalker-ish or coercive?

→ When will you know if reuniting is off the table or an unhealthy choice for one or both of you?

→ How will you know whether your desire to reunite is really about pursuing a healthy relationship, or a natural response to being sad and lonely after a breakup?

Talk to Your Boys About Heartbreak, Anger, and Revenge

If you haven't been dumped in a while, you may have forgotten how angry it can make you feel. This is natural and doesn't mean you (or your boy!) are messed up or deviant. It also doesn't mean you have to act on that anger. Preparing kids for this wide range of emotions can help when the time comes that they have to deal with them.

Try saying: "Just so you know, it's normal to feel like you want to yell at the person who hurt you or say things to make sure they're hurting as much as you are. As tempting as that may be, it doesn't help people get over heartbreak any faster and, in the end, just makes it all feel worse."

This same conversation can be had about taking sadness or anger out on parents, friends, and siblings. It's tempting, but if we can "name" that feeling and its cause, it's easier to make sure not to displace it and make someone else suffer for pain caused by a breakup or rejection.

Relationships can be hard, but everything is easier when you have someone reliable to turn to for advice and comfort. Parents can be a source of comfort and healing for a kid going through a breakup or dealing with rejection. This may involve keeping him busy, distracting him with activities, maybe a weekend away where there's no cell service, etc. Balance the effort with making sure they know you don't expect them to "snap out of it" and continuing to be emotionally available for them to talk or cry.

REMEMBER THIS:

❶ Because of the way they are socialized, boys often are not prepared for romantic relationships in the ways girls are. This can cause them to feel a wide range of emotions upon realizing that romance usually means feeling vulnerable: from anger to jealousy to dependence. We need to prepare them to handle all these feelings in a healthy way.

❷ The world often discourages boys from being vulnerable, and if they've been hurt before, it may be challenging to let themselves be emotionally open. We can prepare our kids to be vulnerable in a healthy way, and emphasize how wonderful it can be to feel that with a partner.

❸ Boys need guidance and support during all the phases of relationships, and parents can prepare them to show up for each stage in the healthiest way possible.

❹ Teen heartbreak is real, even in boys. He's not being "dramatic," he's feeling big feelings and that's OK. Don't minimize them!

❺ Lots of people think getting back together with an ex is the best plan when they are lonely or feeling heartbroken. Talk to your boys about what that really means and the realities of reunion, so they don't have to go through the roller coaster of being in an on-again, off-again relationship.

"I think being aware of sexuality in a more practical way can prepare you more for real life. For a lot of boys, 'The Sex Talk' doesn't really extend past the sterile biological discussions, which leaves them hanging on how to handle themselves in their sex lives as they develop."

—Wade, age 21

Chapter 5

Talk to Your Boys About

SEX AND SEXUALITY

"Be responsible"

"You'll be safe, right?"

"Just don't get anyone pregnant!"

In some families, little directives like this are about as detailed as the conversations about sex get, at least with boys. Parents sometimes say that they are waiting for their son to ask questions, or that they don't want to make anyone feel awkward. Maybe they assume school covers things in a sex ed class.

Why does this matter? Well, sex is one of the fundamental ways that humans connect with one another, and can be a source of great pleasure, joy, and fulfillment. Of course, it also carries a relatively high degree of risk—it can contribute to heartbreak, infections, and unplanned pregnancies. It is also only one piece of the bigger puzzle that is the topic of sexuality. Sexuality includes things like attraction, desire, orientation, gender, and behavior, all of which deserve some attention.

These topics can be complicated. And a lot of parents were raised with a lot of shame around sex and sexuality, making it harder for us to talk as openly as we wish we could.

We know our children deserve better. They deserve factual information about their bodies and their sexuality, and they benefit so much from having supportive, empathetic adults on their side as they move toward adulthood.

When talking about sexuality, you'll get lots of opportunities to address misconceptions and biases, and you and your boy can practice learning together as novel topics come up.

Through these talks you can address common concerns boys have, such as fear of rejection, fear of not being "good at sex," fear of harming someone. You can help boys learn how to recognize their sexual feelings and desires without letting those desires control their lives. You can practice raising boys who can communicate clearly and without shame, and work to help them become good "sexual citizens." You can talk openly about gender identity and sexual orientation, and you can let them know that you'll love and support them no matter what.

CHECK IN WITH YOURSELF

Before starting to talk to a boy about sexuality, it's wise to spend a little time reflecting on your own beliefs and biases.

> Do you think sexuality is an important component of life?

> How did you learn about sexuality when you were growing up?

> Where do you think boys should learn about sexuality, and who should teach them?

> Do you think schools do enough to teach about sexuality?

> How do you feel about LGBTQ+ inclusion?

> What are some problems you think might develop if boys don't learn much about sexuality from trusted adults?

Own Your Discomfort

If you were someone who was raised never talking about sex with the trusted adults in your life or encouraged to feel ashamed or even "dirty" when discussing it, you will likely start out with some discomfort around this topic. That's OK! You're not wrong for feeling this way.

Joanna, who was raised in a highly conservative Evangelical community in the era of purity culture, grew up with a lot of shame around sex and sexuality, and wondered if she would ever be able to talk to her kids about sex without shame or embarrassment. She wanted them to feel empowered, to learn that their bodies belong solely to themselves, and to know that feeling desire is healthy and natural.

But that feeling of shame lingered. It felt like part of *who she was*, and she wondered why some people could so thoroughly own their sexuality and she couldn't. Why did it all feel like such a dirty secret for her?

Then one day, she heard Dr. Laura Berman on the radio discussing the shame she'd witnessed in many of her clients. She advised parents to own their shame and embarrassment and practice talking about body parts and sex—and their shame and embarrassment—before they even start the process of talking to their kids about sex.

She also advised parents to start naming children's genitals correctly from day one. Not a "pee pee" but a penis. Not a "down there" but a vulva or vagina. Dr. Berman advised that, as they grew up, sharing science-based facts about sperm and eggs was a great place to start. As the kids get older, you share more information, and it goes from simple biology to human sexuality.

Joanna followed this model and, after a while, she realized she wasn't embarrassed anymore. Talking about sex and bodies and desire and love with her kids started to flow naturally, an idea that would've been preposterous during her own teen years.

Changes like these, which so many of us have to make, disrupt generations of shame and silence—and we hope to empower you to have your own shame-free, empowered conversations with your tweens and teens.

How to Get Started

Ideally, conversations about bodies and sexuality happen throughout a child's life, with the level of information gradually increasing over time in an age-appropriate way. Realistically, we know these conversations often happen in fits and starts.

Before beginning these talks, it can be useful to think about your ultimate goals. Here are a few you might consider:

→ Reinforce the concept that sexuality is an important part of being a human.

→ Normalize having questions and concerns related to different aspects of sexuality at different times of life.

→ Establish ourselves as "askable adults" who are available to field questions without shame or embarrassment.

→ Connect them to resources in the community they might need, like reproductive health care or therapy.

→ Make sure that boys understand the importance of consent and how to put it into practice.

→ Make sure boys understand the basics of sexual health care—how to take care of their bodies and reduce the risk of STIs and unplanned pregnancies.

→ Provide space to learn about and discuss phone-based and online sexual interactions.

→ If you feel awkward, own it by saying something like, "I wasn't raised with a trusted adult to talk to about things like this, but I want you to feel safe to talk to me about anything."

Human sexuality is a fascinating and important topic, and it deserves ongoing attention. Don't try to fit everything you want to discuss into one talk. A better strategy is to plan for a series of talks. One great thing about having these talks today, unlike in prior generations, is that there are so many resources available. There are countless books, podcasts, newsletters, and YouTube videos available on the subject of sexuality, so if you want to learn more about a topic you have lots of places to turn. Some adults use these resources to do research before talking to teens, and others look for media they can share with their teens to prompt discussion. These are both good approaches!

The Big Picture of Sexuality

As a high school health teacher, Christopher has taught classes introducing the concept of sexuality to thousands of students in San Francisco's public schools. One tone-setting activity he's used a lot is to have students create a "human sexuality person." Using five pieces of paper, students create a person that reflects some of the big influences and concerns that come up when people talk about sexuality. It doesn't capture everything, but it gets across the idea that "sexuality" is a big topic that affects all humans, and each of them experiences it a little differently.

Here's how he introduces it to students:

Many people think sex and sexuality is just about body parts and sexual behaviors. But our sexuality is so much more than that. Each person has a different perception, connection, and understanding of their own sexuality.

The sexual decisions we make in life are not only connected to whether we are attracted to someone or not, but are also related to the different values we hold, what we have learned from our families and our cultures, how we feel about our bodies, and more.

By looking at the "big picture" of sexuality we can begin to explore all of our ideas around these topics. This can help us understand our values and beliefs about being sexual and how they relate to who we are and how we behave.

The students then answer prompts on five different sheets of paper, each with a different focus:

Name Your Values, Beliefs, and Norms:

→ What have your parents/caregivers taught you about sex?

→ What beliefs about sex, dating, and relationships does your family have?

→ What have you learned from the media about sex?

→ Where else have you heard people giving advice related to sex? What did they say?

Sexual Orientation:

→ What sexual orientations have you heard of?

→ What have you heard about these?

→ How are people of different orientations portrayed in the media?

→ Are there expectations for people with different sexual orientations? What are they?

→ Where do you think these expectations come from?

Gender Roles:

→ What is gender?

→ How do we learn about gender?

→ What genders have you heard of?

→ What expectations do you think society has for people of those genders?

→ How do you feel about gender and gender roles?

Communication and Relationships:

→ What types of relationships have you heard of?

→ How do people start relationships? How do people end relationships?

→ Are these healthy or unhealthy ways of starting/ending relationships?

→ What kind of qualities makes a "good" partner?

Body Image and Body Parts:

→ What body parts do people associate with sexual development?

→ What different ideas do people have about these body parts?

→ How do people learn more about their bodies?

→ How does our image of our bodies affect us?

→ According to TV, movies, and music, what types of bodies or what body parts are valued or considered beautiful/desirable? Do you agree with the media on this? If not, what do they get wrong?

Once the students have recorded their answers on each page, the papers are put all together—one head, four limbs—to create a unique Human Sexuality Person. Although this was designed for the classroom, it would be easy to do at home. A parent and child could learn a lot by doing this exercise together.

Boys Need to Understand Birth Control

Our society often tells women in heterosexual relationships that preventing pregnancy is primarily their responsibility. If we want more men to step up to share in this effort, we must start explaining that to our boys. We also need to start teaching them about the many options now available to prevent pregnancy.

Condoms remain the easiest method for boys and young men to access and use, and they have many benefits—they're inexpensive, can be used spontaneously, and they are effective at dramatically reducing the risk of both pregnancy and sexually transmitted infections. Boys should know where to get condoms and how to use them well before they become sexually active. You may also want to make sure they know to get lube, which can make condoms more slippery, reducing friction and making accidental breaks less likely.

In addition to condoms, boys should be able to explain how other common contraception methods, like the Pill, the Patch, and the IUD, work, and how to access them in your community. It's important for boys to understand how they work, how effective they are, and how much effort it takes to use them well. Birth control needs to be seen as a shared responsibility!

Sex: The Ground Rules

Some boys may be having sex with different people. Some boys may be having sex with just one person. Some may start having sex in their younger teens, others not until college or later and some may choose to wait until marriage. We can make sure our kids understand that even though it might feel like "everyone is doing it," that's not always the case. But there are a few fundamental ground rules that all kids need to know, no matter how sexually active they are:

→ All sex should include partners who are enthusiastic, excited to participate, and are enjoying themselves.

→ Sex (and all intimate touching) requires consent. That means asking for a "yes" before proceeding, rather than waiting for someone to say "no" to unwanted touch (see more on consent in the next chapter).

What do you wish adults understood about dating and relationships today?

"Talking to boys about differences in sexuality at a younger age will make them more comfortable being themselves. I think parents should say in explicit terms that it's OK if you're not straight or if you're not cis."

—Wade, age 21

"I wish adults knew that guys get stressed about relationships, too. Like, it's not just girls. The first relationship I was in was with a girl who liked me a lot but I wasn't sure if I liked her. She wanted to be with me all the time and was very needy, and I felt like I didn't know how to say no to her. I was super anxious because I was so afraid of hurting the feelings of this girl, and I didn't even like her that way after a while. It was like being carried away in a riptide and always feeling like a bad guy because I didn't like her enough, and (in her mind) I was doing things wrong all the time. I really didn't know what to do."

—Cam, age 16

"Be open-minded about who your child chooses to date because judging someone by appearance may deprive you of knowing an amazing human being. Please don't punish your child for wanting to date but make sure that they are safe and absolutely have consent."

—Jake, age 20

"I wish adults understood and taught kids that communication is everything. Consent is not present enough. Some people enter relationships with the intention of short-term fun, others enter with the intention of something permanent, and some don't have an intention in mind. Both partners should agree on the same intention, or else there will be HURT at some point or other."

—Nat, age 17

→ If any partner, at any time, appears to not be enjoying themselves, the sex should stop—even if the partner hasn't asked for it to stop—so a conversation can be had about whether they want to continue. Remember, even if you said "yes" to something, you can always change your mind, take a break, or stop.

→ Pressuring someone to have sex with you is called coercion. If someone is coerced into saying "yes" or agreeing to an activity, that is nonconsensual sex and can be considered rape or sexual assault.

→ Sex should happen when both teen partners are sober, and regardless of how old the participants are, sex should never happen when one or more partners is drunk, high, or otherwise incapable of making a clear decision.

→ This also means both partners should be awake. Touching someone who is asleep or passed out is not OK and can also be considered rape or assault.

What If My Son Is Gay?

Experts agree that you don't need to change too much about how you talk about sexuality, relationships, or even sex just because a boy might be attracted to other boys.

Michael Payne, a therapist in the Washington, DC, area who specializes in men's issues, LGBTQ+ identity, and sexual orientation, suggests that the most important thing to do is create a home where open conversation is encouraged and feelings are validated. If a kid feels safe talking to you about his feelings in general, he is more likely to feel safe talking to you about his sexuality.

"It's about creating an environment where you want to get to know your kid—rather than them having to teach you who they are," Payne advises.

He does caution against a few common traps that even the most well-meaning parents can fall into:

Don't put them in a corner with their sexuality

"Never ask them directly 'Are you gay?' before they introduce the concept themselves," Payne told us. He went on to explain that he's heard of people who have been put on the spot like this—even with well-intentioned parents—who felt they couldn't tell the truth. Maybe they didn't know for sure how to name their feelings or maybe they simply weren't comfortable talking about it yet.

"They may become uncomfortable and say something just to stop the conversation, like, 'Oh, no, I'm not,'" Payne says. "After that, it gets a lot harder to go back and say his truth, to eventually tell you, 'Actually, I am gay.'"

Ultimately, we want to avoid associating our boys' sexual identities with shame or secrets, which could easily happen if a boy felt backed into a corner, conversationally, before he was ready to talk it.

Don't immediately associate gayness or bisexuality with sex

"When I came out in 2001, the first thing my mom did was take me to get an HIV test—and that was really scarring!" psychotherapist Brian Spitulnik told us.

Just because your son has come out doesn't mean he's having sex. While you should eventually talk about consent and safe sex, it shouldn't be the first point of conversation. Instead, we can ask about the person he likes, talk about the type of dates he'd like to go on, and learn more about what's happening in his social circle as far as dating and sex.

Don't reward people-pleasing or emotional conformity

"For gay kids, it's about normalizing," Spitulnik says. "So many of the boys I see were these sad, sweet boys [growing up]. But boys are not supposed to be sad and not supposed to be sweet. Many of these boys were told 'stop being so sensitive,' which can be incredibly harmful to a kid regardless of gender or sexuality. For gay boys, it can be hard to not associate this repression of emotion with their sexual identity—which only furthers feelings of shame and inadequacy."

Similarly, Payne told us that a lot of gay kids become people-pleasers after a childhood where they may have felt isolated in their experiences.

"Think about families who are ethnic or racial or religious minorities," he says. "The family is having the shared experience of being a minority. [Kids in these families] can talk about it and relate to it because they have that common ground with their family members.

"But for sexual minority kids," he continued, "when they start to realize that they may be gay, it can be alienating."

This can even happen in a family where a boy is loved and accepted— at least on the surface. But that child may still feel different, like he's not masculine enough or that he makes his family members uncomfortable.

In response, he may tamp down some of the most vibrant parts of himself in order to please others and feel more accepted.

How to show acceptance for your queer kid's sexuality

Showing up for your queer kid is about a lot more than putting a Pride flag pin on your jean jacket—though that is a lovely show of support. It also requires "validating every single thing your kid feels," according to Spitulnik. Just listen and let them know you hear them and you're listening and that their feelings are worth your time.

In addition to validating their emotions, Payne suggests showing your kid acceptance in your actions as well as your words. Here are a few ways to do this:

→ Watch TV and movies where characters are LGBTQ+, and talk positively about them.

→ Be inclusive of the LGBTQ+ folks in your community and speak positively of the queer folks you know.

→ Talk openly about your support for equality-based policies in politics or within your faith.

→ Shut down homophobia if it arises in your home or with your family.

→ Ask your kid what TV or movies he'd most like to watch with you, and follow his lead without complaints.

→ Apologize if, in the past, you've made some mistakes in talking about LGBTQ+ issues and pledge to keep learning and doing better.

➜ Support them if they want to learn more about PrEP, the preventative medication that can lower people's chances of contracting HIV. Be sure to add that it's also OK if he's not sexually active or feels like he's not ready for sex, yet, just like you would with a straight teen.

Talk to Your Boys About Homophobia

When Joanna's oldest son reached middle school, he shared how many guys in his class casually used the word "fag" at school. She was shocked. She truly believed that casual-but-overt homophobia in progressive areas had gone the way of the dodo. She also knew the parents of many of the boys routinely saying it—and many of them were proudly and openly pro-LGBTQ+. How did this happen?

That's when she realized that there were words parents told their kids not to say, including swear words, blasphemous words, and bigotry-based words, but they'd never separated "naughty" words from hurtful, hate-based words. That meant there were a whole bunch of kids who had no idea about the history or impact of words like this one (as well as racist and sexist ones). So talk to your boys about homophobia. Here's a sample script:

> It wasn't that long ago that discrimination against LGBTQ+ people was legal. Until 2015, only male-female couples could get married, which meant gay and lesbian couples didn't have any of the same rights to care for each other or inherit property as straight couples did. It was really sad.
>
> Throughout much of our history it was also really dangerous to be an out LGBTQ+ person. Someone might attack, beat, or even kill you simply because you were gay. What makes it even worse is that homophobia also meant that you weren't protected, so people who attacked and even murdered LGBTQ+ people for no reason sometimes just walked free.
>
> Even though a lot has changed today, there are still places where it's dangerous to be queer, and lots of LGBTQ+ people carry some trauma from how unsafe it was for so long. On top of all that, lots of LGBTQ+ kids fear that their parents will stop loving them if they are open about who they are. Many

of these kids are still told that being gay is a sin. Some kids are told that they cannot live with their parents and may lose their parents entirely if they are queer while others may be told their parents will always love them, but will hate the "gay" parts of their identities. This often causes profound emotional distress for kids who feel they cannot simply "cut out" their gayness from their identity.

Now ask:

Now that you know that history and how some LGBTQ+ kids feel, how do you think it makes them feel to hear people using words like "fag" in the locker room or at school? Do you think that makes them feel safe? What else might they be feeling when they hear it?

Finally, find solutions together.

Try saying: "It's good to know that you won't say those words. It's always better to err on the side of not hurting people who haven't done anything to you."

What can you say when other kids are doing it? I know you don't want to draw their hate, or become the target. Are there things you've seen popular kids do, or older kids, that has worked in the past to diffuse an awkward situation regarding homophobic slurs?

Sometimes it's as simple as saying, "Hey, that's not cool" or just "Knock it off" or "Don't be rude."

Inspire empathy:

When kids throw around homophobic slurs in the locker room, they often don't stop to consider how an LGBTQ+ peer might feel hearing this. It's likely they believe there are no gay kids around, as they assume everyone who is gay is already out. Young people today are coming out publicly younger than ever—but the average is still around age sixteen. That means there are many who will not come out until after high school.

Remind your boy that we don't always know someone's history or full identity, and they can't truly know who is going to be hurt, scared, or offended when they participate in homophobic jokes or use hate-based slurs.

It doesn't take much to simply not be hateful. It's easy to just not say those words. Use other words without such a painful history. Even better, imagine being the kid who's hearing that word and feeling scared or sad—and imagine how you'd feel knowing that there are guys in your school who would never say such things. And imagine how great it would feel to hear someone tell those guys to knock it off.

Wrestling with Hard Questions

Researchers at Harvard University's Making Caring Common project say they've found that high school and college students enthusiastically engage with ethical questions such as:

→ What do I do if I know my friend is cheating on his girlfriend who is also my friend?

→ Is cheating ever justified?

→ Is it exploitation when a high school senior hooks up with a college freshman?

→ Is it OK for one person to pay for everything in a relationship if they have more money than their partner?

You can discuss questions like this with your son and share answers together. It might be useful to try to see things from the perspective of each of the people involved. You can also talk about methods to resolve the situation in a fair, honest, and caring way.

Big questions like this force kids to work through these ideas and can help on many levels:

→ They develop complex thinking and problem-solving skills.

→ They cultivate the ability to consider multiple perspectives and sort out their ethical obligations to others, which is a big part of developing empathy and decreasing tendencies toward impulsiveness.

→ They practice ethical reasoning when dealing with conflicting loyalties.

→ They learn how to take up questions about human rights and dignity.

Myths About Boys and Sex

Sometimes when people are talking to boys about sex, stereotypes show up unintentionally. Here are a few:

MYTH: All boys are interested in having sex and want it all the time.

MYTH: All boys start out straight and are interested in girls.

MYTH: Boys aren't interested in love or committed relationships.

MYTH: Boys are only interested in partners who look like models.

MYTH: Boys need sex and have physical pain when rejected.

MYTH: A boy would never say "no" to a girl or woman who wanted sex or physical intimacy.

It's important to remember that every boy is unique, and we need to drop our assumptions about what they desire and care about. Strive to accept them just as they are, even if it doesn't fit with stereotypes. Reject and debunk the myths that end up putting some boys in danger.

In an article, "Five Tips For Guiding Teens and Young Adults in Developing Healthy Romantic Relationships," the Making Caring Common Project encourages adults and teens to pay attention to the relationships they see in the media and in real life to observe how couples deal with stress and problems:

"Maintaining healthy relationships requires a range of skills, including the ability to communicate honestly and effectively, to jointly solve problems, to manage anger, and to be generous. Healthy relationships also greatly benefit from the ability to zoom in—to take another's perspective in a real and deep way—and to zoom out—to step back for a more wide-angle view of the relationship and its dynamics, strengths, and challenges."

REMEMBER THIS:

❶ Talking to boys about sexuality is important to their emotional development.

❷ Sexuality is about a lot more than sex. It includes gender roles, relationships, sexual orientation, values, and more.

❸ Don't try to fit everything into one talk. Try to make it an ongoing conversation that deepens over time.

❹ Use books, videos, and social media as learning aids.

❺ Encourage your boy to get critical about media.

❻ Don't let slurs and hurtful words go unaddressed. Be clear with your expectations around the kind of language that's off limits, and explain why it's important to you.

❼ Don't assume all boys want casual sex.

❽ Encourage teens to think philosophically about relationships and use situations you see in the real world or in the media to fuel these discussions.

"One of the most important interpersonal skills for everyone to master is consent. To say I feel strongly about consent is an understatement— particularly when talking about sex. A relationship cannot be considered healthy if those involved don't have equal say or don't feel comfortable saying no; communication and mutual respect are crucial for success."

—Rory, age 16

Chapter 6

Talk to Your Boys About

CONSENT

C onsent is a powerful way to introduce kids of almost any age to the concept of bodily autonomy. At its core, consent is the principle that people have the right to make decisions about their own bodies and the expectation that others around them will honor those limits. This is a concept that we can start teaching our children in toddlerhood, and one that will evolve in complexity as they grow into teens.

In the past, conversations about consent largely focused on a "No Means No" standard—the idea that if someone is touching you and you're not into it, you should be able to say "no" and expect them to stop. Recently, there's been a movement to shift to a "Yes Means Yes" standard, sometimes called "enthusiastic consent." Essentially this means that before kissing, touching, or other types of sexual contact, the people involved should give an affirmative "Yes!" if it's something they really want to do.

Expanding the definition of consent can prompt a lot of meaningful—sometimes even philosophical—discussions, and we think it's likely to lead to safer, more trusting, and ultimately more pleasurable and fulfilling encounters. This shift also presents us with a tremendous opportunity to have deep discussions with our boys about how to articulate their own wishes and desires, how to respect other people's boundaries, and how to make connections that feel good to everyone involved.

Writer and activist Jaclyn Friedman is one of the people who helped popularize the "Yes Means Yes" standard. She is the executive director of EducateUS, an organization focused on "a complete transformation of K–12 public sex education in the United States." In a 2022 essay, Friedman explained the personal reason she's so passionate about sex ed advocacy:

"When I was twenty years old, I was sexually assaulted by someone I knew. He wasn't someone I was dating or even liked, but we were at a party together, and he followed me back to my room uninvited.

"In the aftermath, it became clear that this was not a guy who was used to thinking about how his actions affect other people, a guy who had never once considered the concept of consent, and one who definitely didn't think he would face any consequences if he just took what he wanted. In other words, the guy who hurt me had been failed by his sex and relationships education, and I have been forever harmed by the education he didn't get."

We are so grateful to Friedman for sharing her story—reflections like this have real power to make change. The messaging here is a strong call to action for better sex education in our schools. It is also an opportunity to make sure that all of our boys receive clear messages about consent in schools and at home.

These conversations are increasingly happening in schools. A number of members of our boys' panel mentioned studying consent in school, and several told us they learned about FRIES, an acronym popularized by Planned Parenthood that's used to teach the elements of a consensual interaction (see box on next page).

Shafia Zaloom, who teaches health courses at the Urban School in San Francisco, tries to get students thinking deeply about these issues: "When I teach about consent, I always encourage students to think of it as a 'vibe,' an orientation to relationships, and not just a legal responsibility or the very low bar of 'not a felony!'

"Consent laws are important because they protect people during moments when they may not be able to themselves," Zaloom told us. "Consent is the essential foundation. It's what holds everything up. And it's a pretty low bar for a positive and pleasurable sexual experience. There's so much more to think about, to take into consideration, to be attuned to, if we're talking about promoting healthy sexuality and relationships that are grounded in mutual respect, empathy, care, and dignity."

Consent Is as Easy as FRIES

Freely given

Consenting is a choice you make without pressure, manipulation, or under the influence of drugs or alcohol.

Reversible

Anyone can change their mind about what they feel like doing, at any time. Even if you've done it before, and even if you're both naked in bed.

Informed

You can only consent to something if you have the full story. For example, if someone says they'll use a condom and then they don't, there isn't full consent.

Enthusiastic

When it comes to sex, you should only do stuff you WANT to do, not things that you feel you're expected to do.

Specific

Saying yes to one thing (like going to the bedroom to make out) doesn't mean you've said yes to others (like having sex).

You get the final say over what happens with your body. It doesn't matter if you've hooked up before or even if you said yes earlier and then changed your mind. You're allowed to say "stop" at any time, and your partner needs to respect that.

Consent is never implied by your past behavior, what you wear, or where you go. Sexual consent is always clearly communicated—there should be no question or mystery. Silence is not consent. And it's not just important the first time you're with someone. Couples who've had sex before or even ones who've been together for a long time also need to consent before sex—every time.

She talks to students about "ethical sexuality," which considers the well-being of everyone involved in an encounter. And she challenges students to think about what "good sex" would mean to them. This is a higher standard than just "was it consensual?"

"You can have a consensual sexual experience that is boring, embarrassing, disappointing, or that feels like a waste of time," Zaloom says. "And not that that isn't a part of life. It certainly is. But we want to aspire to something more than that. So there's legal, there's ethical, and then there's what's 'good.'"

We asked boys:

How do you define consent?

"Asking someone for permission to do something."

—Isaiah, age 17

"The best definition of consent I've heard is noted as: 'an enthusiastic, informed, and sober yes.' It's necessary to know that a drunk or otherwise inhibited person cannot give consent. A mumbled yes or tiny head nod is similarly void. If you're not one hundred percent sure the person is saying yes, the answer is no."

—Rory, age 16

"I use the FRIES definition, and I always ensure that I have consent for so much as touching anyone, because you can never know how someone will feel."

—Jordan, age 19

"A CONFIRMED and INFORMED decision that is agreed upon between two people. Following the rules of FRIES, consent with respect to sex and relationships is reversible and can be given up if a partner decides."

—Nat, age 17

How to Know When It's Time to Talk About Consent

Unlike some other topics, you don't have to wait for boys to get older to start talking about consent. There are lots of opportunities to practice consent skills that don't have anything to do with sex.

This can look like teaching a toddler to ask before giving someone a hug. It can look like telling a middle schooler that they don't have to share their lunch with others if they don't want to, and that their peers should respect that limit.

Consent is a topic of discussion in many classrooms, so it's likely your boy already knows something about this topic.

> **Try saying this:** "I've been reading about consent, and I understand a lot of schools are teaching about it. Have you had any lessons at your school about this?"

You can follow up by asking what they have heard about consent, and whether they agree with those messages.

To start a more in-depth discussion, try discussing a scenario. These can be drawn from real life, from TV or movies, or something you just make up. Here are two examples based upon real conversations we've had with teens. Have your teen read this (or read it aloud if it wouldn't be too cringey for your teen), and then ask questions like the ones we supply below:

Jamil and Cass's Story

Cass, who is new to her high school, and a group of her friends are hanging out at the house of a girl, Bella, who is known for having parties when her parents are out of town. When Bella plans a party, one of the main topics of conversation is about who is going to hook up with whom—in addition to who is going to bring the booze. Before this party, Cass made sure to tell the most gossipy kids that she wanted to hook up with Jamil, a very popular athlete and the class president—hoping he'd hear about it and tell someone that he wanted to hook up with her, too.

By the time the party rolls around, everyone in their group of friends knows that Jamil and Cass are planning on hooking up, and Bella has a bedroom reserved for them. Cass, who feels inexperienced compared to others, starts feeling nervous when Jamil walks in. She grabs a shot of tequila and downs it, then pours another. Her friends laugh and push her toward him, tequila cup in hand.

Cass is starting to feel drunk by the time Jamil smiles and asks what she's drinking. She wobbles, smiles, and tells him she's buzzed. Before he can say anything else, Cass kisses him, then grabs his hand and leads him down the hallway to Bella's room.

A few questions to consider about Cass and Jamil at Bella's party:

→ How can intoxication affect a person's ability to make good decisions and give enthusiastic consent?

→ How truly ready is Cass to hook up with Jamil if she needed to down two shots of alcohol in order to approach him in this way?

→ If you were Jamil, what questions would you have in your mind knowing that Cass is newer to the party scene than you?

→ Does Jamil have more social power than Cass given that he's very popular at their school? How might this impact the dynamics of this situation?

→ What responsibility does Jamil hold in making sure Cass is truly comfortable in the setting and with him, overall?

→ Would this be different if Cass had been in the party scene and popular group for a long time, like he had?

→ What potential issues might there be with Cass kissing Jamil immediately after saying hi and then leading him down the hallway?

→ Jamil told mutual friends that he wanted to hook up with Cass—but is that the same as consent?

→ Is "Yes Means Yes" as important for guys as it is for girls?

→ What unique social pressures that go along with this hookup might Jamil experience as a boy?

→ Do you think a healthy, consent-based conversation could help these two prevent any misunderstandings or problems from arising?

→ What responsibility does Bella have in this situation? How about her parents?

Micah and Hayden's Story

Micah and Hayden have been friends for a long time, and only recently admitted that they have crushes on each other. They decide to hang out alone one night, away from all their other friends. They plan dinner at their favorite restaurant and then a movie night at Micah's.

The dinner goes great, and the flirty vibe increases steadily until they're on the couch with a movie in front of them. A few minutes into the movie, Hayden grabs Micah's hand—the first more-than-friends move between them. Micah smiles back and gives Hayden's hand a squeeze.

A few minutes later, Micah leans over and starts to kiss Hayden, who kisses back. As they make out, Micah goes to put a hand under Hayden's shirt, which Hayden pushes away, casually. They continue making out and Micah tries reaching for Hayden's backside. Hayden doesn't resist this move, but seems less enthusiastic and responsive afterward.

A few questions to consider:

→ What sorts of conversations could Micah and Hayden have had before they started kissing?

→ What are some less-obvious ways to ask for consent for a kiss? Can you talk about a kiss without being dorky?

→ In what ways could Micah have prevented any discomfort or awkwardness while kissing Hayden?

→ What are the risks of "going for it" with sexual activity without asking for consent—for both Hayden and Micah?

→ Are there ways to ask for consent before you get to a point where someone has to move your hand away? Can this be done in a sexy or romantic way?

→ How could Hayden and Micah's parents have prepared them for a more comfortable first romantic and sexual interaction? What conversations might have helped prepare Micah to consider Hayden's feelings before pushing a boundary?

→ What should Micah have done once Hayden stopped being as enthusiastic in their kissing?

→ If Hayden isn't asking Micah to stop, should Micah stop anyway—why or why not?

→ What might Hayden be experiencing in that moment? Why might someone not speak up directly? How does the fact that the couple are at Micah's house, alone, affect the power dynamic?

Ignoring "No" Isn't Romantic

We sometimes hear teens—and even some adults—telling boys that they have to be very persistent if they want to get a date or hookup. They try to be encouraging by saying things like "Keep trying—maybe they're just playing hard to get!"

If we're trying to build a culture of consent, we should make clear that pushing past a "no" isn't charming or "earning" someone's affection. It is a violation of a person's limits.

There's nothing wrong with boys feeling attracted to someone. There's nothing wrong with boys being "horny." There's nothing wrong with asking someone out, in a respectful way.

Here's what's not fine: asking someone out repeatedly or trying to wear them down until they agree to go out or hook up. This can feel like coercion or harassment.

> **Ask:** "Do you really want someone to go out with you because it's the only way they can get you to stop bothering them?"

It's also important that we don't inadvertently teach our boys to blame victims of sexual assault for what someone else chose to do to them. This can happen when we repeat outdated, harmful myths about why sexual assault happens.

> **Don't say:** "That girl shouldn't have been in his dorm room if she didn't want to have sex with him."

> **Instead, say:** "It doesn't matter if she went to his room or not, anyone can change their mind at any point and only 'yes' means yes."

Don't say: "If that boy didn't want to be bothered in the locker room, maybe he should try to be more masculine."

Instead, say: "There's no excuse for harassment or sexual assault, ever. It doesn't matter what the setting is or if the people doing it say they were joking."

Don't say: "That girl doesn't realize that when she wears revealing clothes, boys think she's 'that kind of girl' and will make her a target."

Instead, say: "It doesn't matter what someone is wearing, nobody 'asks for' harassment or sexual assault. That's not a real thing. What other people wear isn't anyone's business."

We asked boys:

Has anyone ever talked to you about consent? What did they say?

"I've been taught about consent from a really young age, even not in the context of sex. It's a very important lesson to learn."
—Sam, age 15

"The Puberty Ed teacher said it means you agree to, for example, be hugged by someone."
—Elie, age 11

"Yes, my mom taught me that no means no, even if someone changes their mind."
—Carson, age 14

"They told me that if the person says no then it is an absolute and immutable no. No ifs, ands, or buts."
—Jordan, age 19

Boys Can Be Victims, Too

Anybody can be a victim of sexual violence, and anyone can be a perpetrator of it.

Upon learning that up to one in six boys will be a victim of unwanted sexual contact before age eighteen, we've heard men say, "I thought we didn't have to worry about that with sons." Sadly, we need to worry about it with any child.

After generations of cover-ups and minimization, male survivors of sexual violence are finally finding the support they've always deserved. Revelations of the abuse, cover-ups, and systemic silencing of victims within the Catholic Church and the Boy Scouts of America in the last few decades have opened people's eyes to this reality.

But there are still relatively common types of sexual assault and harassment that go unaddressed, including various "hazing" and bullying environments, like locker rooms.

Many parents fear predatory adults looking at or making inappropriate contact with their boys in locker room settings, but it appears that peer-to-peer sexual assault may be an even bigger locker room concern. Our sons could become victims—or perpetrators—of sexual violence, often framed as hazing or bullying. When Jamie L. Small, PhD, a professor of sociology at the University of Dayton, researched the prevalence of peer-to-peer sexual assault in locker rooms and other athletic settings, she discovered how incredibly hard it is to track. This isn't a new problem with sexual violence data, as it is an area where people have tended to underreport. While this may change with our post-#MeToo generations of children, for now we must assume that many stories of boys assaulted have gone untold.

In the cases Small examined, the violence went well beyond the "horseplay" coaches and other supervising adults claimed to have witnessed, and included restraining the victim, punching him, touching his genitals, and even forceful penetration—oftentimes with a foreign object.

In an article for *The Conversation*, Small wrote about another barrier to getting an accurate sense of how much boy-on-boy sexual harassment and assault is occurring. "Although victims of all genders may be reluctant to report that they've been sexually assaulted due to the stigma of being a rape victim," she writes, "men and boys face a different type of stigma in disclosing experiences of sexual victimization because men are expected to be strong and fight off physical attacks. For that reason, male victims of sexual assault may be reluctant to report their experiences of victimization."

Homophobia also plays a role in keeping male survivors quiet—whether the attacker was an adult or a peer. A report by 1in6, an advocacy and support organization designed to help men who are survivors of childhood sexual abuse, explains how:

"In our interviews with survivors, one client reported that his father asked him if he was gay after being a victim of child sexual abuse. This myth—that exposure to sexual abuse causes one to become gay/lesbian—can cause tremendous pain and confusion for male survivors. Not only does it assume that sexual orientation is [a] choice or purely dependent on life experiences, it perpetuates a spirit of homophobia and a fear/stigma around survivors of child sexual abuse."

In her research, Small discovered that in one small town where a very serious series of violent locker room sexual assaults occurred, the primary concern of many of the witnesses, as well as coaches, was whether the attackers would be seen as gay. She writes:

"What I found is that the community—mainly the boys' school administrators, coaches, and the boys themselves—were more concerned about whether what the perpetrators did was 'gay' than they were with the effect it had on the victims. No one disputed the facts of the case, only whether or not the actions were criminal. They also expressed anxiety about how it would affect the community's reputation as a whole if what the boys did was seen as a homosexual act."

Sexual violence is sexual violence, regardless of who the victim or the perpetrator is. Gender and sexual orientation do not make someone less of a perpetrator or less of a victim in locker room crimes. It is our job to teach our boys that nobody deserves to have their bodies touched, restrained, or harmed in any way—regardless of whether the person doing it is a friend or it's supposed to be funny. Roughhousing can be fun if everyone consents to participate and if everyone enjoys it equally.

In order for locker room or any other type of sexual violence to stop, parents need to make clear that locker room harassment or hazing in any setting is never appropriate and is likely a crime if it does happen. Parents should also never assume that their child wouldn't participate in assault—or that he would never become a victim. Sexual violence is not normal, and it's not something boys just do as part of growing up.

Brainstorm with your boys what they could do if they see someone targeted for abuse or assault in a locker room (or other similar setting):

A few ideas of what they could do include:

→ Telling the abuser/s to knock it off

→ Standing next to the victim to get between them and the group or individual.

→ Pulling the "lead kid" aside casually and telling them that they could get in big trouble for this or appealing to their empathy and sharing that the kid seems uncomfortable or scared.

→ Distracting the lead kid or group away from their target with a joke, story, or even something fake

→ Leaving and immediately asking for help by calling the police and/or getting help from an adult, depending on the severity of the targeting

→ Asking an adult to come into the locker room or wherever the situation is happening, even if you don't tell them why or report who is bullying or being abusive

→ Being a friend to the kid being targeted and helping them find a solution, someone to report to, or simply a number or website to reach out to for help. (The Rape, Abuse & Incest National Network (RAINN) and 1in6 are both high-quality organizations with staff trained in supporting male survivors of sexual violence)

Finally, remind your kids that they never have to keep a secret from you, and that nothing they could ever tell you would make you stop loving them or make you abandon them.

Talk to Your Boys About Sexual Harassment, Assault, and Abuse

In order to help prepare your boy for dealing with potentially harmful or even dangerous situations, start with a few simple reminders:

→ Anyone can be a victim of sexual assault, regardless of their gender or sexual orientation.

→ Sexual assault against boys and men is just as serious, harmful, and dangerous as sexual assault against women—and it's probably more common than we realize.

→ Be wary of any time a big group of people chases, targets, or restrains one person at a time, as it is likely to be (or become) a situation of sexual assault, standard assault, or, at the very least, bullying.

→ Just as with romantic sexual interactions, "no" or "stop" and other similar words are clear indications that a person is not consenting—whether it's to horseplay or sexual acts. It doesn't matter if the person is laughing, smiling, or trying to defend themselves—"no," "stop," or other similar phrases mean to stop, immediately, no questions asked. In every situation.

→ The lack of a "no" doesn't equal a person saying "yes." Sometimes people are too afraid to say "no"—some may find they simply cannot say "no" because of a trauma response, their mouth being covered, or simply how loud the room is or other similar factors. It's best to default to "no" when you haven't heard a clear "yes."

→ Acts of sexual violence are often more about power than "getting off," so watch out for people who seem to have a need to dominate others physically—especially if they seem to be immune to others' sadness or fear (or if they seem to enjoy making people feel that way).

Few topics are more potentially shame-filled than those covered in this chapter, and that can lead teens to keep secrets. While we may assume they know they can talk to us about anything, kids need regular and specific reminders that we will always love them and help them find solutions. As Joanna tells her kids, "We can solve pretty much any problem together once we know what it is."

Alcohol and Consent

Even when they're sober, young men often struggle to accurately read other people's social cues. This ability almost always worsens with alcohol consumption. Multiple studies have shown that men who are drinking regularly misperceive women's friendliness as sexual interest.

That's part of why we emphasize clear verbal consent with teens—we don't want any confusion or ambiguity. It's also one of the reasons we think it's important to emphasize sobriety for teens who are thinking about hooking up with other people. Drinking and drug use can make negotiating consent much more challenging, because they interfere with both decision making and clear communication.

In addition, young people should know that someone who is incapacitated *cannot* legally consent to sexual activity. Make sure your boy knows the common signs of incapacitation, which include: inability to speak clearly or coherently, inability to walk without assistance, and passing out. If they see a person who is this drunk, the best thing they can do is to help them get to a safe place, position them on their side, and stay with them.

REMEMBER THIS:

❶ Talking to boys about what this means can prompt a lot of meaningful discussions. "Yes Means Yes" is the new consent standard.

❷ It doesn't just apply to romantic or sexual situations! You can teach consent at any age.

❸ Example scenarios can be a powerful teaching tool.

❹ Ignoring a "no" isn't charming or romantic, even if it portrayed that way in movies or songs. Learning to hear and accept a rejection with grace is an important life skill.

❺ Young men can help prevent sexual assault.

❻ Boys can be victims, too, and we should take them seriously and help them find support.

"Porn is best thought of as a
movie: actors playing a role
that, while fun to watch,
would be highly unlikely in
the real world."

—Rory, age 16

Chapter 7

Talk to Your Boys About

PORNOGRAPHY

"I looked at the computer's browser history, and it looks like Jesse has been checking out porn sites. I know I need to talk about this with him, but it's so awkward. What should I say?"

"Ugh—I caught Aaron looking at porn last night, and I am so mad. I feel like I want to keep him away from the internet until he's thirty!"

We know that porn is a big issue with teen boys because we get so many questions from other adults about it.

Online porn has become so widespread that it's no longer realistic to think that we'll be able to keep boys from seeing it entirely. That's why we recommend talking about porn with boys before they stumble upon it or seek it out themselves. Experts suggest starting these conversations in age-appropriate ways early, around age ten or eleven, but you should plan on bringing it up again as your boy gets older.

Human beings are naturally interested in sex and sexuality. People have shared erotic images with one another since the days of cave paintings, and have continued to throughout the ages via sculptures, drawings, postcards, books, magazines, films, VHS tapes, and DVDs. Sometimes these materials have been labeled as art; other times they've been called erotica or pornography.

When young people say the word "porn" today, however, there's no mystery about what they mean. They are almost always talking about what's available on adult streaming sites—giant collections of explicit scenes, organized for quick clicking and viewing. Imagine YouTube with a lot more exposed flesh.

These sites are available to anyone with access to a smartphone, tablet, or computer. They usually don't require a log-in or any real proof that the viewer is over eighteen. Young people who land on one of these sites can start watching immediately and for free.

Common Sense Media surveyed more than 1,300 teens from across the US for its 2023 report "Teens and Pornography." Here's a look at the findings:

→ Of the teens surveyed, 73% said they have watched porn, either accidentally or on purpose.

→ The average age when they started viewing online porn was twelve.

→ Most (54%) said that they first saw online porn when they were thirteen or younger, and 15% said they had seen porn before they turned eleven.

The reality is that if your kid has access to the internet, there's a strong probability that they will see porn. The good news is that there's a lot you can do to help them navigate this terrain, and if you can stay calm and curious, talking about this topic can help bring you closer to your son—and ensure that those lines of communication stay open through the teen years.

People often talk about pornography as something that's completely separate from other kinds of media, but the truth is, there are a lot of sexual situations and "sexy" content in mainstream TV shows and movies. This is also true of songs, music videos, magazines, and advertisements. Sometimes researchers group this content all together and describe it as "sexually explicit media."

CHECK IN WITH YOURSELF ▬ ▬ ▬ ▬ ▬ ▬ ▬

Some people think porn is fine for consenting adults to watch, but not for kids. Some people believe all porn is harmful and exploitative.

It's important to think about your beliefs and values about sexually explicit media, and how you want to convey them before you talk to your boys. Some things to consider:

> If you were visiting an art museum with your son and saw a painting that depicted nudity or a sexual situation, would you try to keep him from seeing it? Why or why not?

> If you were watching a TV show or movie with your son, and a sex scene came on, how would you feel about viewing or discussing it with him?

> Advertisements sometimes use titillation or sexual situations to sell products. If you notice your son looking at one of these, how comfortable would you be talking about it?

> Some people think porn should be banned entirely. Do you agree?

> How do you feel about masturbation?

> What do you think you would do if you found your son watching porn? Why?

> Just talking about this issue often brings up a lot of shame and embarrassment for people. Do you think that would be an issue for you? How would you handle it?

How to Start the Conversation

Many parents feel some trepidation about bringing up topics like pornography with their kids. It can feel intimidating, uncomfortable, and scary. But by pushing past the awkwardness, you are making it possible to have ongoing talks about sensitive topics. You are letting your kids know that you won't let shame or embarrassment get in the way of important conversations, and that they can come to you with their real questions and concerns.

Depending on your comfort level and the age of your child, here are some ways to start a conversation about porn.

Try saying:

→ "Many people your age are curious about bodies and sex, and that's perfectly normal. Sometimes people want to look at videos or pictures online to learn more about sex, but porn isn't a great source of accurate information. I wanted to share a book I picked up that might answer some of your questions, and also to let you know that you can ask me questions about anything you see online and I will do my best to answer."

→ "Sometimes people look at pictures of naked people or videos of people having sex—this is called porn. Have you ever heard about this? Have you ever seen anything like this before? Let's talk about it and I can answer any questions you have."

→ "I know this may be awkward, but I think it's important. I've been hearing that a lot of people your age are looking at porn—either by accident or on purpose. I want to make sure that we've talked about it so that I can share some facts about porn and let you know that you can talk to me about this and we can discuss it anytime. You won't be in trouble."

→ "Three of the things that are often missing from porn are connection, respect, and fun. In real life, consensual sex is really fun when you are emotionally and physically ready for it. It's also very intimate. Most of the time, partners smile and connect by looking in each other's eyes. They even talk about what they like and how they feel and sometimes even laugh together. In real life, people often say the most connected sex is their 'best sex ever.' That's because intimacy rewards so many parts of our brains and can create a 'glowy' feeling that can help form the foundation of deep, lasting relationships. You don't usually see that in porn."

What to Do If They See Porn

If your child sees pornography, react in a calm way, and use a positive tone of voice and gentle words. Feelings of shock, frustration, or worry can come across as anger, even if that's not your intention. This topic can bring up a lot of embarrassment and shame for people, and shame really gets in the way of open, honest communication. Avoid judgmental statements and questions like these:

NO: "Why were you watching that?"

NO: "I can't believe you would do that!"

NO: "Don't you feel embarrassed?"

NO: "This is so degrading, does this mean you hate women now?"

We asked boys:

What do you think adults should know about teen boys and porn?

"Every boy has that curiosity, but it can quickly consume someone. Take an open but stern approach about the negative effects it can have on your mind and how an addiction can form."
—Jordan, age 19

"I think it's pretty common for boys to watch porn. I think it's important to give your children space to learn about [it], but I guess in some way you can also help them learn about stuff like that because obviously they are curious."
—Isaiah, age 17

"Teen boys are struck with a lot of hormones, which can sometimes lead to built-up sexual desire. Rather than trying to repress those feelings and create frustration, porn and masturbation give teen boys an outlet to work through their sexual impulses. If you catch your child with porn, please do not punish them—the embarrassment alone will be sufficient."
—Nat, age 17

Instead of being angry, try to stay curious and engaged. It's much easier to have influence on people you keep close. It may be hard but try to stay connected so that the space for learning and discussion stays open. Reassure them that they didn't do anything wrong, and try to ask questions that show you care:

YES: "How do you feel about what you saw?"

YES: "Was there something you were trying to learn about?"

YES: "Is there something I can help you understand?"

How you talk about bodies, relationships, and sexuality can have a profound effect on your children. As much as possible, try to keep shame and embarrassment at bay. By staying relaxed and "askable," you increase the likelihood that your child will trust you and continue to come to you with questions and for advice.

We asked boys:

What would you say to a boy two to three years younger than you about porn?

"If you see a video by accident, tell an adult and don't share or save the video."

—Carson, age 14

"Don't feel guilty for being curious about pornography—those companies know their audience. Just be sure you're accessing it from verifiably ethical sources (and try not to get viruses!)."

—Rory, age 16

"Porn is unrealistic. It creates a glorified caricature of sex and sexual activity, and watchers must always understand that what shows up in porn is not an accurate representation of what sex is actually like, how to appropriately deal with sexual impulses, and how to address consent issues."

—Nat, age 17

Setting Realistic Expectations About Sex

Sometimes tweens and teens watch porn because they are trying to learn something about relationships or sex. As Shafia Zaloom puts it in her book *Sex, Teens, and Everything in Between*, "that's like watching *The Fast and the Furious* to learn how to drive."

Boys who watch porn to learn about sex may develop sexual expectations that are unrealistic or even harmful. There's usually a lot missing from porn videos that is important in real-life situations. The short clips on porn sites often cut right to the sex, so viewers don't see any of the things that typically come first, like kissing, nonsexual touch, negotiation, boundary and consent conversations about what the people involved actually want to do, or discussions about STI status and pregnancy prevention. In heterosexual scenes, there can be an uneven emphasis on male orgasm and ejaculation—women's pleasure and orgasms often seem like a secondary consideration or are completely absent.

Applying a Media Literacy Lens to Sexually Explicit Content

One way to get teens thinking critically about sexual content in ads, movies, or TV shows is to ask some of these media literacy questions. People can also ask these same critical questions about porn scenes.

→ Why was this media created?

→ What are the creators trying to make the viewer feel?

→ What editing and camera tricks are used to keep the viewer's attention?

→ What does the creator want the viewer to think by watching this?

→ What values and points of view are represented? What is left out?

→ Was the production and sharing of this media consensual?

You can also talk about how porn is made. In porn, performers position their bodies for maximum exposure to the camera, not for pleasure or connection. They move in ways designed to keep you watching, not in ways that are designed to make the experience more enjoyable for the partners. Performers are being paid to do the kind of sexual stuff people like to watch—not necessarily the things people like to do when they're sharing a sexual experience together. If something weird or awkward happens, the director yells "cut!" and everyone just stops and resets the scene like they weren't just having sex.

Being able to talk openly about issues like romance, desire, consent, and sex is an important part of what sociologists call "sexual citizenship," and the way you talk about porn with the kids in your life can do a lot to encourage this openness.

These are skills your kids can use in their lives as they get older, when they are talking to partners or possibly raising kids of their own. You are taking steps to help raise humans who are empathic, caring, and who think critically about what they see in the world.

REMEMBER THIS:

❶ The average American youth first sees porn at age twelve.

❷ Porn is not a good substitute for quality sex education.

❸ When talking about porn with boys, avoid anger and shame.

❹ Learning how porn is made can help people look at it critically.

❺ Boys who watch porn might need help resetting their expectations about dating and sex.

"I wish adults understood how dangerous and effective weed vapes are, and how easy they are to hide. All most kids need is a private bathroom to get completely high."

—Sammu, age 14

Chapter 8

SUBSTANCE USE

One of the topics that can seem most daunting to discuss with teens is drug and alcohol use. Adults sometimes worry that if they bring the topic up, they might inadvertently end up promoting drinking or drug use, or that they'll have to field questions about their own personal history with substances.

Despite the fact that not all teens will use drugs or alcohol, some adults see partying, drinking, and drug use as rites of passage for teenagers, something we can't do much to change. Others get so worried about teen substance use that they try to use fear, exaggeration, and scare tactics to keep teens from ever going near drugs or alcohol.

We have a different take. We see substance use as a serious issue that deserves attention and discussion, and we think caring, nuanced conversations with adults can have a lot of influence on teen attitudes and behavior. We also know that not all teens drink or use drugs. In fact, according to the 2024 Monitoring the Future survey, most American high school seniors say they haven't used alcohol, tobacco, or cannabis in the last twelve months. That reflects a downward trend in use that started in the 1990s—a trend that's important to keep in mind as we discuss substance use with our teens.

Talking about this topic can also give you a great deal of insight into what's going on with a young person in other areas of their life.

Discussions about substance use often lead to conversations about mental health, friendships, and relationships. Establishing yourself as someone who cares, who can listen, and who will keep things real can go a long way with a teenager.

In recent years, scientists have learned a lot about how the brain develops, which has helped us understand more about the risks of substance use during the tween and teen years. Connections and pathways between regions are still developing in an adolescent's brain. In many ways this is an advantage: It is why teens can learn new things so quickly. It also means that teen brains can adapt to the effects of substances very quickly.

Research tells us that the earlier someone starts drinking or using drugs, the riskier it can be—in large part because of brain development. In her book *The Addiction Inoculation*, Jessica Lahey writes, "If [a girl]

We asked boys:

How much pressure do boys like you face to vape, drink, or use substances? What does that usually look like?

"Depending on who you are around, there's either extreme pressure to stay sober, or pressure to drink and use substances."
—Sammu, age 14

"It all depends on the type of friends you hang out with. Some friends respect you for not wanting to do things, but some friends try to pressure you into doing certain substances."
—Jayden, age 16

"I know quite a few people who use substances, drink, or vape, and I feel like I am unable to tell them to stop. Oftentimes I feel like I am invading their privacy and that it's their choice, so I shouldn't butt in. I feel pressured not to tell anybody and not to try to get them help, but I don't feel pressured to use."
—Yash, age 16

begins drinking or taking drugs in her mid-twenties, once her brain development is complete, bad things can still happen but she is at *much* lower risk of brain damage or poor mental health outcomes, including substance use disorder." Educating young people about how their brains grow and develop can be very empowering and can help them to make more informed decisions about their own substance use.

Another thing that's important for adults to understand is that, in recent years, there have been some big changes in the actual substances that young people are using. For example:

→ Vaping is now much more popular than smoking.

→ Cannabis (marijuana) is much more potent than it was in the past, and now comes infused into a wide variety of products, like chocolate, candy, and soda.

→ Fentanyl, which is now frequently found in cocaine, heroin, and counterfeit prescription pills, has greatly increased the risk of fatal overdoses. In fact, drug overdoses are now the third leading cause of death among children ages one to nineteen in the US, after firearm-related injuries and motor vehicle crashes.

CHECK IN WITH YOURSELF ▬ ▬ ▬ ▬ ▬ ▬ ▬

Before you start to talk about substance use with a young person, it's good to get clear about your own beliefs and values. Here are some questions to consider:

> How do you feel about people drinking? What about smoking and vaping or even using cannabis?

> How do you feel about people using pills, powders, or other drugs?

> How do those answers change if the "people" are tweens or teens? Why?

> Have you known anyone who has struggled with alcohol or drug use?

> Do you have a family history of substance use issues?

> How might you react if you find out your child smokes, vapes, drinks, or uses drugs?

How to Start Talking About Substance Use

A lot of people wait to start talking to kids about drugs and alcohol until after those kids have come into contact with these substances or their peers have started experimenting.

In *The Addiction Inoculation*, Jessica Lahey writes that it's most effective to start talking about substance use with kids early—ideally while they're still in elementary school. This gives them time to start rehearsing how they might behave around drugs or alcohol *before* they first encounter them. For families with a history of substance use, or for people living in communities where there is a high likelihood of exposure to substances, it's critically important to have these conversations early, openly, and often.

What if your kids are already older? Have you missed the boat? No. Lahey's advice is to start talking as soon as possible. "Today is always preferable to later," she writes. "Talking about personal health and safety is hard, whether you are discussing drugs, sex, consent, mental health, self-injury, or a family history of substance use, and it is not going to magically become easier tomorrow, next week, or next year. Talk now."

When you're ready, give your child a heads-up that you want to have an honest conversation about drinking and drugs. Let them know that this will be the start of an ongoing conversation and that you will continue to check in. Try not to lecture or talk down to them. Instead, treat them with respect and give them a chance to express their feelings or concerns. Conversations around substance use are likely to be awkward, which makes them perfect for long car rides, while working on a project together, or on walks.

As you talk to your child, try to avoid judgment, anger, or fear. Young people may pick up on your tone and tune out or react defensively. An open conversation will disarm the notion that this is a lecture. It will also provide a relaxed environment to discuss ideas without making them feel like they are being blamed or are in trouble.

The ultimate goal is to let them know you expect them to act responsibly, not just because they want to follow the rules, but for their own well-being.

Bite-size conversations, held consistently, work best

Think of this first conversation as just opening the door—you don't need to say it all in one go. Bite-size conversations and information sharing can be very effective. Focus on setting the tone for open and ongoing dialogue. It is not about being right or having your stance immediately embraced.

If you have a partner or co-parent, make sure you have these conversations together with your child so they see that you are on the same page and equally invested in sharing this knowledge and keeping them safe. If you don't have a partner, think about inviting another family member over and having a conversation over dinner so your kids can understand this is a norm that other households share and will reinforce together.

It's smart to start with a simple question like, "What have you heard about vaping?" This will help you understand what they know already, and also give you an opportunity to correct any misinformation. Then you have an opening to share what you know, by saying something like "I've been reading up on it, and think it's an important issue to talk about together."

Acknowledge that there is a lot to learn and you want to share your knowledge and continue to learn together—things change quickly and together you can discuss the most up-to-date information with each other.

Setting Your Expectations with a Younger Boy

Here are some key points to emphasize when you start talking about substance use:

→ There's a lot of research that says kids who start using substances like alcohol, drugs, and nicotine have an increased risk of addiction later in life.

→ The brains of teenagers are still growing and developing—people's brains aren't fully developed until they're twenty-five!

→ Because teens' brains are still developing, substances sometimes affect young people differently than they would adults.

→ Certain drugs—including alcohol—affect the way our brains work in harmful ways—especially when we use them a lot.

Share Your Expectations Clearly

When adults share their substance use expectations with young people, they sometimes say things like "stay safe" or "make smart decisions," which can be misinterpreted. For example, a parent who says, "Make smart decisions" may think they are asking their child not to drink, but the child may think they mean, "Don't drink enough to black out." It's better to be specific. If you mean, "You can go out with your friends as long as you can assure me you won't drink, smoke, or vape," then say that.

If you haven't already, get clear with yourself about the rules and

We asked boys:

Do you worry that people you know might develop problems from substance use? Why or why not?

"I'm worried about my dad, who is a smoker. I already got my mom to quit, after a very long time—she smoked for twenty years."
—Octavian, age 11

"I have seen boys my age try substances and some grow dependent. I had a friend in eighth grade start smoking weed for a short time, and when his parents caught him they decided to homeschool him for the rest of the semester."
—Sammu, age 14

"Yes, I have lots of friends who abuse substances and constantly are needing a hit, and I worry about problems they could develop."
—Jayden, age 16

"People generally won't report substance abuse because they don't want to get their friends in trouble. There should be a way to quickly and anonymously report that doesn't lead to the person getting in trouble, but rather leads to them getting the help they need to quit."
—Yash, age 16

expectations you plan to set around substance use. Then clearly communicate those rules and the specific consequences for breaking them.

Teens will be more receptive if you can lay out the reasoning behind your rules, which may include concerns about their health and safety and making decisions while under the influence, legal issues, or negative impacts on school performance.

Emphasize to your child that their health and safety are your top priorities. Many parents do this when discussing drinking and driving—making a strong declaration that they should *never* drive after drinking or get in a car with an impaired driver. You may want to modify your rules in a way that reflects those priorities. Will a child who's broken the rules but asks for help face the same consequences as they would if they had hidden their behavior? You may want to put rules in place that make it less likely that they will put themselves at risk to avoid punishment. For example, many families tell teens, "If you are ever somewhere where people are being unsafe and/or you feel uncomfortable, you can call home for a ride with no questions asked."

His Values Matter the Most

Substance use is a complicated issue. Trying to address it with simple messages like "Just Say No" is not sufficient. Instead, share some simple, true information, and give lots of time to practice communicating about it.

Asking teens to clarify their own values around substance use is a critical part of this conversation. Encourage them to focus on ways they can make positive choices and navigate risky environments. To keep it as realistic as possible, you can ask open-ended questions about what their peers are doing and how they feel about it.

Once they have started to clarify their values about substance use, it's time to think about how they're going to communicate them to other people.

Ask them to think about the reasons behind their limits, and then practice stating those limits out loud, like they would in a social situation when someone is asking why they don't want to drink or get high.

Maybe they are on a sports team and would face penalties if they were caught. Maybe they have a family history of alcoholism or drug addiction and they don't want to take chances with themselves. Maybe they simply want to stay sober so they can drive themselves home when they're ready to leave a party.

Just like shooting baskets or solving algebra equations, setting limits gets easier with practice. They can practice saying things like "That's cool if you want to do it, but it's not for me," "I promised myself I wouldn't _____ until I'm done with high school," or even "I would love to join in, but my mom is really, really strict, and I can't take a chance on her finding out."

Addressing Your Own Use

Sometimes young people ask questions like "Have you ever used drugs?" How you answer is a personal decision. It's OK to say, "I'd rather not talk about that" or "I don't think today is the right day to get into my life history."

You might say, "I promise to tell you one day, I just don't feel ready to right now." That way it doesn't feel like you are shutting down the conversation, and it also gives you time to consider your answer. If you do choose to share, think about how what you say can help you connect with your child and deepen their understanding of the issues involved.

You may want to talk about how the fact that fentanyl is present in so many illicit drugs today makes it more risky to experiment with drugs than it was in the past. You can talk about other things that have changed as well, saying something like "When I was growing up, we did not have the brain scanning technology that we do today. We didn't understand the risks of using drugs when we were teenagers. We were told not to use, but were not given science-based explanations about how it might affect us."

Parents with a history of substance use sometimes say that they regret some of the choices that they made and they are trying to help their child avoid making similar mistakes.

What Should Parents Know About Harm Reduction

Bonnie Halpern-Felsher, PhD, is a professor of pediatrics and adolescent medicine at Stanford, and the founder and executive director of the university's REACH Lab, which focuses on understanding, preventing, and reducing substance use among teens and young adults. She supports a harm-reduction approach to talking about drugs with youth that encourages them to abstain from drug use, while also providing them with information to reduce their risk of addiction and death if they do choose to use.

"The first tenet of harm reduction is that the most important way to reduce your harm is not to use in the first place," Halpern-Felsher explains. "The second is if you are using, let's work on trying to either stop or cut back. And if those aren't working, let's talk about using in a way that at least keeps you safe from addiction, health-related harms, and death."

People may be more used to this kind of conversation in relation to alcohol or sex. Parents often say things like "I'd rather you didn't drink at all, but if you do, I definitely don't want you driving, where you could kill yourself or someone else. Please order a ride or give me a call" or "I really hope you wait to have sex, but if you can't, I want to make sure you know how to use condoms and birth control to avoid pregnancy and STIs."

Halpern-Felsher says she knows that a lot of parents aren't having these kinds of conversations about drug use with their kids. "They shy away. They worry that if they have a conversation, they're going to be encouraging use. But I want to normalize drug education communication, not normalize drug use."

She likes to remind parents that it should be a conversation, not a confrontation or a lecture:

"*Try saying* to your teenager, 'Hey, I just learned about _____, or I'm reading about _____, or I went on a website and learned about alcohol, tobacco, or other drugs. Can we have a conversation to learn from each other about it? Can we do this together? Can we learn? Can we teach each other?' That's the most important thing. Just talk to your kids."

The REACH Lab manages a high school drug education curriculum called Safety First. Although designed for use in a classroom, parents can easily adopt the ideas for use in conversations at home. Safety First emphasizes messages like:

→ If you're using drugs, the healthiest choice is to stop using, or at least cut down on how much and how often you use.

→ Ideally, you're using drugs only as recommended by a doctor or a pharmaceutical label. If not, don't take a lot of any drug. Wait and see how it affects you before taking any more.

→ Consider your mindset before using drugs. What you're thinking and feeling before and during substance use can affect your experience.

→ Consider the setting. Where and with whom you're using drugs can reduce your chance of injury or death.

→ Check the substance before you use it. Test strips aren't always 100% accurate, but testing a drug for things like fentanyl can reduce the risk of poisoning. Many pills and powders, including cocaine, are now contaminated with fentanyl and other substances. This significantly increases the risk of death.

→ Don't mix drugs. The effects from combining drugs may be stronger and more unpredictable than one drug alone, and can be deadly.

→ A stimulant like Adderall or cocaine does NOT sober you up. It may wake you up, but it likely only makes you more impaired.

→ Know how to respond in an emergency: Be ready to give CPR, call 911, administer an opioid reversal medication (such as Narcan), and move people into the recovery position.

When to Reach Out for Help

Teens may use substances to help manage anxiety, relieve stress, distract from unpleasant emotions, or connect socially with peers. Being curious about those reasons can help him feel less judged. It may also give you a window into your teen's underlying struggles, help him develop insight into his own behavior, and point to problems that may need professional support.

On the other hand, these conversations may be challenging for a parent to have with a child, and some young people have limited understanding as to why they use substances. Teens who use substances regularly and/or who have had a problem associated with substance use may be on a trajectory for developing a substance use disorder. It is a good idea for them to have an assessment with a professional who can support them in changing their behavior.

What Can You Say When You Learn Your Son Is Drinking, Smoking, or Vaping?

You might discover this information when you walk in on them, when you get a call from law enforcement, or when school calls home. They might even tell you about it themselves. When this happens, what's the best way to respond?

First, take some breaths and try to retain a sense of perspective. It's natural to be angry or disappointed but leading with those feelings may push a teen away. Remember that the goal is to stay connected and help them stop using or reduce their use.

When it comes to drinking, smoking, or vaping, keep in mind that these industries target teenagers like crazy, so save some rage for the corporations who push these products at our youth.

Sometimes parents panic or catastrophize, imagining that this incident will set their son on a downward spiral. Remember that not everyone who tries drugs or alcohol as a teen experiences a negative, life-altering outcome.

REMEMBER THIS:

❶ Talks about serious subjects like drinking and drugs are best delivered in low-pressure, "small bite" conversations.

❷ Not all teenagers use or even try drugs and alcohol.

❸ The drugs that young people commonly encounter have changed and are likely more dangerous due to impurities.

❹ Don't just lecture—try to be curious and create a dialogue.

❺ Set your expectations clearly, but communicate that you're always available for help.

❻ Work with your child to help them set their own limits and practice asserting them.

❼ Reach out for professional help if you're worried about a young person's substance use.

"I find that the majority of the boys' interests at my school have nothing to do with the school curriculum, which makes them less engaged in school. I've noticed that many of the boys want to work in professions deemed as less academically professional, fields like songwriting or sports. This is different from the girls at my school—the vast majority of them desire to pursue careers such as biological studies or medical school."

—Preston, age 16

Chapter 9

Talk to Your Boys About

SCHOOL

Want to get a teacher talking? Ask them what they notice about the boys in their classes. Here are a few things we've heard over and over:

"Boys can't sit still."

"The boys in my class are not serious students. They're so immature."

"Boys just can't pay attention, and they distract everyone else."

"Boys are so disrespectful— to other kids and to adults."

"Boys are lazy, won't do any work, and don't care about grades."

"Boys don't know how to do anything for themselves anymore."

"Boys are violent and so full of rage— they scare me."

That's a lot. And while each of these statements may be true for some boys, we can't help but wonder if these stereotypes are keeping boys from being fully seen.

The boys have their own thoughts about school. Here are some of the things we've heard from them:

"School is boring."

"No one at school cares about me."

"All teachers do is talk—it's never any fun."

"I wish we still had recess."

"I only care about one or two classes."

"It's so stressful and overwhelming!"

"My teachers are so mean."

"I can't wait until I'm done with school."

"None of what I'm learning is relevant to real life."

Some of the things people say about boys and school are exaggerations or stereotypes, of course, but there is solid data that says boys *are* struggling more with school these days. At the same time, a lot of girls are finding success in school, and more of them are choosing to continue their education after high school. There are now 2.4 million more female than male undergraduates on US campuses (8.9 million women compared to 6.5 million men), according to a 2024 report from the American Institute for Boys and Men.

This disparity is enough of an issue that some advocates are proposing big, sweeping changes to the education system to try to address these differences. Author and scholar Richard V. Reeves suggests that because boys typically mature a little more slowly than girls, they should start kindergarten a year later. Others are calling for redesigning schools to be more "boy-friendly," or pushing for a massive recruiting effort to hire and train more male teachers.

We love that people are talking about these big ideas, but structural reforms can take years to implement, if they happen at all. Our focus here is on how to talk to the boys in our lives about the importance of education, how to help your school best serve the unique needs of your boy, and to encourage them to share their own thoughts about school.

CHECK IN WITH YOURSELF ▬ ▬ ▬ ▬ ▬ ▬ ▬

Before talking to your boys about education, it's important to spend some time reflecting on your beliefs about education.

> Think hard about what "success" in school means to you. Does your son have to get a 4.0, take as many Advanced Placement classes as possible, and get into a specific college for you to feel proud of him?

> What are your expectations around school attendance? How would you feel about your son skipping classes or leaving school early?

> When you think about how your son talks to and treats other people in the school, what are your expectations? Are they different if he's talking to peers than if he's talking to teachers or administrators?

> Is participation in extracurricular activities important to you? What about sports? If so, what will you say if your son asks "why?" and what you will do if he refuses to participate?

> How does your partner or co-parent feel on these issues?

Regardless of how you answer these questions, the key is to remember that your own experiences with school may be vastly different from your kid's. The best thing we can do is show up, listen, and support our kids, regardless of what their school experiences are.

How to Talk to Your Boys About School

For many families, discussions about the importance of education often start with the same common question that kids ask their parents: *Why do you care about school so much?*

Education is often called "the great equalizer" because it can (at least in theory) make the same opportunities available to everyone. Of course, the learning conditions are dramatically different from school to school and community to community, which may make it hard for things to ever be truly equal. However, education is crucial for helping children develop skills, build understanding, and create connections. Schools attempt to build a common, foundational knowledge base among all students, with the understanding that those students will soon (we hope!) become active, engaged citizens who work, volunteer, and vote.

What do you like and dislike about school?

"I like seeing my friends. I enjoy gym class because I get to play sports. I do not like state testing because of how much time it takes up out of our schedule. I also do not enjoy the homework because it's time-consuming and I'd rather be hanging out with friends or playing video games."

—Carson, age 14

"I like the structure of days, the learning environment, and meeting new people. I dislike the stress and anxiety it gives me."

—James, age 21

"What I like about school is seeing friends and learning new, important stuff like economics. What I dislike are the constant assessments we have in each class that give us no time for our own life."

—Isaiah, age 17

"What do I like? I enjoy the school environment and connecting with my classmates; they all come from diverse experiences and viewpoints that are informative and challenge my daily thinking. I enjoy being around others, and education has been my main method of developing close relationships. My connections with my peers are the primary reason I look forward to class each day. What do I dislike? School is my main source of stress and trauma, which I believe is prevalent among many current high school students. Thinking to myself, 'Only a few more years of this and I can graduate' isn't enough. Every day, I feel so much pressure to meet society's expectations."

—Preston, age 16

But that lofty reasoning only helps so much with the everyday challenges and frustrations of being a student.

As almost every parent knows, asking kids "How was school today?" doesn't usually generate much more than single-word answers. How can you encourage your son to share more about what is going on? Here are some better ways to spark conversation:

→ What were people talking about today?

→ Can you remember anything funny that happened?

→ How are you feeling about math class these days?

→ Who did you sit with at lunch?

→ Tell me about the best minute of your day.

→ What was the hardest thing you had to do today?

→ Tell me about what you read in class.

→ Who did you hang out with today? What did you do?

→ What's the biggest difference between this year and last year?

Sometimes our investment in our kids' education can unintentionally create stress. For example, if you are always asking about grades, your son will learn that grades are really important to you. That might just add to the pressure he's already feeling.

One of the dilemmas of modern parenting is knowing how involved you should be in day-to-day school activities and assignments, especially since many schools now use digital gradebooks that send almost constant updates about homework and class progress.

For day-to-day concerns, like a question about an assignment, we recommend having your child lead that communication, while you provide as much background support as they need. That may mean overseeing the digital gradebook and reminding your child to follow up or communicate with their teacher. Some kids may need a little guidance for how to properly address these issues, but small interactions like this are a great way to teach communication skills and personal responsibility.

For bigger concerns—things like school refusal, absenteeism, bullying, or harassment—it's important to start addressing them as soon as possible. The same is true if you're worried that your son is experiencing anxiety or depression related to school.

Remind Your Kids: Perfection Is a Myth

Say something like "Nobody is perfect, and you never need to be perfect to be loved and accepted in this house."

Make space for him to try new things and then drop them simply because he does not enjoy them. Encourage him to attempt new activities because he's curious or thinks they sound fun, not just because he thinks they will look good on an application.

Resist the urge to keep him "productive" 24/7. Let him listen to music and lie on a hammock, play some video games, or hang out with his friends.

Make space for him to get a B or even a C, even if you think he could manage an A if he studied harder or slept less.

Learning to Play the "Game of School"

Lisa Damour, PhD, explained on an episode of her *Ask Lisa* podcast that "When students thrive, it's not necessarily because they're very smart. It's because they know exactly where, when, and how to get work done."

Boys often need help with "planning ahead" skills, like anticipating how much time they need to spend studying for a test. If boys are slow to learn these skills, it can greatly interfere with their academic performance.

In her book *Erasing the Finish Line*, academic adviser and early career development expert Ana Homayoun details some of the skills and systems she teaches students to give them a firm foundation for success in school.

"'Executive functioning' is an academic term that has recently, relatively speaking, made it into the parenting lexicon," Homayoun writes. "It describes the abilities we need to focus, concentrate, and complete tasks effectively and efficiently—tasks that are not automatic and instead require focus."

It's probably no surprise that Homayoun sees a lot of boys in her practice. After all, executive function skills generally improve as children get older, but on average they develop more slowly in boys.

When she's trying to help students get on track academically, Homayoun focuses on developing and practicing six key skills. When she's working with someone new, she starts by asking them to self-assess how they do in each of these areas:

- → Organizing
- → Planning
- → Prioritizing
- → Starting tasks
- → Completing tasks
- → Adaptable thinking

"I begin with these six initial focus points in part because they provide a framework that feels useful and manageable to most students," Homayoun tells us. "From there, we expand our system building to include greater self-awareness around identifying and accessing resources and recognizing what strategies work best."

She's not providing therapy, but her interventions can make a big difference in how students see themselves.

"Feeling disorganized or overwhelmed about academics can really affect boys' mental health," she says. "They can lose confidence in themselves, which decreases their intrinsic motivation, increases their anxiety, and can make them feel like they don't belong. My work is around helping these students, individually or as a school community, to solve these issues."

"Hope is what keeps me going," Homayoun says, noting that she spends a lot of time reassuring parents that things can improve. "Provide time, structure, and support, and build routines, and they will catch up. It can and will change."

When Boys Disconnect from School

If a boy is saying that he "doesn't even see the point of school," try saying:

> "School matters, and staying in school and doing your best there is important. It's a place where you can learn, build habits, and make friends. We don't expect it to always be easy or fun, but it shouldn't feel overwhelming to you. If you are ever having problems with school—with peers, with

classwork, with teachers, or anything else—we want to know what's going on."

Note that you're not promising to sweep in and fix every problem. You won't be able to do that, and not all problems are best solved by parents. But you *can* always be a good listener, and you *can* help identify the problems that would benefit from adult support.

You can also try to encourage some culture change at the school by pushing the staff to work harder to connect with boys. You can ask them to speak up about the kind of norms they are trying to instill for

We Need More Male Teachers

Why don't more boys feel like school is a place for them? It may be partly due to the lack of male teachers in their classroom. Men now account for just 23% of the US elementary and secondary school teachers, down from about 30% in 1988, according to "Missing Misters: Gender Diversity Among Teachers," a 2024 report from the American Institute for Boys and Men.

Over a quarter of all US students are boys of color, but only 6% of teachers are men of color.

How can we reverse this trend?

→ We could do a high-profile campaign to encourage men to become teachers. It will require a big effort: even returning to the 1988 gender ratio would require more than 230,000 additional male teachers.

→ One option to consider: removing barriers for "career changers" coming into teaching after doing other types of work.

→ We can start actively encouraging boys to consider teaching as a career. In the same way we've developed outreach programs encouraging girls to go into math and science careers, we can roll out campaigns encouraging boys to think about becoming educators.

boys' behavior and conduct and encourage them to intentionally create a social environment where boys are free to express a wide range of emotions, show love and caring, or feel safe being vulnerable or asking for support.

If a boy is struggling to connect with people or groups at school, try saying:

"It sounds like you really want to find your place in the school. I think that's such an important thing to do, and it will probably make school a lot more fun for you. Let's think about this together. Can we look at the list of clubs, sports, and activities the school offers and pick a couple that sound worth trying?"

You may want to talk about how to follow up with potential new friends, like exchanging phone numbers or social media handles, inviting people to hang out or do an activity with you, making concrete plans and following up on them. Some boys really need to be walked through all of these steps.

School and the Man Box

In school, boys take in messages about masculinity all the time. Even if these lessons aren't spoken aloud, boys quickly learn the "rules" about masculine expression in their schools. It's almost like a second curriculum, one that boys learn by observing their peers. They may not realize it, but they learn answers to questions like:

→ What can I wear?

→ Is getting good grades celebrated or will I get roasted?

→ What hobbies or interests are likely to be mocked?

→ What kind of talk about relationships is acceptable?

→ How much are we supposed to be interested in sex?

→ Is violence allowed? Is it encouraged?

→ What kind of people is it OK to say you're attracted to?

A restrictive view of masculinity can get in the way of academic engagement and performance. If boys latch onto the idea that "being a man" means always being right, they may stay quiet in class unless they are absolutely sure of an answer. This separates them from one of the

We asked boys:

What do you think makes a great teacher?

"They get to know their students well and they are cool, calm, and collected. They are not all over the place—I like to know what I can expect."

—Carson, age 14

"I think what makes a great teacher is having the ability to joke around with the students and be fun and funny. But then also having that mood where you're serious. Those sorts of teachers help out the best because when you have those two sides they remind you that high school doesn't have to all be that boring and not all teachers are strict, rude, or not fun."

—Isaiah, age 17

"In my opinion, a teacher is someone who helps you along your educational journey. Not someone who holds your hand every step of the way, but someone who can support your needs and devotes time in and out of class to help you expand on concepts you didn't understand in class. A teacher is not hired to be a personal friend, but it is still important they form personal relationships with their students so the students feel the connection and have motivation to come to class."

—Preston, age 16

"A teacher that is open and honest. One that is fun and can connect with the kids. These all give a sense of respect that then makes it much easier for students to reciprocate."

—James, age 21

main ways that humans learn—by making guesses and then sharing ideas and talking them out with other people. Boys who embrace this narrow definition of manhood may also stay away from activities that they might enjoy—like choir, dance, or theater—out of fear that they might be teased or called "gay." They may stand by silently while witnessing bullying or harassment—or even join in—rather than violate an unspoken "bro code."

Too Much School; Not Enough Play

Adults sometimes think about high school as merely a stepping stone on the path to college, and frame getting into the "best" college as the most important goal for young people. Yet kids are being pushed harder than ever, often with little consideration as to the quality of a student's life in the present time.

If you look at the homework and studying schedules of your average high-achieving student and consider the demanding schedules of varsity sports, you can see that it is nearly impossible to fit in anything else. Sleep often ends up being compromised, along with unscheduled creative or self-care time.

Teens need "playtime," even if it looks different than it did when they were small. Drawing in a sketchbook, shooting hoops, playing pool with a friend, plucking out a tune on a guitar, and riding bikes with friends all count as "play" to our teens.

As much as we want our kids to succeed in school, it's important to remember that a kid who is sleep-deprived, overstressed and overcommitted, and lacking "me time" is usually not enjoying life. If the goal is perfection (or nearly so), we are setting these kids up to fail. Worse, we're building their self-esteem on a very shaky foundation.

Psychologist Patricia A. O'Gorman, PhD, suggests making a conscious effort to remind our kids that they are human *beings*, not human *doings*: "We need to help our kids build internal self-worth based upon who they are, what is important to them, and what their values are, as shown by what they give, what they make happen, and not just what they can achieve."

Help kids learn and express who they are by diversifying their experiences with activities that cannot be "won" or even accomplished in a traditional sense. Dr. O'Gorman sees particular benefit in activities that are about serving others when it comes to helping kids develop a balanced sense of self. She offers some ideas, suggesting you build upon your child's own interests:

→ Volunteering at the local animal shelter

→ Helping other kids after school with homework in a subject they enjoy

→ Working with disabled adults

→ Teaching Sunday school or another class at your family's house of worship

→ Leading or helping organize meditation class

What Makes a School "Boy-Friendly"?

Because every boy is different, there's no one universal answer to what makes a school a good fit for boys. Here are a few things we consider when thinking about schools:

→ How does the school support students' taking care of their mental health and seeking help when they need it?

→ What does the school do to help kids make friends?

→ How much time do students at the school spend practicing communication skills and connection-building skills?

→ How does the school support kids who need to get up and move around?

→ What is the school's policy about taking away recess, PE, or movement during the day?

→ How many male teachers or counselors does the school have? Are those educators able to actively teach social/ emotional skills? Some schools—especially if they have only a small number of men on staff—lean on those men to be taskmasters or strict disciplinarians.

→ Which students are publicly celebrated, and what are they celebrated for?

→ What kind of programming does the school have specifically for young men? Do they offer boys' groups or a similar targeted program to support discussion of healthy masculinity?

➜ Being part of a local community activity, like helping with little kids' tee-ball or soccer, or participating in beach clean-up day, trail maintenance, or another outdoor project

We asked boys:

A lot of boys say they don't like school. Why do you think that is?

"I think a lot of boys say they don't like school either because they might not have a good social life in school, the constant schoolwork, and sitting in a chair all day when we want to do something else."

—Isaiah, age 17

"I think boys find a lot of joy in being up and about. Sitting for long periods of time can be really difficult. There is a reason we look forward to sports and the gym so much."

—James, age 21

Getting Support with Learning Differences

Sometimes issues in school can be a sign of a learning disability or difference. Nearly 14% of kids in the US between the ages of twelve and seventeen have been diagnosed with ADHD, according to the Centers for Disease Control and Prevention. Boys get ADHD diagnoses more than twice as often as girls and are nearly four times more likely to be diagnosed with autism.

When dealing with potential learning differences, it's important to know your rights—and your child's rights. One place to start is to get familiar with the Individuals with Disabilities Education Act (IDEA) and to reach out to parents' groups as well as the counselors and administrators at your child's school for more information.

According to Sharon Saline, PsyD, author of the book *What Your ADHD Child Wishes You Knew*, "When a tween or teen is struggling with a learning difference, the best place to start is by talking about his experience and validating it. You want to normalize what he is going through first and then brainstorm options together afterwards.

"Listen and reflect back what you hear but don't reassure him that everything will be okay," she told us. "He won't believe you and he'll feel like you are minimizing his troubles. The most important thing he needs is to feel heard."

The 5 A's of Helping Kids with Learning Challenges

As a parent of a child with a learning difference, Joanna knows the emotional toll these challenges can have on kids, especially when they reach middle school. She quickly discovered that she was most helpful to her kids when she did the following:

1. **Accept** the reality of the challenges—without accepting that the challenge means a child cannot succeed.
2. **Adapt** your plans when necessary, in both big and small ways, without setting low expectations for your kid.
3. **Applaud** your child's successes—especially when they are meaningful to him.
4. **Acknowledge** progress whenever and wherever you see it.
5. **Appreciate** that everyone learns and achieves differently. Some types of differences have names while others—even among the most successful people in society—may go unnoticed or unnamed.

A few years after his diagnosis with an auditory-based learning difference, Joanna's son found himself struggling in the Spanish classes deemed necessary for a well-rounded college-prep high school curriculum. He knew that the University of California schools—his dream school system at the time—strongly encouraged four years of language classes and he was overwhelmed by the idea of two more years. He was nearly panicked over how his grades would further decline. Following the five rules above, Joanna's family did the following:

→ They accepted that learning a language in a classroom setting using prerecorded audio tracks was not optimal for him and that his highest grade would likely be a C.

→ They adapted to the idea that only two years of Spanish may take him out of the running for some of the most competitive schools and expanded their list of target colleges. They applauded his 75% test scores rather than pushing him to turn them into A's or B's.

→ They acknowledged some new skills he was developing in order to achieve his C grade, and gave extra attention to the classes he loved and that made him feel good about himself.

→ They helped him appreciate that everyone learns differently, reminding him that most people learn languages best out in the world talking with native speakers and that may work for him in the future.

"Ultimately, what I hope parents are able to do is offer compassion for their son's challenges (and for themselves) and collaborate on any solutions," Dr. Saline told us.

And don't forget to celebrate his wins, big and small. After all, as Dr. Saline explains, "It's the progress and the efforts that matter most for building confidence and competence."

Rethinking College for Some

When it comes time to apply to college, it is easy to get swept up in competitiveness. Young people sometimes worry that their whole life will be ruined if they don't get into a super-competitive school. It's important to remember that fewer than 1% of all college students in the US attend an Ivy League school. The vast majority of undergraduates go to public universities, and more than 40% of US undergraduate students attend community colleges. These can be an attractive (and more affordable) option for many students. Community colleges often have organized programs for students who want to transfer to a traditional university later.

If you are hearing from your boy that "college isn't for them," you should first make sure they are exposed to various options for college—not just the ones you hope they will attend. This can mean doing formal college tours and looking for public events—presentations, open houses, summer camps, etc.—at a campus near you. But we also encourage you to be open to the fact that college right after high school isn't necessarily the best path for everyone. Some young people really benefit from taking a "career year," as author Hannah Maruyama calls it, to do work, volunteer, travel, or gain some life experience or maturity.

For some boys, training or apprenticeship programs may be a better match than college. These structured, work-based learning opportunities offer young people the opportunity to learn specialized skills that they can use throughout their career. They are popular options in countries like Denmark, the UK, Australia, and Germany. The American Institute for Boys and Men has been calling for the United States to make more investment in apprenticeship programs, which are often promoted as a way to help young men find their way to a career if college isn't a good fit.

When talking to kids about after-graduation plans, it's important to let them know that they have lots of options for the future. Many boys think they have only two choices: starting a job they will be stuck in forever, or attending a four-year college or university. This is a false binary.

Maruyama, coauthor of *The Degree Free Way*, suggests brainstorming with kids first, making clear that there are no bad or wrong answers. "First, ask questions so you know what he's imagining for his future. Make sure you don't interrupt or try to 'help' them with their answer. And remember, there are no wrong answers!"

Here are few questions we suggest asking your teen, based on Maruyama's guidance:

Ask: Imagine your life in fifteen years. What does it look like?

→ What are the highlights of your life at this age?

→ Who is around you (spouse, kids)?

→ Do you have pets?

→ Where do you live? In a city, on a farm, in a cabin, or maybe on a boat?

Gauge what type of job he would like to have. Say: We all have to work. With that in mind . . .

→ What sort of expenses do you imagine you'd have?

→ If you could choose when to work, when would you work in a week?

→ What do you think is a good amount to make every year?

The question at the beginning is a reality check. Many kids have no idea what type of income they'll need or want. The goal is to get an answer, even if you don't like it or feel it's "wrong."

Determine if you really need a college degree to fund this future— and decide if you need to pursue it right away.

→ Ask: Do you need a college degree to make that amount? Does the type of job you are interested in legally require a degree?

You need the answer to the first question to see what they know about degrees and work. For the second question, they most likely will not know. That's intentional. Then, look up the answer together.

Maruyama explains that this is "vocational creativity" in action—and it won't happen in just one conversation. It is something you can explore over time, together. Let them find things you didn't know. Letting them be "smarter" than you gives them stewardship over their future path.

There are benefits to waiting until a person is older to start college, especially considering that the brain isn't fully developed until a person is twenty-five. In addition, when they file for financial aid as a slightly older student, their (likely lower) income, not yours, will be considered, dropping the price dramatically.

Of course, some kids will do better going straight to college after graduation. We aren't here to tell you which is best, but rather to help you talk to your boys about their options.

REMEMBER THIS:

❶ Many boys are struggling in school, which can affect their long-term health and happiness.

❷ School is a place where rigid rules around masculinity are often reinforced by peers.

❸ It's possible to find schools that are more "boy-friendly," and it's possible for schools to change.

❹ Work to make sure boys know that college is a "place for them," but also be open to ideas like a "career year."

❺ For some school issues, like a missing homework assignment, it's best to let boys handle it with some coaching from you. For more serious concerns, like repeated absences, it's important to seek support ASAP.

❻ You and your child both have rights regarding education. It's important to know these and fight to have them fully implemented—especially in regard to special education services.

❼ Boys often need support in learning organization and study skills and learning how to "play the game of school."

"I wish parents and other adults involved understood that, for the most part, sports are about making and being with friends. I also wish they understood that their arguing and yelling is just embarrassing.

"Sports are about being healthy and social. It's where a lot of kids learn a lot of their teamwork skills, the importance of hard work, how to socialize, and how to work with someone like a boss/coach. It's not about winning the Little League World Series."

—James, age 21

Chapter 10

Talk to Your Boys About

SPORTS AND EXTRACURRICULARS

When Joanna's first baby was due to arrive, she and her husband, Ivan, decorated his nursery entirely in a surf theme. A surfer since he was eight years old, Ivan even bought baby Izac some teeny tiny board shorts. He was sure Izac would love to surf.

Izac did not, in fact, love to surf. Instead, he tried lots of different things (lacrosse, basketball, theater, cross-country, and more) before discovering a passion for track and field, specifically the javelin. This was far from Joanna and Ivan's only experience trying (and failing) to nudge their kids toward their own interests. Their middle son became entranced with a sport they hated at the time—baseball—and pursued it with such commitment they couldn't help but fall in love with it.

Sports and extracurriculars are fantastic for our kids, but, like anything else, they are most beneficial in moderation, when kids are challenged but not exhausted, and they are particularly great for our kids when we let them try things without burdening them with our own expectations.

CHECK IN WITH YOURSELF — — — — — — — — —

> What dreams did I have that weren't fully realized?
> How have these experiences affected me as an adult? As a parent?
> What pressures and expectations might I unfairly be putting on my child?
> What do I most want my child to get out of his hobbies and sports?

In her two decades of parenting, Joanna noticed that the kids who are pushed to fulfill a parent's dream tend to be the most likely to rebel against that dream as they grow. The parents who are engaged and encouraging, but not too pushy, tend to create kids who happily commit to activities.

There were a few families with parents who were retired athletes or successful actors in Joanna's community in suburban Los Angeles. After years of observing how these parents with a high level of success treat their children when they play sports or engage in activities, she realized that they're the least likely to put pressure on their kids to be the best. One dad, a retired Major League Baseball player, told her, "I'm raising a young man, not a baseball player."

It occurred to Joanna that parents like her MLB friend don't need their kids to be big shots in order to feel good about themselves. Their kids get to explore their interests without the weight of making their parents happy.

Loving What They Love

As parents, we have an opportunity to show our kids that we value them for the unique people they are by joining in on what they love. This can be challenging when our kid's interests are vastly different from our own.

One family we interviewed experienced this exact thing with their son, Jake, now sixteen. Larry, Jake's dad, was a college swimmer who loved competitive sports and other activities considered typically "masculine" during his Generation X childhood. Larry even built a batting

We asked boys:

What sports, hobbies, or activities do you like? What do you like about them?

"I like rock climbing and gymnastics. I like them because they are not very competitive."

—Gavin, age 10

"Baseball, surfing, shoemaking, video games, sketching, snowboarding, pickleball. Most of my hobbies and activities are very hands-on or outdoors. These things offer me an escape from my anxiety that I can find temporary peace in and are usually creative or a workout."

—James, age 21

"Biking, Ultimate Frisbee, and longboarding. I like them because they aren't very competitive."

—Ezra, age 15

"None, but I play guitar a lot."

—Sam, age 15

"Swimming because it's relaxing and I'm good at it."

—Elie, age 11

"I like to compete in swimming, math, and robotics. They're really fun because I get to engage my brain and think critically in a way that is rare in school. I also like to play music, read books, and play video games for fun."

—Jeff, age 16

cage in their backyard, but Jake was only mildly interested. While Jake is a fantastic swimmer like his dad, it was clear from a young age that he loved singing and performing as much as, if not more than, swimming.

"Based on my own competitive-swimming experience, I can share suggestions and tactics with Jake for helping with his nerves before a race.

------ No Wrong Answers: Questions to Get You Talking ---------

When a boy starts playing a sport or doing an activity his parents love, it can be hard to determine the source of his motivation. Is he pursuing this because he's genuinely passionate or because he feels he may disappoint you (or another adult in his life) if he does not?

A good way to know is to ask him open-ended questions about what he loves and how he feels when he's doing various activities. Here are a few ideas:

→ What is your favorite thing to do?

→ What can you see yourself doing even as you get older?

→ When you close your eyes and envision a perfect day, what are you doing?

→ How do you feel after practicing, performing, or a game?

→ When was the last time you felt really, really proud?

→ Do you think you get a lot out of [the activity the parent loves and pushes]? What sorts of things do you get from it?

→ If I wasn't so into this activity, would you still do it?

→ What's the worst part of this activity?

In these answers, watch for signs that he's not enjoying it for himself. For instance, if what he gets out of it is seeing your face in the stands or audience when he looks up, and not much more, it's likely he's doing it only for you.

Of course, there's nothing wrong with kids trying new things based on a parent's encouragement. Many kids discover they share a passion or aptitude with a parent. The trick is to monitor a teen's overall well-being, stress levels, and life enjoyment when they do.

These answers can also help guide you toward emphasizing the things he does love, the things that bring him peace, joy, and pride.

I can also give instructions for a change to a turn, or something for a specific stroke, and he'll do it. And he'll get a great time," Larry told us.

"On the flip side, he gets into all this performing and singing—stuff I never did. There, I focus on two things," Larry says. "First of all, I'm present. I'm there. I don't miss it. Second, it's about work ethic. I don't know anything about singing, but I know you have to practice. I know you have to work hard at it and be motivated. It doesn't make a difference what it is, it's about applying those same lessons.

"I never had to have Jake follow in my footsteps exactly," Larry explained. "In fact, he wasn't going to do the musical last year and I was like, 'Why wouldn't you do that?!' I was shocked."

Jake tried to explain that he was busy: swimming and the musical were at the same time. Larry sensed there was more to the story.

"I kind of felt like he was not doing the musical because he wanted to make me happy by swimming. I was like, 'That's bullshit, I know you love to sing and perform. You should try out. We'll worry about the rest of it if you make it.'"

Jake did get a part in the school musical, and, with his mom and dad's encouragement, Jake worked with his coach to make both possible. School rules didn't allow kids to do two big activities in one season, but Jake was motivated enough to make it happen. He even helped his swim team win a state championship.

Jake was also nominated for a big award for the musical performance and was invited to an award ceremony in Hollywood.

"Nominees sit in front with only one parent," Jake's mom, Heather, told us. "He asked Larry to sit with him because he never would have auditioned if Lar didn't push him."

The Risks of High-Pressure Youth Athletics

Sports can be fantastic for kids at any age. Younger kids benefit from the social aspects of their activities as well as the physical activity associated with sports and other movement-based extracurriculars. In addition, sports teach kids lessons about hard work, being a good teammate, following instructions, and how to win and lose while being a "good sport."

By middle school, kids tend to know whether they enjoy the sports they've tried or if they would prefer to focus on other interests like theater or robotics or even competitive gaming. For some kids, sports continue to play a balanced, fulfilling role throughout high school and possibly even into college and adulthood. For others, high-level sports become more of an obsession—not just for the kids but also for parents and coaches. Some feel more pressure to perform in these sports than in school, a level of pressure that can become unhealthy when unchecked.

In 2022, Damian Mendez was a promising wrestler who had just graduated from high school. Before he could make it to college, where he was going to join the wrestling team, Damian died running in the summer heat while wearing a sweat suit, a common practice among wrestlers trying to "make weight."

Sang Ho Baek, an NCAA Division I pitcher, died in 2021 from complications after an ulnar collateral ligament (UCL) reconstruction. Casually known as Tommy John surgery, in athletes this procedure is most often needed after years of damage to the elbow due to throwing, and was once reserved for the pros.

Dr. Mark Cohen, a team physician for the Chicago White Sox, told Rush University's orthopedic publication that this is no longer the case. These days, the fastest-growing population needing Tommy John surgery are fifteen- to nineteen-year-olds, primarily due to overuse from early single-sport specialization and year-round throwing.

When we were in school, even the best high school athletes played their sport in school during the season and moved on as the seasons changed. They may have enjoyed other activities in their downtime or worked an after-school job. The most intense youth players may have joined teams in the summer, but nothing from that era compares to the intensity of club sports today, where kids often specialize in their sport in middle school and then spend twelve months of every year practicing and playing. They have very little time to truly relax, be creative, or explore other interests.

In Joanna's experience, it's not just year-round competition causing the problem, it's the for-profit tournament and showcase model itself. While nonprofit youth sports organizations (like Little League or the American Youth Soccer Organization) and for-profit sports groups and teams may have similar rules, plenty of parents agree that for-profit youth sports teams are less likely to prioritize protecting their athletes from overuse or risky-use injuries. Why? Because more wins means more invitations to high-status tournaments, more membership for their teams, and overall better profits for their owners.

While tragic deaths like Damian's and Sang's are relatively rare, many kids are experiencing incredible pressure under today's high-demand sports schedules and suffering injuries and burnout at a startling rate. It's our job as their parents and caregivers to help them find balance so they can thrive without having to adopt an adult-level set of liabilities and responsibilities before they are truly ready.

Talk to Your Boys About
Reasonable vs. Unreasonable Risk

Here are a few conversation starters and questions to ask your son about his activities:

→ How long do you hope to be able to do this activity? Is the way that you're participating in it now helpful in achieving that outcome?

→ What do you hope to get out of this activity? Is this for fun, to help you get into college, or for some other reason?

→ How would you feel if you could no longer do this activity?

→ What would you do if the activity you loved required you to participate in a way that felt unsafe or even immoral to you?

→ What will you be giving up in order to participate?

It's important to note that it's totally normal and can be healthy for some kids to hyperfocus on one activity at a time. For instance, if a kid loves theater and his whole life centers on his theater friends and productions, that may be perfectly OK. But if their behavior seems at all maladaptive, it's our job, as parents, to help them find balance so their self-esteem isn't solely based on one area of success—and to help prevent injuries.

Teaching Kids to Advocate for Themselves with Coaches

One of the biggest challenges parents face as their kids grow is the issue of the "bad coach" (or theater director, band instructor, etc.). A few different issues can make this situation tricky:

→ You fear the coach or leader may "punish" the kid with fewer opportunities.

→ Your kid may not be objective about the source of a pressure: Is it, at least in part, coming from himself?

→ You fear being "that parent" who acts like they know more than the coach or leader and ends up embarrassing themselves or their child.

First, we should make clear that certain situations demand parental intervention, such as the risk of physical danger, unnecessary health risks, racism/sexism/homophobia or other biased practices (including using bigoted words), physical or sexual abuse, or sexually inappropriate language or behavior.

Rory Poplion, a baseball coach and player-development specialist who trains high school and college players, says that in a "bad coach" situation—such as when the coach is repeatedly being demeaning to the point of bullying—then parents *should* step up.

"They're 'youth' for a reason," explains Poplion. "Even if they're a young man, they're still a kid, and parents have to step in and have a conversation with Coach about what they expect, making sure no lines are crossed."

When He Wants More Game Time or a Better Position

"If there's ever a time when a kid feels like they should be playing more," says Poplion, "the very first thing they should do is make a plan to go out and earn it."

Poplion suggests practicing a conversation like this with your son:

"Hey, Coach, I noticed I'm not playing as much right now. What do I need to do to get better? Am I not doing something? Can I stay after practice? Can I come early? Can I come work on my game? Because

I want to be one of those guys on the floor. I want an opportunity to showcase my skill set. What do I need to do to get there?"

The coach may or may not be receptive, but most of the time, coaches are amenable to a kid's interest in improving, and will help him figure out how. Beyond that, it's up to our kids to do the work.

Growth mindset do's and don'ts:

Regardless of what type of extracurricular activities your son enjoys, adopting a "growth mindset" can help keep him motivated and working toward his goals. Growth mindset is a great exercise in resilience that can help kids in their careers and relationships as adults, too.

Don't focus on talent—regardless of whether he has it or not.
Do praise him for effort and growth.

SCENARIO: He's frustrated that he's not getting enough playing time in basketball games.

> **Example:** "I see you out there practicing that layup again and again. It's a lot of work, and I'm proud of you for that. And I know you didn't play much in the last game, but when you were in, your layups showed so much improvement."

Don't frame strengths and weaknesses in absolutes.
Do focus on the possibility of improvement.

SCENARIO: He's annoyed that a new type of clay isn't working as well as he'd hoped in his art classes.

> **Example:** "Maybe you're just not as good with porcelain as you are with the clay you're more used to, yet. That doesn't mean you never will be."

> **Note the use of the word "yet."** Why is this important? First, you're telling him the truth. He knows he's not as good with porcelain as he is with the other clay materials. Denying that reality doesn't boost his self-esteem; it makes him question your honesty. Adding that "yet" says there's a strong likelihood he will get there.

Don't worry about other people's jobs.

Do help determine what is mostly within his control, and practice letting go of what's not.

SCENARIO: He's down on himself for walking so many batters when he pitched the last game.

> **Example:** "You don't have to strike out every batter or throw top-speed pitches. For this game, don't worry about winning or striking kids out. Just focus on getting the ball into the strike zone and let your defense handle the hits."
>
> **Note that neither the umpire nor the coach (or any other player) is mentioned here.** That's because you can't control anyone else—only your own choices and response.

Don't set perfection (or even winning, necessarily) as the goal.

Do set small, realistic goals for improvement.

SCENARIO: His turns are slowing him down in swimming, and in trying to catch up with them, his stroke form is being thrown off.

> **Example:** "For now, all I want you to think about is the turn you've been practicing. You don't have to win, you just have to feel good about your turns. Then do the strokes the way you know they work best and let your times be what they are for now."

Locker Room Culture

For kids who haven't had a lot of locker room experience (and even some who have) the process of changing for PE or a sport can be intimidating. Many adult men have stories from their locker room days—some of which qualify as legitimately traumatic.

Remember this: Younger kids are often intimidated to change in front of older ones. Physical development happens to kids at vastly different rates, leaving some ninth graders with muscles and a mustache and others with the physique of a ten-year-old. All of this is normal, and it's important to remind your son of this fact.

Reassure your son that it's OK to cover up while changing, if that makes him more comfortable. He can practice the "surfer's change" (how surfers change out of soggy wetsuits and into dry shorts on the beach) by wrapping a towel around his waist while changing pants or underpants, so he feels comfortable and confident doing it for the first time in the locker room. This is a common practice in many school locker rooms and a great option.

Foul Mouths and Sexist Comments in the Locker Room

Another locker room scenario experienced by many boys and men is "locker room talk"—the types of conversations that happen when boys forget about manners and respect when talking about sex, girls, and even other guys in the locker room or other all-boy situations.

"No one can hear you in the locker room; you are with all of your friends and it's private," one fifteen-year-old athlete told us. "It's hilarious most of the time, though I do remember one kid was saying some pretty pig-y stuff about a girl I'm friends with and I was so pissed off. I called him a little boy and told him he's only mad because he can't get her."

"I saw so many fights in locker rooms in middle school and high school, it's crazy," a twenty-year-old college student shared. "You're all in this room together and there are no eyes on you. Everyone feels invincible. Lots of times they're also hitting off the weed pen and shit just gets out of hand."

For her book *Boys & Sex*, author Peggy Orenstein interviewed one hundred boys and young men over the course of two years about a wide range of subjects. She reports that the topic of locker room culture appeared to make her interview subjects incredibly uncomfortable.

"They would rather talk about porn use, erectile dysfunction, premature ejaculation," she writes, "anything but admit to a woman the truth about 'locker room banter.'"

Talking to Our Boys About Locker Room Behavior

Don't start with threats like "I better not hear that you're talking badly about girls."

Instead, try saying: "I know this is common in some locker rooms or in groups of guys and I want to discuss our expectations for how you talk about girls and women."

Don't make it seem like all boys or men are bad or sexist or that inappropriate locker room behavior is unavoidable.

Instead, try saying: "I know not all guys do this, but sometimes it might feel like they do, because the loudest and most 'edgy' voices tend to stand out more. But that doesn't make them common or normal. Notice how many guys in the room are not saying such extreme things."

Ask: "How would you feel if a girl you liked or who trusted you as a friend found out you were saying something degrading, objectifying, or offensive about her or a friend of hers behind her back? Do you think she would like you after that?"

Remind him: "Don't forget that you never know when something is being recorded or will get back to others—a coach you admire, your favorite teacher, your parents, or even college admissions boards or future employers."

Brainstorm with him: "Sometimes it only takes one voice to stop a hurtful pattern. Is there something you can say to interrupt degrading talk when you hear it?"

When Should You Let a Kid Quit a Sport or Activity?

Dr. Harold S. Koplewicz, a child and adolescent psychiatrist and founding president of the Child Mind Institute, suggests that gentle pushing in some situations can be good for kids: "We know that being able to tolerate discomfort is a wonderful life trait, and in addition to that, it makes them grittier and more resilient," he shared on the CMI website.

That's a good reason to make sure they aren't quitting just because they hit a rough patch, had a quarrel with a teammate, got a new coach

We asked boys:

Have you ever had a hobby/sport you loved and suddenly not wanted to do it anymore?

"Yes, swimming. I want to stop because I was being told what to do by a teacher and I would just like to swim freely and be myself instead of being told how to swim."

—Octavian, age 11

"Yes, swimming hurts. It hurts so much, I regret every hard training session. But I do it because it's a challenging sport and it's not something you can just do on a whim."

—Jeff, age 16

"Some things I just get bored, so I stop."

—Ezra, age 15

"Most of the time I've had to stop due to time constraints. Though there have been times when I've been in slumps in a sport and not wanted to play as much or I mess up a project and get discouraged."

—James, age 21

or teacher they don't like as much, or aren't improving at the same rate as others. We want them to push past mild discomforts and even big challenges *so they know that they can*. This is a skill that will come in handy for the rest of their lives.

"I think most parents want their kids to avoid the mistakes they made," says Dr. Koplewicz. "Are we encouraging or pushing our kids because it's in their best interest, or is it something we're doing for ourselves?"

If they have a sudden change of heart, it's possible they're being bullied, intimidated, or even harmed by a coach or teammate. So the first thing we need to do is hear them out and make sure their safety and emotional needs are being supported.

Why let a kid quit or pause an activity: a simple rule of thumb

Does he want to quit when he wins—or just when he loses?

If he wants to quit when he's had a rough workout, made a big or embarrassing mistake during a recital, or had a big loss, it's likely situational. Finding ways to work with the problem, like improving a certain skill or practicing more, will likely help.

If, however, he wants to quit after the wins as well as the losses, after the fun practices as well as the tough ones, he's likely thought this through and is truly ready to let this activity go. He's clearly lost his joy and his passion, and that is totally OK. He's probably ready to try new things, and that is wonderful for kids!

As Phyllis Fagell, author of *Middle School Superpowers: Raising Resilient Tweens in Turbulent Times*, told *Good Housekeeping* magazine:

"Resilience doesn't come only from sticking with something that's hard or persisting at something you hate. Resilience comes from taking a risk, such as learning a skill or participating in an activity with people you don't know. Resilience also comes from developing self-awareness—from understanding where your strengths and interests intersect and having the confidence to know when and how to pivot and try something new."

REMEMBER THIS:

❶ Our kids are not a vessel for our dreams or unfulfilled plans.

❷ Sports and activities are a great way to teach our kids how to persevere despite challenges and to develop the "grit" that can help them be successful in life, but pushing youth athletes too hard, too far, and too fast can result in serious burnout, serious injury, and even death.

❸ With sports comes the risk of exposure to sexist and other bigoted, degrading language in the locker room, but our kids don't have to become part of it.

❹ When we hyperfocus on college applications and building a "perfect application" with lots of sports and extracurriculars, we can miss an opportunity to know the child we actually have in front of us. We also risk increasing their stress levels and put them at risk of serious stress and anxiety later in life.

❺ A sport or activity doesn't need to be part of our kids' lives through college or even all the way through high school in order to be beneficial. Kids can and should quit when they're truly done—but it's not always simple to determine when they're quitting for the right reasons.

"I wish parents understood that on some games there isn't a pause button and you can't always save where you are. That's why sometimes kids are asking for extra time when parents tell them to finish a game, because they can't save, and their progress is very important to them."

—Octavian, age 11

Chapter 11

Talk to Your Boys About

SCREEN TIME AND TECHNOLOGY

S creen time. The phrase alone is enough to make parents shiver. Whether you've given your children unlimited access to screens or restricted them to the point that other parents raise an eyebrow, somebody out there thinks you're doing it wrong.

To make matters worse, there isn't one screen time recommendation that is easily applied to all kids in all situations. Technology changes so fast, it's hard for parents to keep up, a fact that also creates major challenges for scientists trying to conduct long-term research about how screen time impacts our kids.

While we cannot recommend one certain technology plan for your family, we can help you talk to your teens about technology, screen time, and the media.

One of the most effective ways to push a teen or tween away is to openly judge something they love—and when it comes to social media use and gaming, it's easy to find ourselves condemning our kids' choices.

When we, the authors of this book, were growing up in the '80s and '90s, we didn't have internet access at home, there was no social media, and video games were simple, like *Super Mario Bros.* and *The Legend of Zelda.*

It's all too easy to feel overwhelmed by how different our kids' experiences with technology are from ours, and simply give up. The problem is, we cannot adequately prepare kids to have healthy relationships with technology if we aren't at least trying to understand and relate.

Things have changed so much that it has created a generational divide and a gap between parents and kids. As foreign as some of this new media may be to us, parents have to help kids navigate.

We don't have to become masters of modern gaming in order to have great conversations about tech use. It's more important that we resist bringing our own assumptions and baggage into these conversations. The best way to do this is to be honest with ourselves first.

So, where do we start? And how do we set rules and standards for our kids' digital behaviors when the use of these apps and devices doesn't necessarily come naturally to us?

The one thing pretty much every expert on parenting and tech suggests is that parents listen to their children's perspectives before judging their screen use. That means resisting the urge to snark at kids or say they'll "rot their brains" staring at their screens. Instead, be open-minded and model for them how to listen respectfully by doing so yourself.

CHECK IN WITH YOURSELF

A few questions to ask:

> What was my emotional relationship with media and tech when I was a kid?

> How did I feel about my caregivers' rules around media and tech use?

> Do I have any traumatic or upsetting experiences or bad memories around media use?

> What are my biggest fears when it comes to my kids' media and tech use?

> How willing am I to learn new tech or engage with the media in order to bond with my kids regarding their interests?

> How much value do I put on my child's ability to "do what other kids do" or relate with them about their games and/or social media use?

We asked boys:

What do you wish adults understood about games, phones, or technology?

"That technology can feel hard for us to control. So they should teach children to regulate themselves from the start."

—Jeff, age 16

"I wish they understood that I talk to people while gaming and can talk about big things even while doing something else."

—Ezra, age 15

"That lots of kids rely on video games to keep in contact with real-life friends."

—Sam, age 15

"I've noticed that a lot of parents just say yes to their kids about a lot of stuff. I also wish that more parents would set a healthy amount of restrictions for their kids around tech, because playing too many violent games can develop violent habits, and not having a time limit on social media can make it harder for kids to entertain themselves."

—Xavier, age 15

What Experts Say About Screen Time

We wish we could provide you with some all-knowing guide to screen time rules. But no such definitive guide exists. Why? Because every kid is different and develops at a different rate, every family has different rules, and every parent has varying abilities to supervise on a close level as their kids use screens.

We believe all of these factors matter greatly in setting rules and limits for kids, but that means there's a lot of confusion out there.

"It's not just parents who are confused," Anya Kamenetz writes in *The Art of Screen Time.* "The experts are talking past each other. And they disagree, often dramatically."

Dimitri Christakis, a professor of pediatrics at the University of Washington and director of the Center for Child Health, Behavior and Development who has led multiple studies about the impact of screens on children, told Kamenetz, "The real challenge is finding what constitutes healthy screen use and a healthy amount of it."

That means we have to make decisions on a family-by-family or kid-by-kid basis, based upon open and collaborative conversations.

The one recommendation most experts agree on? The fact that we should consume media *with* our children, at least part of the time.

Social Media

When is a kid ready for social media and unsupervised online time? That's the million-dollar question, with yet another complicated answer. Even the experts often don't agree.

There is a growing parent-led movement called "wait until eighth," which encourages parents to keep their kids off social media until they've reached eighth grade. The effort has gained some prominent supporters, including well-known psychologist Dr. Laura Berman, whose sixteen-year-old son, Sammy, died of fentanyl poisoning after buying a pill via Snapchat.

Teach Healthy Tech Use
Like You Teach a Healthy Diet

"When families come together to share a meal, positive values can be communicated and bonds strengthened," Anya Kamenetz writes in *The Art of Screen Time*. "In addition, balancing appropriate screen time is similar to making sure your kids are getting enough nutrition in their diets."

Will consuming media together and learning more about what our kids are into take up more of our time? Yes. But good parenting tends to take effort and time.

"The stakes are high," Kamenetz writes. "We owe it to our kids to do more than get freaked out. We have to get smart."

Other experts say that kids shouldn't use social media until they're at least sixteen. Not everyone agrees, though. The counterargument is that, while some kids may genuinely need a later starting age, in most cases it's best to introduce kids to social media at an age where they are likely to accept your guidance and give a lot of weight to your opinions.

Finally, banning all social media, especially for older teens, is about as realistic as pretending social media doesn't exist. "Social media has rapidly become integral to teenage identity and self-worth. We don't have to appreciate this reality, but we do need to recognize and accept it," writes John Duffy, PsyD, a clinical psychologist, in his book *Parenting the New Teen in the Age of Anxiety.*

When Should Kids Start Using Social Media?

"When teens are saying they want to use social media to stay connected to friends, that's a good sign," writes Christine Elgersma for Common Sense Media. "If their answer is more along the lines of trying to get famous or 'showing off' in some way, it's more problematic—and could lead to risky behavior in their search for online fame."

Ultimately, parents will have to decide on the limits that make sense for their kids. Here are some guidelines to consider:

Kids who are ready for social media will:

→ Show impulse control and the ability to pause before saying or writing things they may regret.

→ Be able to handle hurt feelings and negativity that can be hard to escape online by using coping skills, like talking to a trusted adult or taking a break.

→ Have the maturity to understand that digital fame is very rare, is fleeting when it happens, and comes with baggage and consequences.

→ Demonstrate a consistent, age-appropriate ability to follow the rules and make choices that reflect their values.

→ Have a strong understanding of how sexual consent works online, the rules around privacy, and signs that someone intends to harm them.

A few simple ways to monitor a younger adolescent's social media use:

→ Buy a phone designed for monitoring behavior, which allows a kid to gradually get more freedom as he grows up or demonstrates responsibility.

→ Allow him to use social media only on a parent's phone or device so all accounts can be closely monitored, and time spent online can be tightly controlled.

→ Install software that monitors usage of troubling words, threats, and other key safety warning signs and sends parents reports.

→ Share a login and password for various social media accounts of the child's, so a parent can watch all activity from their own phone.

→ Set up "mirroring" between a child's phone and a parent's so the parent can see what the child is doing on their phone without having to be in the same room.

Rules and systems like these can be incredibly helpful—but there will always be kids who know how to subvert the system. That's why monitoring cannot replace regular conversations and a solid set of rules and expectations.

Do's and Don'ts for talking about social media:

Don't say "no" to a child's request before fully investigating what they are interested in.

Do let them get their feelings out and make their case. Then reflect back what you hear from your child, so he knows he is being heard and that you are considering his perspective. This is empowering and encouraging.

Don't exaggerate or share urban legends about online behavior.

Do share stories of real quandaries other kids have found themselves in after fact-checking their veracity.

Don't tell your child he can't be trusted to make good decisions.

Do share that you'd like to help him practice making good choices, and that every skill—including how to use social media appropriately—takes time and support to develop.

Don't say or even imply that you won't look at their phone or accounts and then snoop on them in secret.

Do explain that part of learning to use social media and the internet appropriately is having someone keep an eye on things while we learn and grow.

Do be specific about the level of supervision you will impose and what you do and do not expect from your child. Explain what choices can cause him to lose his privileges with his devices or apps.

We asked boys:

Have you ever interacted with scary people online?

"I was on a *Minecraft* Discord server and I started talking to these neo-Nazis and I was so intrigued. I always wondered, 'How could someone justify being a Nazi?' Like, let's say I didn't like Asians or Black people, what would make me feel strongly enough that I'd go out and talk about it?

"I was bewildered and honestly sort of amazed that I could just talk to neo-Nazis. I told them that I'm Asian and they liked that, almost like a model minority. But it seems like, at the core, they're definitely afraid that white culture is disappearing.

"My parents taught me that the 'us versus them' mentality is false, so I could see that this stuff was all just 'us versus them.' Like, if I said something ignorant as a little kid my parents would always tell me to look beneath the surface and explain how I was wrong. They didn't get mad, they just showed me that you can't take everything at face value. If I hadn't had that, I can see how in that Discord channel I could've fallen for what they were saying."

—Michael, age 16

Expert Insights: How to Help
Kids Use Critical Thinking

Here are a few questions to ask kids when looking at any form of media, adapted from Project Look Sharp at Ithaca College:

Ask:

→ Who made this and for what purpose?
→ Is this fact, opinion, or something else (like fiction, satire, etc.)?
→ What are the sources of the ideas or assertions?
→ Is this a trustworthy source about this particular topic?
→ How might I confirm this information using reliable sources?
→ What are the messages about this?
→ What do they want me to do, think, or feel?
→ Who is the target audience?
→ Who paid for this? Who might make money from it?
→ What is left out that might be important to know?
→ Whose voices are included? Whose might be left out?
→ What aspects of historical or cultural norms are relevant to consider?
→ Who might this message benefit? Who might it harm?
→ How and why might different people interpret this differently?
→ Do I have an open mind about this? Why or why not?
→ Will I share this? If so, how and with whom? If not, why not?
→ What kinds of actions might I take in response to this?

Using this list of questions, find a piece of media that you can examine together. Bonus points if it comes from his or your social feed. Practicing these questions when kids start using social media can arm them with important tools to keep themselves and others safe.

Social Media and Exploitation

In the two decades that Christopher has been teaching health and sexuality education, he's seen kids with unsupervised social media access deal with a lot of consent and privacy issues. Most parents don't know much about this world, and aren't clear on how to supervise it.

Some things that parents should be ready to help their kids navigate as they join social media platforms:

→ Sexism, homophobia, racism, and other anti-equality ideas are often spread through memes and funny videos—boys might dismiss these as "just jokes" without guidance from trusted adults about the impact of "jokes" that make hatred and discrimination seem normal.

→ Sometimes offensive content or offensive comments that boys post online get shared with people beyond the intended audience. Some experts suggest that kids ask themselves: "How would I feel if my grandmother or favorite teacher saw this post?"

→ Young people sometimes see sexual content on social media that they aren't ready for or won't fully understand.

→ Adults sometimes use social media to interact with or exploit minors. It's important to talk about how to recognize predatory behavior and what to do about it.

→ It is common for people, especially young people, to share photos that are sent to them, even if they promise not to. This is true even for things that are shared privately or via a "disappearing media" app—and they should not participate in this bad (and possibly even illegal) violation of privacy.

→ There can be a lot of pressure for young people to send nudes to others. It's important to talk to boys about how to handle this pressure, and how to make sure they aren't pressuring others to share things they don't want to share.

→ It's smart to talk about "sextortion," which is a scam in which someone builds up trust with a victim and gets them to send nude photos or videos and then threatens to release those images publicly unless the victim sends money or meets other demands.

Video Games

Knowing when to introduce video games can be simpler than figuring out when a child is ready for unsupervised social media use. That's because a kid can play an all-ages game like *Mario Kart* with a parent in a controlled environment.

We asked boys:

Is gaming social for you?

"Yes, a lot of my friends and all of my family play games, so it gives us something to share time with and talk about together!"
—Xavier, age 15

"Yes, I like to meet people with common interests, and I have met some lifelong friends through gaming."
—Sam, age 15

"Yes, because I bond over video games with my friends."
—Crosby, age 12

"Gaming shows your friend's true colors. Also, I like socializing online with other people just for socializing experience—like in other countries and other races, just to be one together. But unfortunately toxicity does exist."
—Max, age 15

"I've had this one friend named Joaquin for almost four years now. I met him on *Roblox* a long time ago but we still keep in touch all the time. He's genuinely been one of my closest friends for years and I'm very glad I met him. Online friendships can be very valuable to children and it's up to the parents to teach proper online safety to still protect children."
—Vince, age 15

When playing as a family, parents can observe how their child reacts to the stimulating sounds and graphics, how they behave when winning and losing, and how they interact with those they're playing with. How do they react to loss or being told it's time to stop playing? These are signs of maturity and readiness to play more independently.

Although studies of first-person shooter and other violent games have not shown an increased risk of real-life violent behavior, experts and parents alike point to a range of negative outcomes for the kids who use them.

In *Decoding Boys*, pediatrician and mother of two teens Dr. Cara Natterson writes:

"The data doesn't show what I see in my house and what I hear from so many others: that kids on games seem agitated after playing for a long enough time; that they act like they are traumatized, or at least jacked-up on endorphins. Combined with what looks a whole lot like desensitization to shooting and killing, how can there not be at least some link to real-life violence?"

She notes that, despite her observations, data from multiple studies suggest gamers can reap major benefits from playing first-person shooter games, like improved spatial skills, changes in neural processing and efficiency that boost attention, and even enhancement of creative thinking. Still, Dr. Natterson made clear to us that "there's no denying that first-person shooter games turn on the biological stress response."

She, and many other pediatricians, insists we need more research into exactly how all of these outcomes are related so as to prove conclusively whether these types of games ultimately do tie together with real-world violence and desensitization.

Regardless of where or when you start kids with gaming, pretty much every expert suggests gaming alongside your child to be sure he's in an appropriate environment and practicing good digital hygiene.

Other benefits to gaming together include:

→ Teaching him digital manners and gaming etiquette.

→ Helping him spot the signs of a person with bad intentions.

→ Guiding him on how to keep his information private.

→ Modeling or explaining how to handle a destructive or otherwise inappropriate person in a game.

➜ Helping him plan when to stop playing for the day and how to set goals for what he wants to accomplish before logging off.

➜ Modeling or explaining what to do when others are being mean or inappropriate.

➜ Finding online game tutorials, chat servers, and highlight reels that are designed for all ages, rather than spending time on YouTube going from video to video, with no age restrictions.

Confronting Bigotry in Video Game Communities

If your kid has been playing open games, he's likely heard racist, sexist, homophobic, or other hate-based words. It's also likely these words have affected him in some way, especially if he's been the target of hate-based words. Even if he has not, the prevalence of bigoted slurs in gaming can trick kids into believing these words are harmless—which is objectively untrue.

According to a 2024 survey from the Pew Research Center, 48% of teen boys who play video games say they have been called an offensive name while playing, and 15% have been physically threatened.

As parents, it's critical that we intervene with our kids before they become targets—or part of the problem.

> **Try saying:** "Hey, I just read a very upsetting report about racism and other bigotry in video games. Some experts even believe the rise in racism in online games could be contributing to the suicides of people your age. I know you would never want to hurt someone, but I want to state again that our family rules do not allow us to use racist, sexist, homophobic, or any other hate-based words no matter where we are. Not online, not during video games, not at school, and not at home."

Reassure him that you aren't trying to stop him from gaming, but rather that you want to be in a place where he can openly talk about his experiences and ask questions or find guidance for how to handle these situations.

Ask: "Have you ever heard threatening or bigoted language online? Have you been a victim of this, and if so, how did that feel?"

We asked boys:

What do you love about video games?

"I enjoy them for their storyline, expansive worlds, and sometimes multiplayer mechanics. Also I enjoy the stimulation."
—Xavier, age 15

"I like the sense of community and the ability to feel social."
—Sam, age 15

"I love not having to think about other things and also being able to do things with people far away."
—Ezra, age 15

"It's relaxing, like an escape from life."
—Mark, age 17

"They can have a ton of things included in the game, making them fun to play and talk about. It also is very fun to win the game."
—Crosby, age 12

Talk to Your Boys About the Risks of Gaming

While we feel it's important not to overreact when our kids start gaming, we believe it's equally as important to be aware of some of the risks.

Compulsive or "addictive" behavior

Try saying:

"Video games are fun in part because of how great it feels to win or complete a level or overcome a challenge. It floods our brains with happy chemicals like dopamine, and that feeling is so amazing. It's the same feeling we might have after scoring a goal in soccer or getting a standing ovation after a school play. But it can become hard to stop playing sometimes when we haven't had that 'win' because that feeling is so good. Sometimes, even when we win we want more. I know I've felt that before. It might be smart for us to talk about how to walk away—even if we haven't gotten our 'win' yet.

"Social media is designed to give us rewards—not in the typical way, like when you win a game, but in a way that also increases dopamine and other 'feel good' or 'excitement' chemicals in our brains when you find something really funny, weird, shocking, or emotional. I know when I see something really wild or funny I often want to keep scrolling to find more, and when I don't find something just as good, I feel an urge to scroll more and more, even if I'm tired or feeling annoyed by it. Have you ever felt that? What can we do when we get into that endless need for more?"

Bullying or dog-piling behavior

Try saying:

"When someone is being bullied or ganged up on in school, we can see their faces and watch them get sad or angry and we have empathy for them in the moment. But online, most of the time we can't see people's faces. That can cause us to detach from them in ways that we wouldn't in real life.

"What I really want for you is to be able to stay connected to the human on the other side of the comment or the video or post. You don't have to get overly attached to people or suffer with them, but I want you to just remember the person on the other side is a human just like you."

Radicalism and conspiracy theories

Try saying:

"There are people online who believe things that are really dangerous, cruel, and bad for society, like racist or sexist or homophobic things—and they want other people to believe them, too.

"They may have arguments that seem really convincing, but I want to let you know that I'm here to talk about any of these things, no matter how unpopular or troubling they seem. I won't judge you. We can do some research and figure stuff out together. I'm a safe space for any topic you need to discuss."

The Benefits of Playing Video Games with Your Kids

"As a family that's not as much into traditional sports, sharing esports/gaming with my son gives me the opportunity to bond with him, gives me time to sneakily talk to him about the other things in his life he may not share right after school, and gives us a chance to talk about success and failure much in the way that sports families get to. Plus, it's fun to have a hobby you share with your child.

"I have fond memories from my childhood sharing old Nintendo games like *The Legend of Zelda* and *StarTropics* with my father, so having specific games my son and I like to play together lets me know that he'll have similar memories of me, and I love that.

"As a gamer, I think the only thing I do differently than other nongamer parents is that I am able to inhabit the same spaces with my son. I get to join tournaments with my son daily.

"I also played games not only with my son but with his friends when he was younger. And though I'd limit the times I played with my son's friends, being able to walk in that world gave me insight into the kids' interactions, and let me bond with them in ways I couldn't otherwise."

—Zach Rosenberg, father of a teenage son and cofounder of 8BitDad, an early "dad blog" dedicated to geek fatherhood

Dangerous stunts or "edgy" humor and pranks

Try saying:

"Some people on social media will do things that are really dangerous to get views or go viral, but I want to be super clear that not everything you see is realistic. Remember that not everything wild goes viral, and the risk is often just not worth it.

"On top of that, going viral isn't the same as being famous. I think it's way better to be famous for something that makes you unique, or for working hard at something and completing it well."

Signs That Your Kid Needs Help

When we call something "maladaptive" in this book, what we mean is that the behavior itself may not be a problem, but the way in which it is being used is not necessarily healthy. For instance, playing video games can be a very healthy behavior for our kids (and us!), but if we are using video games as a means to avoid problems, ignore anxiety or other health issues, or in ways that prevent us from doing what is required to be healthy and successful (like eating well, getting exercise, attending school/work), then we may be using gaming maladaptively.

Social media and video games are not the only behaviors that can be used in a maladaptive manner. Even things like eating, reading, and exercise can become maladaptive in certain circumstances.

A few signs your kid could use some screen time or tech intervention:

→ Repeatedly sneaking screen time when they know the rules very clearly

→ Struggling to wake up in the morning

→ Frustration or anger when reasonably asked to set his phone down for meals or conversations

→ A noticeable loss of IRL friendships and interests like sports or hobbies

→ Violent or rage-filled reactions to gaming losses (throwing/ breaking objects, for instance)

→ Adopting new, irrational, or ideologically problematic perspectives

If these problems feel persistent or like something that your typical parental interventions aren't helping with, seek help from a trusted mental health care provider, your family physician, or even a school counselor. It's normal to struggle, and it's also normal to seek help.

We asked boys:

Do you ever find it hard to stop using your phone or playing a game?

"Every now and then I try to take a day off from using TikTok or any of those short-form content apps. I find myself subconsciously opening them up, which is pretty scary. But outside of that I just realize what I'm doing and turn it off."

—Vince, age 15

"Sometimes, but it's just because I am trying to finish something up or figure something out."

—Xavier, age 15

"I find it hard to stop playing sometimes when I am building something in *Minecraft*."

—Ezra, age 15

"Yes. Video games do stimulate your brain and they help me warm up, but because of that, they are also a bit addicting."

—Jeff, age 16

REMEMBER THIS:

❶ One of the most important aspects of parenting well in the twenty-first century is to be as nonjudgmental as possible with teens about their hobbies and online habits.

❷ There are various ways to monitor kids' social media use, including phones that allow gradually increasing access to social media and the open internet.

❸ Video games have changed a lot in the last twenty years, and the best way for parents to understand the games and their kid's involvement is to play with kids and/or coordinate with other parents to help make sure kids are in a safe environment.

❹ The key to success is openness, healthy and regular conversation, and joining together to enjoy tech, media, and various types of screen time.

"Friendships are not only vital, but necessary for good mental health. If you don't have people to reach out to, laugh with, or lean on for support, it's really easy to feel lonely in the world. I consider myself introverted, but I still have that very real, very human need to form connections."

—Nat, age 17

Chapter 12

Talk to Your Boys About

FRIENDSHIP

Picture this scenario. It's Friday, family movie night, a beloved tradition now going on eight years. You're getting out the snacks when your phone buzzes—it's a text from your boy: "I'm hanging out at Luke's tonight. Home by 11." Ouch!

It's normal to feel like you just got dumped by a friend in moments like this. But don't worry, it's also completely normal for adolescents to act this way. It may even be biological, at least according to noted biological anthropologist Helen Fisher, PhD.

A few months before she passed away, we had the honor of speaking with Fisher, who told us that this type of behavior among teenagers is to be expected, noting that the modern brain was "designed" more than 300,000 years ago—well before written history—and it was designed for one reason: survival.

When babies are tiny, they depend upon the adults in their lives to feed and protect them. We met their every need. As they grew, their parents became less directly tied to their survival and they started forming other relationships. They had to. After all, we—their parents and caregivers—are going to get old someday and they will still need community in order to survive.

That's one of the reasons why their brains "urge" them, in a sense, to push away from their families and find new bonds with peers. They need to find people who will hunt, gather, protect, and raise children with them. These are the folks who become their new support system into adulthood, the people who carry on humanity's survival, so to speak. While they may not be consciously aware of the biological reasons why, it is normal and healthy for them to feel a drive to meet new people, explore new lands, and keep that gene pool healthy!

"From an evolutionary perspective," Fisher continued, "they've got something more immediate to their survival than you [as their parents]. And if you can understand this and not take it personally, you can even help them grow into this new role while helping them understand that you want to be of use to their progress, and that you understand that this is their future."

The bottom line for Fisher? "Let them go. They'll be back."

That doesn't mean we let them run wild. Teen friendships can be tricky, and the desire to fit in or be part of a group can sometimes override common sense. But when we accept and empathize with our kids about this new stage of their lives, we can then help them figure out how to handle peer pressure and the drive to belong. That way, when they encounter risky behaviors or the temptation to break rules or go against their own moral codes, they will have tools—and the knowledge that they can come to their parents and trusted caregivers for support and advice.

Now back to imagining the time you got ditched on your pizza night for your boy's friend, Luke. One thing that may alarm you is realizing that Luke is a new friend—a boy you barely know. You may also find it alarming when you realize how much time he spends with Luke and other new friends—and how little he spends with Dante, his best friend since first grade.

As it turns out, it's totally normal for adolescent friendships to shift—and sometimes they shift dramatically. That doesn't make it any less potentially heartbreaking (to the kids or the parents!), but it can be a comfort to know that it's not typically a warning sign.

While it's natural for friendships to shift, we also need to help our boys develop and maintain meaningful friendships during adolescence in order to help protect them against the type of loneliness that harms men and boys.

In 2023, Equimundo published its *State of American Men* report, a survey of more than 2,000 men ages eighteen to forty-five of various

races and ethnicities. Some of the statistics around friendship and loneliness are startling. Here are a few examples:

→ Of men ages eighteen to twenty-three, 65% say that "no one
  really knows me well."

→ Nearly half of men (48%) say their online lives are more
  engaging and rewarding than their offline lives.

→ Only 22% of men have three or more people in their local
  area they feel close to or depend on.

→ Almost 30% of men ages eighteen to twenty-three reported
  not spending time with someone outside their household in
  the past week.

We asked boys:

What do you think can be done to help alleviate loneliness?

"Many people have recently shared the idea of a 'male loneliness
epidemic,' and though most discussion about it has been a lot of
political finger-pointing, I think it's important to acknowledge that
this kind of thing has gotten worse over the years largely thanks to
polarization in internet cultures. While online friendships are very
real, it is good to also try and limit exposure to the internet climate
in general. Please encourage your sons to mostly make physical
friends; it may be a struggle, but it will help!"

—Nat, age 17

For an increasing number of men and boys, the majority of their
friendships happen online, in digital communities, via social media, or
while gaming. While these friendships are certainly meaningful, many
teenage boys find themselves wishing they had more IRL friends and
struggling to fit in with communities outside of their online experiences.

Whether your boy is at the center of a huge and vibrant friend group or more comfortable with one or two close relationships, friendship is important. Preparing him for the changes that may await him can help him face them more easily, too.

CHECK IN WITH YOURSELF ━━ ━━ ━━ ━━ ━━ ━━ ━━

> What assumptions do I have about boy friendships?

> What was friendship like for me at his age? How might those experiences bias me?

> Does friendship come easily or hard for me? How about for my son?

> What models of male friendship does my boy get to see on a regular basis?

What Boys Need in Order to Be Good at Friendship

Brian Spitulnik, a psychotherapist in New York City, told us he believes parents can help adolescent boys develop deeper, more lasting friendships—a skill that can benefit them for a lifetime. First, he insists, we must teach them how to understand emotions—theirs and others'—and how to be vulnerable with others.

"Teaching boys to express feelings—not just anger, but also sadness and fear and joy—means modeling what it's like to be expressive and hold space for someone else's emotions," he told us. And this is something we simply do not do enough for boys.

Yes, we need to hold space for someone's feelings and express our own in order to build a lasting, deep friendship. But first, our boys need to learn that it's OK to express their emotions and be vulnerable in the first place. And that starts with us.

Spitulnik shared a simple question that can help boys (or anyone!) determine if someone is the type of friend who adds to your happiness and sense of connection: "Who are the friends with whom you can truly say 'I'm sad about this thing, do you have a version of that?' If they can say 'Yes, I have a version of that,' then you have a friend."

This may seem obvious to those of us who grew up with great friends, but the world is different now, with lots of kids connecting with others only online and more and more boys feeling lonely and isolated. If our boys don't have someone like that, we need to help them find at least one friend with whom he feels connected.

Once they make a connection with someone, you may want to talk about how to follow up with potential new friends—exchanging cell phone numbers, inviting people to hang out or do an activity with you, making concrete plans and following up on them. As we noted earlier, some boys really need to be walked through all of these steps—even if it seems silly.

Please also remember that some kids struggle socially, but that doesn't mean they're condemned to loneliness for life. Similarly, a popular boy with lots of friends is not immune to loneliness—now or in the future—and learning how to develop emotionally rewarding friendships can benefit him, too.

Cliques, Popularity, and Finding Your People

Female friendships are stereotypically thought to be emotional and full of drama while boys' friendships are assumed to be shallow and based solely on sports or partying. In her book *Masterminds & Wingmen*, about the social dynamics of teen boys, Rosalind Wiseman urges parents not to be fooled by these stereotypes or to assume boys don't need meaningful friendships. "Boys' social structures are just as powerful and controlling as those of girls," she warns, "especially in moments of conflict or abuse of power."

She divides adolescent boys into four main categories of social status, diving deeply into the structure of each group in her book. For our purposes, we are synopsizing the basics to help parents understand what boy social hierarchies look like today:

The 10 Percenters: Your typical popular guys. They have lots of friends, may have plenty of girls to date, and parties and events to attend. Wiseman notes that contrary to what they may portray, they are not guaranteed happiness, success, or a feeling of security.

The Majority: As the name suggests, this group is the bulk of the boys in school, often divided into groups of five or six boys each.

We asked boys:

A lot of boys today say they don't have many close friends. Does that feel true to you?

"I think a lot of people don't have many close friends because they might have trouble being social (like it makes them anxious or something) or that they like things or respect certain things that other people might find silly or stupid or something along those lines."

—Xavier, age 15

"This does not feel true to me because I have many close friends. I think regardless of your gender you should have close friends."

—Merow, age 13

"Yeah, I don't have many close friends and I wish I had more."

—Ezra, age 15

"I have a lot of close female and nonbinary friends, and one close male friend, but in general I think that it's really hard to make close male friends. Whenever I talk with my male friends, the conversation usually devolves into memes or jokes about sex and stuff like that. We don't talk about our feelings; we don't open up to each other; we don't get closer with each other. I think that there's some underlying norm that boys and men just don't talk about feelings. Maybe my guy friends don't find it interesting, or it's frightening, or they're just used to the idea of staying distant. Even though all my male friends are really LGBTQ+ accepting, I think that, in general, there might also be some fear of being seen as gay. With my friends back in middle school especially, some used the f-slur in their conversations; I think everyone was afraid of becoming the butt of those kind of 'jokes.'"

—Nat, age 17

"Kind of. There isn't someone I can completely rely on."

—Jeff, age 16

The Bottom Rung: They're not popular, but they're generally not outcasts.

The Outer Perimeter: These are the kids who don't fit into any group. While this may include social outcasts, it also may include kids who are singularly focused on one school subject or sport to the point where they simply don't fit in with—or don't try to join into—any group.

The good news is that boys don't need to be part of the popular crowd or have a whole team of friends behind them to feel happy and fulfilled in high school. Just one good, trusted friend can make all the difference. Each kid must find his own path, and while one best friend may be enough, having a few friends who play different roles and serve different needs is OK, too.

When Your Boy Is Struggling to Fit In

As parents, it's our job to be a soft-landing place for our boys' feelings and to help them process these feelings. If your son says "I just don't fit in" or "I feel like such a freak at school," you may be tempted to dismiss him ("That's not true!") or tell him to stop thinking that way ("Don't say that!"), but that reaction may make him feel even more alone. Instead, offer comfort, remind him you love him and think he's wonderful, and *then* start brainstorming some solutions.

First and foremost, avoid minimizing his desire to fit in.

Don't say: "It's OK if you're having trouble making friends, you've got us, your parents!"

Instead, say: "It can be so hard when you feel like you don't have a good friend you can trust or a group of friends. It happens to a lot of kids your age, and eventually most of us find our people. In the meantime, know that we love you and are always here—though we know we aren't meant to replace having good friends."

Don't say: "You're too good for those kids, anyway. That group of boys are all such little punks."

Instead, say: "I can imagine how much it must hurt to be left out like that. Are there other kids in school who might feel more like your people, or who might appreciate you more or understand you better?"

Research has shown that teens and young adults are more likely to believe they can persevere if they know others have persevered before them. Here are a few examples of how to reframe challenges to help a kid feel hopeful:

→ "Hey, I know the first day of high school can be nerve-wracking and bring up a lot of worries. But I wanted to let you know that lots of kids feel that way at some point, even the ones who seem to have it all together. I think some kids are just really good at hiding it. It usually gets much easier after a few days."

→ "When I was your age, I felt like I was so short and felt like a little kid, and everyone else was so confident. Since then I've learned that most people felt the same way about their own insecurities. If you're feeling anything like that, just know it can get easier and you're not the only one!"

→ "Just know that it's normal to feel awkward and alone when you start at a new school. And that's the reality at first, right? You don't know anyone—or you only know a few people—and it may even feel lonely at first. Most people would feel the same way. Feeling weird or awkward doesn't mean you *are* weird or awkward. In fact, feeling awkward is probably more common than feeling confident in this situation!"

When a child is struggling socially, it can be helpful to start with a few simple questions.

First, determine if your child is actually struggling socially. Sometimes what looks lonely to us is just how a kid likes it. For instance, maybe he has one good friend he hangs out with at school and a few times a month on the weekend, but otherwise he stays home with family or works on things he's passionate about. If you were popular or part of an active social scene at his age, you may be tempted to assume he's miserable, but it may work perfectly for him!

Talk to Your Boys About Popularity

Don't say: "Popularity is overrated. Popular kids tend to fail as adults anyway."

Instead, say: "Popularity often feels really important, and in some ways it is. It can feel cruddy to be left out of a group that seems to be having so much fun. But it's important you know that you don't need to be popular or part of the cool clique to be happy—in fact, some studies show that as long as you have a good friend or two, you're likely just as happy as other kids in high school."

Don't say: "Why aren't you friends with [insert names of boys in a group you think your kid should be hanging out with]? Wouldn't you want to be friends with them?"

Instead, ask questions: "What are the different groups at your school like? Are there popular kids and unpopular or is it more a mix? Where do you fit? Do you wish you were in a different group or are you happy with how it is?"

Here are a few questions that can help you start the conversation:

→ "What's your friendship life like these days?"
→ "Who, if anyone, do you trust most, outside of our immediate family?"
→ "Is there anything you'd change or like more of when it comes to friendships and your social life?"

Note that these questions don't presume something is wrong, but rather offer opportunities for him to share his feelings, untainted by our own expectations.

If you do determine that he's struggling, ask a few specific questions to understand why. Such as:

→ "What part of making friends feels challenging?"

→ "What happens when you start talking to someone who seems like they could become a friend?"

Then, instead of assuming he wants your help, ask if he'd like to talk through some situations or role-play to figure out how to approach them. If he declines, offer an opportunity to talk to someone else—an older sibling, a cool uncle, or maybe even a school counselor or therapist, depending on how emotional he is feeling.

If making friends has been easy for you, it can be hard to imagine your child's perspective when he's struggling. Parenting coach and author Caroline Maguire shared a formula with us that might help parents think more concretely about how to build friendships—and remind us that this doesn't happen overnight.

"Each time you participate and bond and share experiences with someone," she told us, "you collect information and you grow knowledge of the other person; you grow trust and engage in shared experiences."

Instead of encouraging your child to try to break into the "cool kids" group, ask him to consider which groups do things he finds fun or interesting.

→ Does he love watching musicals? How about the theater kids?

→ Is he into cars and motorcycles? What about the kids who take Auto Shop?

→ Is he into films? Check out if there's a school TV station or newspaper. What are those kids like?

→ Does he love '90s metal bands? Maybe there are other kids who wear vintage concert t-shirts.

Once he has an idea of what he's into and what he might find fun to do with other people, he can think about how to meet those kids or get to know them better.

Ultimately, your son has to be the one guiding these friendships, but you can assist him in learning how to "do" friendship better.

We asked boys:

What do you think parents should do if their son is struggling to make friends?

"Try to sit down and have talks with the kid about it and see if they can discover the problem, then the parents should try to help their kids through it, but I don't agree with just inviting random kids over to try and make friends out of them."

—Xavier, age 15

"Talk to your son about their feelings and experiences. Listen without judgment to understand why it is challenging for them to make friends. Then you could encourage your son to participate in activities where they can meet new people in their community."

—Merow, age 13

"Not forcing people to make friends but signing them up to do things."

—Ezra, age 15

"I think that parents should be sensitive to their son's interests and try to set him up with a hobby or group that aligns with those interests. For example, my dad signed me up for a Dungeons & Dragons game group when I was struggling to make friends. Everyone in the group liked what we were doing, so we bonded and got closer over our mutual love of DnD. It was after we all reached that initial level of trust that our friendship became deeper and closer."

—Nat, age 17

Keeping Friendships Going

In addition to making friends, many of our boys need to learn skills to keep friendships going. As adults, many of us have developed systems for maintaining friendships and keeping them alive and healthy. This isn't something we immediately know how to do; we practice over time—often not realizing that we are honing a skill.

Caroline Maguire shared a friendship hack that can work well for everyone: "Do one thing to nurture your friendship every day."

You can encourage your boy to put it on his calendar, if that's how he best keeps on top of things.

We asked boys:

What do you wish adults understood about friendships today?

"It's not easy to make friends, especially as teens, because everyone is just trying to not have their voice crack and trying to impress the next person, so I wish that more adults would talk to their kids about friendships, and not just let them off the hook if they say they have friends. Really try and get to them, because that will also build a stronger bond between the parents and children."

—Xavier, age 15

A few suggestions for growing friendships with daily interactions:

→ Texting, even just to ask what's new

→ Bringing a friend's favorite snack to nutrition or lunch break every once in a while

→ Sharing memes or videos you know a friend will like

→ Setting up a time to play a video game together or meet to shoot hoops (or whatever interests you share)

Ultimately, our boys are the ones who need to decide which friendships to nurture and grow and which to set aside. We can help them feel empowered by their choices and their friendships.

When You Dislike His Friends

We've all been there. Your kid gets in the car at pick-up and shares yet another story about his friend—the one who drives you bonkers—and the hijinks they got into together. This can be cute when they're little, but as they get older, our worries about the company our teens keep grow deeper.

For the purposes of this chapter, we're going to call the friend Robert.

Step One: Don't Bad-mouth Robert

This is hard, especially if you tend to have an open relationship with your son. The two of you likely share opinions on everything, no holds barred. But when it comes to a friend he values, think before you speak.

Nobody likes to feel judged, and that goes double for teens. And nobody likes to hear people they care about being disparaged. Remember, teenagers are hardwired to care deeply about their friends, and he likely feels loyalty toward Robert.

Step Two: Ask Questions

Remember, just because we're adults and they're teens doesn't mean we know everything and they know nothing. Your son might have lovely reasons for hanging out with that kid you're not so into.

Try asking:

→ "Tell me more about Robert, what's he into?"

→ "How is Robert liking ninth grade (or whatever is happening in their lives)?"

→ "What sort of stuff do you and Robert talk about at lunch?"

Remember: Don't judge, just listen!

Step Three: Get to Know Robert (If You Don't Already)

Yes, you need to get to know Robert. Even if it's just offering him a ride home from school or asking him to join you for dinner, inviting Robert into your life is going to give you an opportunity to see his value in your son's life, and help keep your son close. You may even start liking Robert!

Getting to know his parents may help, too, though that can be hard to do as our kids get older.

Step Four: Express Concerns to Your Son

Once you have gotten to know Robert, if you're still concerned about his influence on your son, have a conversation.

A few ideas for what to say:

→ "I've gotten to know Robert a bit and I want to share a few concerns. Maybe you have some of the same ones."

→ "There's an old phrase that says, 'Show me the people you spend the most time with, and I'll show you your future,' and it's got me thinking about some of the choices Robert makes."

→ "I wonder if there's something deeper to why you enjoy being friends with Robert, because, on the surface, it seems to me like he's not very nice to other people. Have you noticed that?"

→ "I know you like having Robert over, but I'm going to be honest with you: Some of the choices he makes concern me. Have you ever felt that way?"

→ "I am thinking about some of the choices Robert makes, and I wonder—do you feel like he has your best interests in mind when you're together?"

A few things not to say:

→ "Don't you have any better friends?"

→ "Robert is a loser/annoying/weird/etc."

→ "Robert is going to pull you down."

→ "Why don't you hang out with those other nice boys?"

Girls Make Good Friends!

Many straight teen boys report that they can have authentic, meaningful, nonromantic friendships with girls. This is something to encourage, especially for our boys who identify as straight. Platonic friendships help boys learn nonromantic relational skills with women, which leads to more respect and less "othering" of the opposite sex.

REMEMBER THIS:

❶ Men are in a loneliness crisis—and part of the reason is a sharply increasing number of men who report not having any close friends. We can help our boys create friendships that are healthy and long-lasting.

❷ Not all of the popular boys are happy—and boys do not need to be popular or "cool" to be happy and fulfilled. One good friend makes a huge difference. Parents often care more about their son's popularity than the teen does.

❸ Making friends isn't always easy, but it is a skill that can be learned.

❹ There are certain tools that can help teens and young adults feel accepted and emotionally secure in social situations, and parents can help.

❺ Sometimes you will dislike his friends. If you must talk to your son about his friend, do so respectfully and without extending judgment to your son.

"Not everyone in society is being treated equally, as there are still wage gaps and more between race, sexuality, and gender. We, as a society, have been working to bridge those gaps, but we need to come a long way before it's 'solved.'"

—Rahul, age 15

Chapter 13

Talk to Your Boys About

POWER, BULLYING, AND INCLUSION

W hile power and privilege in society may seem like a very adult topic, social power is something most of our kids already understand—at least in the context of their own worlds. They've likely sat through several lectures about bullying, even if they haven't seen or experienced it themselves, and they know who has power in their school, who is included in activities—and who is not.

The goal of this chapter is to help parents reframe conversations about bullying, power, and inclusion so they're less divisive. We want to get our boys thinking and talking about power and privilege in ways that increase empathy and inspire them to take concrete steps to make the world more fair, more kind, and more caring.

The world is a very diverse, connected place these days. Growing up today means playing, studying, and connecting with people of different races, people with different abilities, people who practice different religions, and people of varying sexual orientations or gender expressions, both online and in person. This is a great thing, and it may feel very different from how previous generations grew up.

You don't have to be an expert to start these conversations, and you don't have to say everything perfectly. You just have to be willing to talk and learn together.

Talk to Your Boys About Bullying

You've probably noticed that conversations about bullying are often met with an eyeroll or dismissive sigh. It doesn't mean your kid doesn't care about bullying, but rather that the term "bullying" is overused to the point of losing its meaning—and young people know that.

While cruelty and exclusion should be taken seriously and addressed, bullying is a specific type of mistreatment that requires different interventions and solutions.

Bullying isn't just one kid being unkind to someone else. It is a pattern of behavior designed to target someone, hurt them, and make them feel inferior.

"An individual act of cruelty or exclusion can usually be solved in conversations with caring adults," anti-bullying educator Jamie Utt-Schumacher, PhD, told us. "Bullying, on the other hand, typically cannot be solved by talking only to the kids."

Why? Because it's not random and it's not just random kids who are targeted—and it doesn't start with the kids.

"The *American Education Research Journal* did a comprehensive review of literature on bullying," Utt-Schumacher explained, "and they found that the vast majority of bullying behaviors mimic ways in which oppression writ large shows up in their community."

These patterns show up differently depending on dynamics within their community. In one area, homophobia or racism may be the bigotry reflected in that school's bullying while in others, poverty or class issues may be the trigger.

Here's how to begin:

→ Parents and teachers talk a lot about bullying. Is it a problem in your school?

→ When I was a kid, bullying was all over the place and nobody seemed to think about it.

→ When bullying does happen, who seems to be targeted the most?

POWER, BULLYING, AND INCLUSION | 223

Depending on your kid's willingness to talk, you can go deeper:

→ What sorts of things happen in the bullying you see or hear about? Are kids making fun of other kids, or is it more like violence?

→ Do you think purposefully excluding some kids counts as bullying?

→ Do you ever hear about identity-based bullying, like when someone is bullied or called out for being a person of a different race, or about their perceived sexuality or a disability?

In his anti-bullying curriculum, Utt-Schumacher teaches kids that there are three different roles a kid can take in helping:

1. **Interveners/Interrupters:** These are the people who step in when they see someone being unkind. Often, the best way to do this is by distracting: i.e., making a joke, changing the subject, or doing something goofy to draw attention away from the situation.

Utt-Schumacher made it clear to us that it is not the job of kids to educate other kids about why something is wrong. That's an adult's job, and one that adults must do when they intervene. If a kid wishes to and feels empowered to, it can be helpful, but we should let our kids know that simply interrupting the behavior can be enough.

"Everyone has an interrupter role, but not everyone's interrupter role is the same," Utt-Schumacher emphasized.

2. **First Responders:** These are the people who follow up with the targeted person. For kids, this can be as simple as saying, "Hey, I saw what happened and that sucked. I'm sorry," "How can I help?" or "How are you doing? That was rough." First Responders remind a targeted kid that they aren't alone, which can be of enormous help.

3. **Social Normers:** Utt-Schumacher likens these kids to the "influencers" of their school or group—the ones who can start a new trend or deem something "uncool" that others will follow.

In his work with young people, Utt-Schumacher observed that ideas students would've deemed "corny" if an adult had suggested them can be game-changers when brainstormed by or initiated by Social Normers.

In one example he shared with us, students at a high school—along with teachers, administrators, and members of the community—came together to try to solve a bullying problem. Students brainstormed ideas along with the adults and were empowered to follow through on ones that resonated with them.

One of these ideas was to place Post-it notes with kind messages on one another's lockers. The popular kids at school acted as Social Normers and started the trend, which was then followed by others, helping create a new culture of kindness. Utt-Schumacher believes this simply would not have worked as well had the idea come directly from the adults.

"Social Norming by itself is the least effective strategy. It's meant to amplify the efforts of Interrupters and First Responders, and works best when the school and community are making changes at the same time," says Utt-Schumacher.

Questions that focus on solutions can help your kid find ways to feel empowered:

→ Are there people in your school who do a good job intervening? What do they do?

→ What do you think someone who has been targeted might appreciate hearing you say after the fact?

→ Are there adults you trust that you could talk to about this, if you didn't feel like intervening would work?

Remember to use active listening tools to help your kid feel heard and understood:

→ "Let me be sure I understand what you're saying . . ."

→ "I can imagine that might feel _____. Is that right, or something else?"

→ "Wow, it sounds like ____ is happening, does that seem accurate?"

→ "That sounds complicated. Is there anything you think parents and teachers don't understand about this situation?"

We asked boys:

Do you think everyone in society (or even just your school) is treated fairly these days?

"The notion that everyone in society is treated fairly is so laughable that I don't think a sane person has believed this since we first crawled out of the ocean 360 million years ago. No identities are inherently better than others, yet people are treated as though that's the case. Therefore, everyone in society, including and especially at my school, are not treated fairly these days."

—Nadav, age 15

"No, because I feel like it got to the point where everyone tries to be better than the other."

—Anees, age 18

"I don't think anyone will ever be treated fairly. There's always going to be some sort of prejudice and hate in the world. The world isn't going to be perfect where nobody is judged by their race or sexual orientation. I don't think it's possible. Obviously, I wish it was possible. Most people wish everyone was treated fairly."

—Cam, age 16

Your Kid Might Be the Bully

"Not my kid!"

We all want to believe our kids act in moral ways and would never harm anyone else. In her book *How to Raise Kids Who Aren't Assholes,*

Talk to Your Boys About
Assuming Everyone Else Is Happy

Adolescents are smarter than we realize.

Try saying: "I know it feels like those kids at the top of the social pyramid have it all, but did you know that the most popular kid in school often feels much more pressure than other kids? Let me read you a quote from this book."

(Then read him whatever you feel is relevant from this book or any of the fantastic ones we've cited in this chapter.)

Then ask: "Why do you think those guys feel this way? Do you feel like they have to hide it more than other kids?"

Questions that can get him thinking about assumptions:

→ Have you ever met someone and been surprised by what they had going on under the surface?
→ What do you think other people assume incorrectly about you?
→ Have you ever seen a different side of any of those popular boys, something that makes them less perfect?
→ Are there ways that opening up about your own feelings might help others? What if the other guys did?

If your son is one of the popular guys, try asking:

→ Do you think other people are happier than you? If so, why?
→ What are the stresses that come with being popular or high-achieving at your school?
→ Do you feel you have to hide your fears and insecurities? What would happen if you stopped hiding them?

Melinda Wenner Moyer explains why that is a problematic way of thinking:

> "When researchers at the University of New Hampshire surveyed kids and parents, they found that 31 percent of fifth graders admitted to teasing or picking on others, but that only 11 percent of their parents thought their kids ever did such things.
>
> "The parents of kids who bullied were especially unlikely to suspect a problem: When the researchers talked to the subgroup of students who had admitted to picking on peers, they found that only 2 percent of those kids' parents were aware of their children's behavior."

In other words, the parents of so-called bullies are the least likely to believe that their kids are capable of bullying. If you find that your kid has been bullying others, you might feel furious, embarrassed, or defensive. This is natural. But it's important to get back to a calm, steady state so you can approach your boy objectively and rationally. Avoid labeling them (or any child) as a bully. Instead, focus on the behavior.

Many kids who choose to bully are, or have been, bullied themselves, and often their behavior reflects unkind acts they've witnessed or been taught at home. Their behavior is a choice they made, not who they are, and it doesn't need to define them forever.

Ask your kid:

→ Do you think most people who act like bullies or make other people feel bad are inherently cruel people?

→ What emotions do you think motivate kids to be unkind to one another or act like bullies?

→ What cultural changes might need to happen at your school or in your group so targeted kids feel safer and kids who are being unkind can make better choices?

Talk to Your Boys About Hate-based Insults and Slurs

In our experience, most boys say they wouldn't want to harm another student based on their race or identity. But too often, the run-of-the-mill "trash talking" and name-calling that seem to be the hallmark of so many teen boys' interactions can easily slip into something that looks a lot like hate speech. That's why it's so important to talk to them about words and how they matter.

There are a few ways to approach the subject. If you can do this before they hear the words from peers or while playing video games/watching streamers, that's the best bet. And remember that these conversations aren't a one-time-only thing!

→ Always add context when telling a kid that a word is hurtful (racist, sexist, anti-Semitic, homophobic, etc). Add who it hurts, why these words are so powerful, and how the person might feel when they hear these words.

→ Share a short history of what that group experienced that will connect empathy for the targeted group with the word itself.

→ Don't shut down a conversation because your kid said something problematic. Ask questions and appeal to his compassion and empathy.

→ Start by assuming that he didn't know the context for this word and/or why using it is hurtful. Invite him into conversation about it, rather than pushing him away. (If he is participating in a hate-based activity, immediate intervention is key. Reach out to a therapist or counselor for further assistance. We also suggest reading *Breaking Hate* by Christian Picciolini, which is focused on intervention stories and helping families intervene with hate-based indoctrination of a loved one.)

→ Don't call victims of hate-based language sensitive or delicate, or frame why he shouldn't say hurtful words solely as a way to avoid "getting canceled."

→ Keep empathy at the center of your conversation. You can also mention that saying hateful or bigoted words can cause others to see him as hateful or bigoted, and explain how that can affect his future, regardless of whether he meant any harm.

Talk to Your Boys About Power

Power and privilege have become big societal topics of conversation in the last few years, part of a major cultural shift that is likely to continue well into the future. To engage in these conversations, our kids need to understand how power shows up in all areas of society, and they need to be able to talk about these issues with compassion and awareness.

Kids today hear many different perspectives on topics like politics, international policy, gender, and racial issues. Their social media time-lines are full of opinions and "hot takes," but not all of these perspectives are well-informed. Worse, not all of these perspectives will be focused on creating a more equitable society that is safe for everyone. In fact, some of them are designed to create division.

When complicated social issues become oversimplified online and then branch into real life, it can lead to unnecessary division and strife. For example, based on what they've learned online, some kids may believe that having power makes people evil, and that people who have "privilege" never had to struggle. These things are simply not true.

Protecting Your Boy from Ideological Predators

One of the most appealing aspects of gaining power is that it can offer a feeling of control over their life. This is particularly attractive to teen-agers who feel an urge to be independent despite still being under the domain of their parents and caregivers.

Some boys who feel powerless may find themselves lured into hate-based and anti-democracy philosophies by ideological predators—adults who target minors for the express purpose of indoctrinating them into harmful groups.

Most of the boys lured into these hate-based groups didn't set out to do harm. In fact, many of those targeted by ideological predators believe they've found a way to help people. Typically, the boys are made to believe that they are being heroic by adopting extremist views or tak-ing extreme action—even if the outcome is hate-based, anti-democracy, or even deadly.

In his book *Breaking Hate*, Christian Picciolini, a former member of a hate group who has spent decades working to prevent others from falling into the same fate, shared with us the factor he believes makes kids most likely to fall for this propaganda: potholes.

Picciolini explains that "life's 'potholes,' caused by unresolved emotional, psychological, and/or physical trauma, and the weighty after-effects of shame and uncertainty that often accompany trauma, are what push some of us down the road to radicalization."

In other words, while any kid can become a target of ideological predators or extremism, kids who have unresolved trauma or underlying shame are the most likely to sign on. They are more likely to be looking for purpose and less likely to feel as though they can know and trust their family—or their own instincts—to know what is best when faced with challenging concepts.

--- No Wrong Answers: Questions to Get You Talking ----------

Power and Heroics

Ask your son:

→ Who do you look up to—real or fictional?

→ What makes you like them?

→ What aspects of their lives and/or personalities do you look up to?

→ Do you think anyone can become a hero?

→ What might be some of the negative aspects of being a hero?

→ What might happen when a hero or superhero gets too much power?

Note: Be prepared for your child to name someone you don't know—or maybe someone you don't like. The challenge is to be open enough to understand why they admire this person and to resist the urge to shut him down or make him feel ashamed.

That doesn't mean you should keep quiet if your kid's hero is a jerk or someone of poor character. It means you should hear his "why" before sharing more information about this person. When you do, invite him into your perspective like you would with a friend. It's likely if you present info with respect, he'll listen with respect.

POWER, BULLYING, AND INCLUSION 231

Inclusion and Empathy

Just when this chapter starts feeling hopeless, we want to share some good news.

Dr. John Duffy has worked with many adolescents and believes kids today are actually more empathetic than they have been in the past. In his book *Parenting the New Teen in the Age of Anxiety*, he writes, "children today are far more open-minded, accepting of differences, and inclusive [. . .] They are less likely to tolerate bullying or injustice of virtually any kind and they recognize the emotional complexities not only of their own lives, but the lives of others as well."

That makes our job of teaching empathy and inclusion much easier!

Of course, we still need to teach our boys skills of inclusion—not just anti-bullying—so they can be part of a future where people are treated fairly and appreciated for who they are.

Once kids understand how unfair many systems of power and privilege are, they often want to figure out how to help. This is an amazing instinct and should be applauded! The first step? Talk about empathy and inclusion.

Most of us have been teaching empathy since our kids were little preschoolers, when, if they hit a friend, we asked them to imagine how that friend felt when they were hit. When we saw a child excluded at the playground, we probably encouraged our kids to ask them to play. These are the early steps of learning to consider how others feel.

Empathy becomes more of a "big picture" conversation when kids reach adolescence. The challenge is to get them to do it consistently.

In his book *Brainstorm*, Dr. Daniel Siegel explains that teenagers become better at practicing empathy as they mature and their prefrontal cortexes become more actively involved in decision-making. That doesn't mean our teens are condemned to ten to fifteen years of poor decision-making; many are already quite empathetic. It simply means we can help develop their empathy "superpower" as they grow.

In fact, Dr. Siegel explains, parents can help their kids with "the regular practice of reflection and reflective conversation."

"One of the most exciting things to remember," Siegel writes, " . . . is that science suggests that such training of a skill grows connections among our neurons that help create a more integrated set of circuits in the brain. And these integrated circuits support how we balance our emotions, focus our attention, understand others and ourselves, approach problems, and interact with others."

In other words, we can help them "flex" their prefrontal cortexes by using them more. Like a workout for the logical, rational, and empathetic parts of their brains.

What does this have to do with power and bullying? Well, when one regularly practices empathy for others, they become less likely to misuse any power they have—now or in the future.

Being an Upstander

In order to counteract what is often called the "bystander effect," activists and educators often teach a variant of the "5Ds of Bystander Intervention" as a means of inspiring people to be "upstanders" instead of bystanders. (See page 244 for more details on the 5Ds.) Regardless of what method is used to teach intervention, the goal is to reduce violence and bullying by teaching people to use empathy and engage in helping others.

Stanford University's Upstander Intervention training offers a few questions we can ask kids to get them thinking about how to make their world more inclusive:

Ask:

→ "What might change if we lived in a community full of upstanders?"

→ "How do we foster a culture of upstanding to reduce all harms in a culture that has the capacity to passively reflect or actively disrupt violence and oppression?"

The brilliance of Upstander training is to tell bystanders what they should do (stand up) rather than what they should not do. Training kids to intervene offers them opportunities to show the targets of bullies that they aren't alone.

Of course, ending violence, bullying, and other oppression requires more than simply asking kids to step up against people who are acting like bullies or targeting others. As Michelle Icard writes in *Fourteen Talks by Age Fourteen*, "I love the intention behind encouraging kids to stick up for others who are targeted or disenfranchised, but we also need to recognize, out loud, to our kids, that this is not as simple as it seems."

As we noted earlier, ending these harmful behaviors is work that needs to be done by schools and organizations, not children. And while kids can make a difference—and have been since more effective anti-bullying programs were first introduced—the majority of this work needs to be done by the adults in power.

Bystander Effect

"The bystander effect occurs when the presence of others discourages an individual from intervening in an emergency situation, against a bully, or during an assault or other crime.

"The greater the number of bystanders, the less likely it is for any one of them to provide help to a person in distress. People are more likely to take action in a crisis when there are few or no other witnesses present."

—*Psychology Today*

That doesn't mean we stop training people to intervene; it means we recognize that not all situations allow us to walk up to a bully and shout for them to stop.

Most bullying isn't done right out in the open. "When it's subtle, manipulative, and sneaky, a kid can't always tell when to step in," Icard writes.

The best thing we can do is ask questions, listen to their answers, and simply acknowledge and affirm that it's not as easy as parents and teachers like to make it seem. Arming kids with strategies like the 5Ds or the Interrupter/First Responder/Social Normer models can help enormously, but true solutions rarely happen without adult intervention and guidance.

Here are a few phrases suggested by the boys we interviewed that might help. Just remember that every school and even social group are different so these are just a starting point. Your kid will be the best source to figure out what would feel natural.

"Hey, that's not cool."

"Too far, bro."

"You're out of line, [name of kid being rude]."

"Enough."

When Joanna asked her son, a nineteen-year-old college student, a leader in his fraternity and NCAA track athlete, what he thinks kids should say in a locker room or social situation when peers are being unkind or even bigoted, he simply said:

"If I see something inappropriate, I say, 'That's not right. That's racist or homophobic,' or whatever. I don't think it has to be a big deal. Just tell them it's not right. That goes a long way."

Do's and Don'ts for talking to kids about bullying, bystanding, and upstanding

Don't say: "I expect you to be an upstander, not a bystander."

Instead, try asking: "Do you see a lot of bullying at your school?" and then brainstorm together what might work to help the kids being bullied.

Don't say: "Any time you see someone being picked on, I want you to march over there and yell at that bully."

Instead, try asking: "Are there times you might feel comfortable intervening when someone seems to be in need of help with a bully? How will you know when it's OK?"

Don't say: "If someone is picking on a smaller kid, or a kid who isn't as popular as you are, walk up and show them how it feels."

Instead, try asking: "What do you think you could do with the assets you have?" and then think of what your kid has to his advantage that can help him in the situation, like his size, popularity, or ability to be a good listener or advocate.

Remind your kid that school rules likely don't consider pushing or hitting someone else's bully to be self-defense.

Remind kids that even people who seem to "have it all" may be struggling, too.

REMEMBER THIS:

❶ Every society has a power structure, with some people having more power and others having less. That power can be helpful or it can turn toxic, keeping one group down in order to serve the best interests of the people who have the power.

❷ Bullying is an expression of power imbalances in a system, and one of the key ways to help end bullying and create a more inclusive society is to help kids practice empathy.

❸ Even the most popular kids have stress, anxiety, and insecurities. Research shows that some of the most stressed-out boys in school are the ones at the top of the popularity heap—especially if they are also high achievers in academics and school activities.

"I am scared of school shootings, because even if your school has a relatively tight-knit community all it takes is one person who doesn't get the help they need to bring a gun to school and just kill people. I just think about how devastating losing my girlfriend or one of my close friends would be on my mental health—and the fact that literally nothing is being done in some regions of this country is genuinely baffling to me as well."

—Frankie, age 14

Chapter 14

Talk to Your Boys About

VIOLENCE, GUNS, AND FIGHTING

Domestic violence. Sexual assault. School shootings. Bullying. Fighting.

There is a lot of violence in our society, and, sadly, a disproportionate amount of it is committed by boys and men. Boys often grow up surrounded by messages that being violent and controlling is an important part of being a man. Boys learn these ideas when they witness or experience violence in their families, in relationships, at school, and in the media.

Boys also learn these messages directly. On playgrounds and in schoolyards, little boys are regularly told to "be a man!" when they start to cry or show fear. As they grow up, they get more messages about what it means to "act like a man"—these messages often include being big, strong, stoic, aggressive, and ready to fight at any time.

If we can get boys to think more critically about violence and practice other ways of solving conflicts, it will help them have closer, more trusting relationships and feel more connected to the people around them. Helping them pause and connect with the consequences of their choices could have a ripple effect, making the world a more peaceful place.

CHECK IN WITH YOURSELF — — — — — — — — — —

Before taking on this discussion with boys in your life, spend some time thinking critically about your attitudes and beliefs that might come up in that discussion. Here are some questions to consider:

> Do you think it's important for boys to know how to fight?
> How do you feel about boys using weapons like guns and knives?
> In what ways has your life been affected by violence?
> What do you think we should do to stop mass shootings?
> How do you think people who are being bullied should respond?
> What do you consider reasonable in terms of self-defense?

How to Know When It's Time to Talk About Violence

Discussions of violence can be prompted by outside events like school shootings or active shooter drills, protests, crime, or violent police interactions. They can also become necessary when a boy's behavior noticeably changes.

Many teenage boys can be moody, rebellious, or angry at times. When behavior starts to escalate, it's time to start talking about it openly.

Aggressive teenage behaviors can include:

→ Shouting
→ Cursing and name-calling
→ Verbal disrespect, sarcasm, or insults
→ Ignoring limits like curfews
→ Bullying and cyberbullying
→ Gossiping and spreading rumors
→ Property destruction
→ Physical violence

Teen aggression can be related to past trauma, mental health conditions like depression or anxiety, or substance use disorders. Sometimes people differentiate between aggressive behaviors that are impulsive (like grabbing something out of a sibling's hand) and those that are plotted in advance.

Doing Things Differently

"I was a sensitive boy growing up, but I was growing up in a lion's den—so I often had to fight," says Ashanti Branch, founder of the Ever Forward Club. "In elementary school, I fought all the time. I never started one of the fights, and I never wanted to fight. I always fought because it was the rules of the community: 'Don't let anybody talk back to you. Don't let anybody pick on you.' I was hypervigilant to make sure those things didn't happen."

Branch now leads a program for young men that explores how our traditional notions of masculinity are connected to the day-to-day violence boys experience.

"If we are telling boys when they're younger to not show part of their humaneness, then we should not be surprised when they begin to act like monsters," Branch says. "Part of the humaneness of empathy, kindness, respect, and caring begins to go out the window because they've been told that those parts of themselves are not welcome."

Even if they don't use violence to express their feelings or control others, many boys and men don't feel comfortable showing the more tender sides of themselves for fear of being called "gay," "girly," or "soft." Branch says this can set them up for trouble.

"If we don't give boys tools to explore all the emotions they feel, then we're going to keep trying to figure out how to rehabilitate them after they've gotten themselves in some bad situations," Branch says. "We keep building cages for them. We just don't provide enough resources at schools for them."

We need the definition of masculinity to reflect the full humanity of boys and men, not just a narrow range of acceptable behaviors. Not only is this important to reduce the level of violence in society, it is imperative to also support men in expressing themselves fully and accepting all parts of themselves, without fear or shame.

Fighting: No Longer a Boyhood Rite of Passage

For generations, boyhood was marked by violence. If it wasn't at the hands of parents or siblings, most boys encountered violence on the playground or around the neighborhood. Masculinity was enforced through violence, and disagreements were settled with fists instead of words. For some, this may still be an unfortunate reality.

For most teens, however, violence is less common in their lives than when their parents and grandparents were young.

While some dads and grandpas may be nostalgic for their fisticuff days, fighting is objectively unhealthy for our kids. Modern technology has shown how traumatic even relatively mild hits to the head can be to the brain, contributing to learning difficulties and challenges regulating mood. In addition, the stress hormones released when you're constantly under threat of violence have been proven to shorten lifespans, limit academic potential, and increase risk of future crime.

We asked boys:

Have you ever been encouraged to get in a fight? Who encouraged you?

"Yes, I was encouraged by a group of kids that I didn't know too well to get in a fight because I thought they were cool. They were looking for a fight, and we were all bored, so I just went along with it. But I guess I took it more seriously than they did, because I wanted to prove myself. I ended up getting punched, and it was the first time I had ever been hit and I ended up walking away because the guys who had been with me had disappeared. I was alone."

—Michael, age 16

"Not really, but my classmates told me when I was younger that I'm too passive and need to defend myself more."

—Jeff, age 16

Fighting can also be profoundly traumatic on an emotional level, and data show that children who experience multiple traumatic events are at higher risks for mental illness, suicide, and poor physical health outcomes.

In other words, we don't want our boys to have to fight. However, there are times when a kid may need to protect himself. So, how do you talk to him about fighting?

Seek Out Local Laws and School Rules Around Fighting and Self-defense

Establish household rules for when he may be allowed to fight. Have a conversation with your co-parent or brainstorm with another trusted adult about what is a reasonable standard for fighting. Then get together with your son to discuss what he thinks are reasonable.

Share with your son some of the possible consequences of fighting, for instance:

→ The person you're fighting might be carrying a weapon or backed by friends you didn't expect.

→ Even without weapons, fights can lead to serious brain injuries and trauma to your organs that can result in hospitalization or death.

→ If you harm another person during a fight, you are legally responsible for their injuries—and that may mean felony assault charges.

→ Fights are often recorded and posted online, sometimes with names and locations attached.

→ Fights may be documented in your academic record, and could affect college applications.

Talk about what counts as self-defense in your rules. For instance:

→ Is fighting to protect yourself when physically attacked OK as long as the fight is not escalated? (e.g., If someone pushes you, replying by punching them in the face may be considered escalation, not self-protection. The person who escalated the fight may be the one in more trouble.)

→ Does a person insulting you or verbally threatening you justify fighting for self-defense? Or is your family rule that you should never be the one who throws the first punch?

→ Do your family rules require that you walk away from the fight at the first opportunity?

How to Start Talking About Masculinity and Violence

It can be hard to figure out how to start having nuanced conversations with boys about violence and how it intersects with masculinity. Here are some suggestions for getting the conversation flowing:

Listen and Connect

We've found that boys are often eager to talk about issues in their lives once they know that someone is really listening and interested in what they have to say. This is not a lecture or a one-sided conversation. Start with some basic questions like:

→ "What kinds of pressures do you think boys face today?"

→ "Do you see a lot of fights?"

→ "Do you think boys feel a lot of pressure to fight?"

→ "Do you think people expect boys to be violent? Why?"

→ "Where do you feel safe and like you can be yourself?"

Talk About Men They Admire—That They Actually Know

Often when boys are asked to name people they admire or look up to, they think about athletes, musicians, influencers, or celebrities. That's fine, but it can be hard to draw any real-life lessons from them. Instead, ask boys to identify some men they admire that they actually know. You can use some of these questions:

→ "Do you know a man who shows a lot of care for others?"

→ "Do you know a man who people seem to really count on?"

→ "Do you know a man who can solve problems without violence?"

→ "Do you know a man who is really funny, but isn't mean?"

→ "Do you know a man who is really good with kids?"

→ "What do you think you can learn from these men about how to live your life?"

Talk About "Jokes," Harassment, and Intimidation

Some of the precursors of violence can be verbal—things like teasing, bullying, threats, and catcalling. It's important to talk about these with boys—here are some places to start:

→ "Have you ever heard of catcalling? What do you think about it?"

→ "Do you think it's OK for boys to shout out 'compliments' about other people's body parts?"

→ "Have you ever had someone get into your personal space in a way that felt threatening or uncomfortable?"

→ "How do you feel when other boys tell mean jokes about girls?"

Talk About Boys and Violence

Violence and fighting can play a major role in boys' lives, but they often don't have a space to talk honestly and reflectively about these topics. Here are some conversation starters that can help change that:

→ "Have you ever felt like you had to prove you were tough?"

→ "What do people usually tell boys when they fall down or get hurt?"

→ "Have you ever been in a fight?"

→ "How do you feel about fighting?"

→ "Why do you think violence is so common among teenage boys?"

Should Boys Step In?

Fights are often (but not always) preceded by some lower-level interaction, often teasing, rumors, bullying, harassment, or verbal abuse. Young people are good at sensing when things are escalating, and respond in one of two ways:

1. Moving away as fast as possible or pretending not to see what's going on.
2. Rushing toward the situation—often with their cell phones out, ready to record—cheering, yelling, and encouraging the people involved to fight.

Although these actions are understandable, they are usually not very helpful. There is another way to handle these situations, and it may feel very empowering for boys to learn about it. It's called bystander intervention.

Many boys try to avoid violence and fights and stay away from others who are fighting. Parents may send a confusing message when they tell their kids to avoid fights while also saying they should stand up for others. The right answer usually lies somewhere in between.

When should they try to intervene and stop others? Here are some prompts for discussing it:

→ "Have you ever seen people intervene in an argument?"
→ "If two of your classmates were about to fight, and a boy like you stepped in to try to cool things down, what do you think would happen?"
→ "What skills help people de-escalate tense situations?"
→ "Do you think boys who can stop fights are powerful?"

These discussions aren't easy. You may find yourself feeling judgmental or getting upset. Take a breath or take a break and remember that boys are still learning and exploring new ideas.

Try not to be in the place where you're telling them they're wrong or trying to force them to agree with what you believe. Instead, keep gently challenging their ideas and encouraging them to engage in their own critical thinking process about what type of man they want to be. Your goal is to help them see other options so they can consciously chart their own path.

No Wrong Answers: Questions to Get You Talking

Try these conversation starters in order to explore your values around violence.

Share your experiences:

→ When I was a kid, there were fights every day in my high school. Do you see a lot of fights?

→ I remember feeling really freaked out when people were fighting. What's that like for you?

→ I can't imagine if people had cameras to film every fight when I was a kid, like your generation. Do you think cameras have changed the culture of fighting?

Ask him to "zoom out" on fighting and violence by imagining certain scenarios:

→ Have you ever been in a situation where you could "sense" something was about to go down?

→ What did that feel like in your body? What did people around you do? How do you imagine the fighters and the people in the crowd were all feeling?

→ Why do you think people get in fights?

→ Have you ever been so angry you've been tempted to fight? What stopped you from doing it?

→ What do you think happens after a fight? How would you feel? How does the other person feel? What might change about how your friends and classmates feel? What about teachers?

Remember: The goal is to get him thinking about the big picture, not just getting that feeling of anger out.

The 5Ds of Bystander Intervention

The organization Right To Be trains people in the "5Ds of Bystander Intervention:"

The 5Ds are different methods—Distract, Delegate, Document, Delay, and Direct—that you can use to support someone who's being harassed, emphasize that harassment is not OK, and demonstrate to people in your life that they have the power to make their community safer.

Anyone can use the 5Ds! They are designed to be safe and not to escalate situations. In fact, four of them are indirect methods of intervention.

Let's take a closer look at each of the 5Ds, and how Right To Be describes them. It's crucial that these interventions are short and succinct. As tempting as it may be, avoid engaging in dialogue, debate, or an argument, since that is how situations can escalate. Always prioritize safety and consider possibilities that are unlikely to put you or anyone else in harm's way.

Distract:

→ Ignore the person who is harassing, and engage directly with the person who is being harassed.

→ Don't talk about or refer to the harassment that's happening. Instead, talk about something completely unrelated.

Delegate:

→ Look for a delegate who is ready and willing to help. Often, a great choice is the person right next to you.

→ When you delegate someone to help you, try to tell them as clearly as possible what you're witnessing and how you'd like them to help.

Document:

→ Documentation involves either recording or taking notes on an instance of harassment.

→ Assess the situation. Is anyone helping the person being harassed? If not, use another of the 5Ds. Recording someone's experience of harm without ensuring they're already receiving help can just create further trauma for them.

→ *Always* ask the person who was harassed what they want to do with your recording and/or notes. *Never* post it online or use it without their permission.

Delay:

→ Even if we can't act in the moment, we can still make a difference for someone who's been harassed by checking in on them after the fact. We can help reduce that person's trauma by speaking to them after an instance of harassment.

Direct:

→ Sometimes, we may want to respond directly to harassment by naming the inappropriate behavior and confronting the person doing harm.

→ Use this one with caution, because direct intervention can be risky—the harassing person may redirect their abuse toward the intervening bystander. Make sure you and the person being harassed are both physically safe first.

Adapted from RightToBe.org. For more information, visit the Right To Be website.

Boys and Gun Violence

We can't talk about violence, particularly in the United States, without talking about guns. Gun violence is a huge problem overall, but boys are particularly affected. Take a look at the data:

Guns are the leading cause of death for children and teens (ages one to nineteen) in this country:

→ Between 2013 and 2022, the gun death rate among children and teens increased 87%. Both gun homicides and suicides fueled this increase.

➜ Each day twelve children die from gun violence in America. Another thirty-two are shot and injured.

➜ Boys accounted for 85% of all gun deaths among children and teens in 2021.

➜ In 2022, the gun suicide rate among Black children and teens surpassed the rate among white children and teens for the first time on record.

➜ The Black child and teen suicide rate tripled over the past two decades (2003 to 2022). In 2022, Black children and teens were twenty times as likely to die by firearm homicide compared to white children and teens.

➜ Black boys under eighteen are 5.5 times more likely to die by firearm homicide than Black girls the same age.

School shootings are a major concern:

➜ Since the shooting at Columbine High School in 1999, more than 378,000 students in the US have experienced gun violence at school, according to research from *The Washington Post*.

➜ Mass shootings are almost always carried out by boys.

Firearms and an Increased Risk of Suicide

In addition to addressing the issue of guns and boys, we need to look at why boys' suicide rates are so much higher than girls', and are more likely to involve a firearm. "Boys are conditioned not to ask for help, to not express their emotions," licensed clinical social worker Stacey Freedenthal said in an interview with *The Washington Post*. "Boys tend to mature and develop at a slower rate than girls," she explained, which makes them more likely to act impulsively.

According to the American Foundation for Suicide Prevention, "most people in suicidal crisis who don't have easy access to a lethal suicide method will not simply find another way to kill themselves."

Freedenthal suggests that removing firearms from your home can dramatically reduce suicide risk. Locking up guns is not as protective as removing them from the home, Freedenthal said, as motivated teenagers can figure out how to get past locks.

We asked boys:

What do you think should be done to stop/reduce mass shootings?

"A supportive community (which is not necessarily easy to come by in a high school setting—which may be the reason why many administrations don't take the necessary steps to prevent these tragedies—but it is not impossible)."

—Frankie, age 14

"Remove guns from everyone."

—Jeff, age 16

"More armed law enforcement in dangerous areas or arm and inform/train citizens. Fight fire with fire."

—Cormac, age 16

"You shouldn't be able to buy a gun unless you're a police officer."

—Octavian, age 11

What to Watch Out For

Sandy Hook Promise is an organization focused on preventing gun violence, especially school shootings. They point out that in four out of five school shootings at least one other person had knowledge of the attacker's plan but failed to report it.

The organization trains people to recognize those signs and get help. Through its Say Something Program, students learn to recognize signs and get help when their classmates show they may be in danger or need help. Those warning signs can include things such as thoughts, feelings, actions, and behaviors. At-risk people can show significant or sudden changes in behavior or personality:

→ Suddenly withdrawing from friends, family, and activities (including online or via social media)

➔ Bullying, especially if targeted toward differences in race, religion, gender, or sexual orientation

➔ Excessive irritability, lack of patience, or becoming angry quickly

➔ Experiencing chronic loneliness or social isolation

➔ Expressing persistent thoughts of harming themselves or someone else

➔ Making direct threats toward a place, another person, or themselves

➔ Bragging about access to guns or weapons

➔ Recruiting accomplices or audiences for an attack

➔ Directly expressing a threat as a plan

➔ Cruelty to animals

How to Talk to Your Boys About Guns

With all of this in mind, it's good to start early when talking to kids about guns and gun violence. Parents should work together with their kids to make easy-to-follow plans for what to do if they see a gun or other dangerous weapon. While thinking about these scenarios may be scary, it can be empowering for kids to have a plan in place—especially when they know it's one their parents approve of.

We are going to share a few examples of how to make a plan with your kids, but these conversations may look different depending on your community (rural versus metropolitan, for instance) and your family.

> **Try saying:** "Hey, I know guns and other weapons are a scary reality in some kids' lives these days. I wish it weren't this way, but the best I can do right now is come up with a plan for what to do when you see a weapon somewhere it should not be, like laying out at someone's house, at school, at a party. I also want to talk about what you could do if someone you know might be a threat to others or themselves. Even if you think they might be joking, it's better to talk about it with me or another adult you trust."

If you live in a home with firearms, for instance if you are a law enforcement officer or if your family regularly hunts, you almost certainly already have a strict set of rules and procedures around when and where it is appropriate to handle weapons. If this applies to you, we urge you to revisit the conversation regularly as your boy grows up so that he knows there are still rules in place, exactly what the rules are, and the consequences for not following them.

While rules will vary family by family, here are some examples of how to be specific and direct with your expectations:

→ "You may never touch a firearm without a parent or another trusted adult present." (Explain who these adults are, like: Uncle Randy, Aunt Belinda, Grandpa Smith, etc.)

→ "In the case of low-powered guns like Airsoft, paintball, or BB guns, you are only to handle them in appropriate settings, like at a range or another approved setting, and only when everyone nearby is wearing adequate eye and skin protection for Airsoft or paintball."

→ "You may not use firearms to shoot at any living creature outside of a licensed hunting situation supervised by adults that we trust. This includes Airsoft and BB guns."

→ "You may not talk about what firearms we have on our property or tell others where we store our firearms."

Even kids from the most experienced military, law enforcement, and hunting families may find themselves in situations where a weapon is used illegally or in unsafe ways. Kids of all ages and levels of experience should be prepared for what to do when a variety of situations arise, including:

→ An unsecured weapon in a home, barn, garage, or any other inappropriate setting

→ A friend or another peer handling a firearm recklessly, illegally, or inappropriately—or hiding any weapon from their parents or caregivers (including someone who has a firearm in their car)

→ Any firearm or weapon at school, ever

→ A child or peer who appears to be obsessed with guns or violence, or any person making threats

→ Attending a party or other big event where a weapon is revealed—be it a gun, knife, or anything else

While we are not firearm or safety experts, Joanna found it helpful to explain to her boys that there is never a safe situation where a firearm is handled by a minor, outside of a well-supervised firing range or while hunting with licensed, experienced adult hunters. In most social situations, knives and Tasers (and even bats or other objects, when misused) should be considered potentially dangerous. Kids should immediately leave these dangerous situations and report them to a trusted adult as soon as they are in a safer place.

REMEMBER THIS:

❶ Anger, sometimes accompanied by violence, may be one of the only emotions that boys feel comfortable showing to the world. To access their full humanity, boys need to be able to access and show a full range of emotions.

❷ Learning and practicing the 5Ds of Bystander Intervention—Distract, Delegate, Document, Delay, and Direct—can be empowering for young people who want to know what they can do when a conflict is escalating.

❸ Clearly articulate your family's feelings about fighting with the boys in your life.

❹ Talk frankly with your boys about guns and what to do if they encounter a gun or see someone with a gun.

"I wish adults understood that everyone is human, that kids deal with racism every day. I also wish they would teach their kids about racism so their kid doesn't accidentally say something racist and end up regretting it."

—Isaiah, age 17

Chapter 15

Talk to Your Boys About

RACISM AND PREJUDICE

Throughout this book, we've encouraged you to have conversations about lots of topics that may feel awkward. We also understand that racism can be one of the most uncomfortable and even painful subjects to discuss. So much so, many people avoid talking about it at all.

In his book *How to Raise an Antiracist*, Ibram X. Kendi, PhD, admits that when his daughter, Imani, was born, his instinct was to try to shield her from the realities of racism for as long as possible, wishing he could pretend it was possible to create a life where she would never have to feel its effects.

The desire to avoid talking about racism sometimes leads people to say things like "I don't see race." Many white parents fear saying the wrong thing or maybe weren't taught to talk about race, so they avoid the conversation entirely.

"When I was growing up in the 1980s, we were taught that the way to be a good person was to swear that race didn't matter, at least not anymore," writes Heather McGhee in *The Sum of Us: What Racism Costs Everyone and How We Can Prosper Together.*

"We now know that color blindness is a form of racial denial that took one of the aspirations of the civil rights movement—that individuals would one day 'not be judged by the color of their skin but by the content of their character'—and stripped it from any consideration of power, hierarchy, or structure," McGhee writes.

Trying to ignore race and racism is not the answer. After all, you can't fight something while pretending it doesn't exist. Instead, we want to encourage you to talk openly about racism and its effects, and encourage the boys in your life to be part of the battle against it.

"Raising our children to be antiracist is like dressing their minds in armor before we send them out into the world," writes Kendi. As parents and as authors, we want to help arm our children for the battle of making the world a fairer, more just place for everyone.

We know that people have very different lived experiences with racism. As parents who are white, we know we can offer only our own lived experiences, so, to capture multiple perspectives, we invited two educators who are also men of color, Jeff Perera and Artnelson Concordia, to contribute their expertise to this chapter. We are so grateful for their wisdom and insights, as well as those of the experts we interviewed for this chapter, but we also know that a few pages from one book cannot capture the lived experiences of everyone who will read this. We hope this chapter is a starting place—just as the other chapters are—to more exploration, learning, and conversation.

CHECK IN WITH YOURSELF

Before diving in, we recommend taking a moment to consider the following questions:

> What do you feel when you hear the words *race* or *racism*?

> How did your family or community talk about race or racism?

> Do you agree with these perspectives now?

> What changes do you hope can happen regarding race in your lifetime?

Shame-Free Talks About Race and Racism

We all have biases. It's part of being human. The way we overcome acting from our biases is to recognize them when they come up. The problem is, thinking about our biases can make us feel ashamed, so we resist the conversations.

Donald E. Grant Jr., PsyD, a psychologist, sociocultural analyst, and author of *White on White Crime*, shared with us a tool one might not immediately associate with fighting racism: mindfulness. Briefly, mindfulness is a nonjudgemental awareness of one's inner state.

"Think of it as upgrading from denial mode to growth mode, with a side of humility," Dr. Grant explained. "Mindfulness acts as a gentle referee between our experiences and our reactions, preventing shame and guilt from landing cheap shots on our self-awareness," Dr. Grant told us. "When you practice mindfulness, you make a conscious effort to take judgment out of the equation—essentially giving your inner critic a coffee break—so you can actually learn from what happened.

"Normally, when faced with our own unconscious biases, our first instinct is to leap to our own defense like a lawyer on overdrive," Dr. Grant said. "But with mindfulness, you're invited (read: required) to take a pause, own up to your actions, and dig into why what you said or did was problematic, even if you don't immediately grasp the full impact of your words." As Dr. Grant notes, letting go of shame is one of the best ways to grow as people. The same also applies to our children.

We asked boys:

Have you ever been treated unfairly because of your race, ethnicity, or religion?

"Yes, I've definitely been treated unfairly for my race because I am a Black male and people just see me as less and not as smart just because of my race."

—Isaiah, age 17

"I haven't been treated unfairly per se, but I have been treated differently due to my race."

—ML, age 15

"Probably, but that's just a part of life and some people have it far worse."

—Sam, age 15

How to Talk to Boys of Color About Racism

Jeff Perera is a speaker, writer, and the founder of Higher Unlearning, an online platform dedicated to exploring issues around men and masculinity.

Before you start the conversation, do some self-reflection in preparation by considering:

→ Your own experiences with racism at different stages of your life. How have these impacted you and how did you manage these feelings and sort through it all?

For white parents raising kids of color, consider:

→ Your own history of holding disappointing views in your youth or early adulthood. What lessons can you pass forward around how we begin to unlearn, grow, and do better?

→ Your own understanding of the realities of facing and navigating racism. What have you learned? From whom?

Opening the door—and keeping it open

→ What would you like to continue doing better?

→ What would you like your child to feel when talking to you about race and racism?

These conversations are simply opening the door to many more over the course of your lifetime. It's important to create an environment in which your kids can feel good about sharing what they might have witnessed or experienced. They might share with you in that moment, or it might be later on, when they are ready. The goal is to convey that the door is open, and that it will be open throughout your lifetime together.

In the past, they might not have told you about what they are going through or have been through. They might be trying to protect you, just as you might withhold stories of facing and experiencing racism with the intent to protect them. That's why it's important to reassure them that they can feel heard, believed, and validated through your comforting and active listening—even when the issue is painful or potentially triggering.

It's also possible that they might hold or have held racist attitudes or beliefs about other people of color. For instance, a Black teen might believe a harmful stereotype about Latinx folks—or vice versa. Be open to unpacking and discussing these with as little judgment as possible, while holding firm to your values and sharing the truth.

How to talk to your boys about race and racism

→ Determine your intention for how you will approach the conversation, the impact it will have, and the ways you will have it together as a family.

→ Create space to listen, and give them time to find their words and go deeper into the issue with you.

→ Model curiosity. Start by asking questions. Racism has been an issue for generations, but what is different about the experience for them/their generation? Let them guide you.

→ Model vulnerability. Open up as a parent and talk about some of the racism you've experienced. Share a story, how it made you feel, what happened after, what you learned or are still learning.

→ Talk about the pressures to fit into outside expectations to be "The Man."

→ Discuss the pressure to be twice as good at tasks and activities in order to overcome racist misconceptions about their ability, to overcome stifling conclusions about their value and humanity.

→ Acknowledge the pressures your son is experiencing as valid and real.

→ Talk about staying safe: explore ways to navigate or help de-escalate a situation when possible.

→ Make sure they know their rights—both civil and personal.

→ If you live in a predominantly white community, share specifics on how they can find support or community—online or in person.

"Different like me, not different from me"

When talking with your son, explore their experiences compared with those of their peers. Unpack how their unique ordeals or situations are similar to and/or different from boys of color from other races and cultures.

Note: It's not about creating a hierarchy of lived experiences with racism, but to see how we can support or further build community with other boys of color.

Recognize that their experiences may be different from yours.

Try saying: "This experience is not unique to you, but your experiences will be unique to you. We are here to hear about it, listen, love, and support you."

Remember: Boys of color experience a distinct and unique reality today versus that of any other generation. We can share our own experience and paths to healing while also creating space to hear, recognize, and validate what they are navigating as a boy of color and a member of their unique generation.

Remind them: You are not alone.

Remind them that they are loved—and not just by you. Tell them that there are many people across your community and the country who care deeply and are working to make things better. Show them who is helping and how.

How Memes, Jokes, and Videos Can Be Used to Recruit Our Kids into Hate

When Joanna's sons were early adolescents, she spent time looking at their Instagram feeds just to keep in touch with what was going on. Usually it was silly: *Minecraft* and *Fortnite*, funny animal videos and nonsensical memes. Then, one day, she saw a historical photo of Hitler zoom through as her son scrolled, and her son "liked" it without even stopping to read it.

She panicked, asked him to scroll back, and together they read the meme. It was a photo of a man leaning down and whispering something in Hitler's ear, which had been meme-ified in all sorts of ways through the years—most of the time to be absurdist, but clearly anti-Nazi. But this one was tipping Hitler off so he would win the war, instead of the Allies.

Her sons had zero clue what they were looking at. When she explained, they were horrified. When she dug more deeply into their "Explore" pages, she saw a few more veiled racist, sexist, homophobic, or otherwise bigoted "jokes." These weren't things her boys had shared; they were things the social media platform was suggesting to them.

After a conversation about the importance of paying attention to what you interact with online, they went through and checked to see if they had "liked" other problematic posts. Fortunately, their histories were pretty clear (if inane in that special way early teens' feeds tend to be!). However, when she started doing some detective work, she saw a troubling pattern: content that was popular with young teenage boys (think: ages twelve to fifteen), like *Minecraft*, *Roblox*, *Fortnite*, pranks, scatological and absurdist low-brow memes, etc., was often followed by ads for or related content pushing kids toward bigoted and anti-democracy ideologies.

These problematic memes weren't about politics, they were simple extremist propaganda. Worse, she noticed that her kids' consumption of what they called "edgy" jokes had numbed them a bit to unkind online content.

That's when she launched a Twitter thread that went massively viral, informing parents that certain adults appeared to be targeting boys (especially white boys) with anti-democracy and hate-based ideologies.

A lot has changed since 2019, when Joanna's Twitter thread went viral. Parents are now aware that social media can be dangerous, not just because of the adult content, but also because of those ideological predators looking for young minds to shape. And of course, racism and other hate-based ideologies still thrive online, including in video games. As we noted in our screen time and tech chapter, 48% of teen boys who play video games say they have been called an offensive name while playing, and 15% have been physically threatened, according to the Pew Research Center.

"Some worry that being subjected to racism in a space that many turn to for leisure could play a role in a troubling rise in suicidality rates among young Black people," Marc Ramirez wrote in a 2023 *USA Today* article. "According to the Centers for Disease Control and Prevention, suicide rates among young Black people ages 10 to 24 rose 36.6% from 2018 to 2021, the largest percentage jump among any demographic."

Talk to Your Boys About "Edgy" Online Jokes and Memes

Start the conversation with questions and reassure your son that you just want to get a feel for what's going on out there, rather than find out if he's done anything wrong.

Try asking:

→ "Do you hear a lot of jokes, like memes or in videos, or even at school where someone says something shocking or offensive just for shock value?"

→ "Do you think the people making those jokes or trying to be edgy know it can be hurtful? Do you think they mean for it to be?"

→ "What do you think makes a joke funny? If someone gets hurt, does that make it less funny?"

Remember: Try not to shame or blame him if you disagree with something he says. Instead, help him understand your perspective and the experiences and perspectives of others.

Try saying:

→ "When we hear something over and over again, it does start to become normal. It's like when one kid in your group of friends says something funny and then it catches on."

→ "It's been found that some groups and organizations post controversial content online or even troll people to make people more divided or to misinform them. I really want to make sure you are aware this is happening so you're on the lookout."

→ "I want you to know that you can bring anything you see online to me and ask about it. Just like we've discussed with bullying or sexual content, I'm not going to be mad at you for asking about it. We can discuss it or figure out what to do together."

Ideological Predators

Ideological predators teach kids that a group of "others" is to blame for the scary or upsetting things they see on the news or experience in their own lives. These skillful adults find kids where they're already hanging out, choosing their recruiting grounds carefully. They look for kids who may be isolated, less socially skilled, and/or victims of bullying; kids who may have more pain and less supervision than others. They have even targeted kids in autism-related online gathering spaces, according to reformed former hate group leader Christian Picciolini.

These online predators lure kids with seemingly logical explanations of how getting rid of those "others" (or simply silencing them) will save those they deem worth protecting in society. The targets of this othering are usually people of color, immigrants, and queer folks—but that list is far from exhaustive. Often, these groups misuse Christianity to support the idea that these "others" don't deserve equality or representation, despite the core message of Jesus, which was to love your neighbor.

Picciolini told us that extremist groups "do a good job 'empowering' those who feel like they have no agency. It's part of the recruitment process." He says that at the core of these hate-based groups are people who are "finding a sense of identity, community, and 'purpose' [with these extreme online organizations] after an inability to find those three important things in the 'real' world."

Picciolini told us that one of the most important ways to protect our kids (and others) from falling prey to ideological predators is a two-fold approach:

First, he insists adults need to do a better job listening to kids. This involves not just listening to, and truly hearing, our own kids, but also listening to what is happening with young people in general. Take a scroll through social media and look at their mental health, how they're doing in school, what they post about online that is challenging them. We need to hear and respect the pain points of their generation. And then we need to believe them.

Second, watch out for what he calls "potholes." As we explained in our chapter on power, "potholes" are unresolved trauma or trauma that feels unnavigable to kids. It's the type that makes a kid feel trapped, as if there is no way out and nobody who can help him.

We asked Picciolini what we can say to our kids to help them when they're stuck in a pothole, and his answer was startling: "What can be said [to them] is often too late. That's why we need to do better at listening."

That doesn't mean we give up on children who are already slipping into hate. If anything, it means we need to intervene with these children more. Talking about these ideological predators, as well as racism and other bigoted mentalities in general, can help prepare kids to spot them early. If we can do that, as well as staying aware of and compassionate to kids' pain, loneliness, and traumas, we can help prevent them from being recruited in the first place. We'd like to add a final step:

Third, teach kids about confirmation bias and help them become aware of it in our own lives.

In their book for young readers, *How to Be a (Young) Antiracist*, Ibram X. Kendi and Nic Stone explain that confirmation bias is "[t]he tendency to interpret, recall, or search for information in a way that supports one's existing beliefs."

We all experience confirmation bias to one degree or another. For instance, nearly everyone who watches cable news chooses to watch the networks that align with their current political beliefs. Most people don't flip between MSNBC and Fox News, for example, even if they want a balance of different opinions.

Here's a sillier example of confirmation bias that might be good for kids:

Imagine believing that zebras do not have stripes, that it is all a myth, and that zookeepers paint stripes on horses and donkeys to fool people.

As a "Zebras Are a Myth" believer, you won't seek out objective facts like historical animal biology books, you will google "how zookeepers turn horses into zebras" or something similar. If a photo of a zebra being born with stripes comes across your social media timeline, you will not think "Here's some proof that zebras are real, I was wrong!" Instead, you will think, "This is fake, more lies from the zookeepers!"

This is a silly example that has nothing to do with racism, but sometimes it takes a silly example to show how silly we can be, as humans, even with very serious subjects.

Social media makes confirmation bias even worse because the algorithms are set to show you more of what you have interacted with. It's important that our kids understand how this works so they will notice when a stereotype or racist trope is being pushed on them.

Talk to Your Boys About Social Media, Confirmation Bias, and Racism

Start the conversation:

Hey, I've learned a lot lately about how stuff shows up on our social media timelines and FYPs; can we chat about it a bit?

Share your perspective:

I've noticed on my own timelines that the more I watch videos about motocross, the more videos come up about it and other related things. I've seen a lot of content about street bikes and new stuff with gravel bikes. I'm sure that's because of how much I'm interacting with motocross content.

Ask:

Have you noticed this with your stuff? (Listen and confirm you're hearing him.)

(After listening): That's interesting, so you're saying that the more *Roblox* videos you watch, the more you see *Minecraft* and *Fortnite*? That does make sense. Do you like that stuff, too?

(Then listen to his answer, of course!)

Make the topic more broad:

So that got me thinking, what if what someone was watching wasn't so healthy or was based on something harmful? I bet the algorithm would show them more of that stuff. And that's what I really wanted to talk to you about.

For instance, what if someone sent you a video that felt like it was racist or making fun of something about a group of people, and you watched it? I bet your FYP would start filling in with more stuff like that. What do you think?

Listen and confirm you're hearing him, then explain further:

(After listening): I'm relieved nobody is sending you videos like that. But at some point, you'll probably come across racism or other harmful stuff on your timeline and I want you to know that the more we see content that is problematic or even just untrue, the easier it is for us to believe it—even if it's hurtful or far-fetched.

Sometimes people share stuff because they want people to believe a lie or join their perspective—and lots of times that stuff is really dangerous for society and hurts people.

Remind him you are available to talk, judgment-free:

Remember, you can show me anything you see online that feels weird, icky, inappropriate, hurtful, or offensive and I won't get angry with you. We can always just discuss it.

Talk to Your Boys About
Race, Ethnicity, and Nationality

Talking about race can happen during everyday teachable moments. Of course, these questions are just suggestions, and every family will have a different conversation based on their own identities and experiences.

About himself:

→ How do you think your race affects the way the world sees you?

→ How about your ethnicity? Does anything about it change or affect the way people see you? In what ways?

→ What about your nationality? How does it change the way people here, where we live, see you? What about if/when we travel outside the USA?

About others:

→ How do you think race affects the way people are treated—in big ways or little ways—in our community or at your school?

→ If you've seen someone being targeted or discriminated against, why do you think the person doing the discrimination did it?

→ If you're in a position to help in the future, what could you do to stop the interaction or help the person being targeted?

About the world:

→ What would the world look like if it were fair and perfect?

→ How would that change your life or other people's lives?

→ (Then share your own feelings and opinions, hopes and dreams. If you've never experienced racism, it's good to admit that and explain why you think that is the case. If you've witnessed or experienced racism or any other form of bias, explain what it was like, how you felt, what you did—or what you wish you could've done.)

We all see weird and confusing things online sometimes. I even send some things to Uncle Nathan when I don't know what to think of them and need to discuss it with someone I trust, and you can always do that, too—with me, Uncle Nathan, Aunt Maria, or another adult that we really trust.

Race, Ethnicity, and Nationality

Part of understanding bigotry and racism is understanding these terms.

Race: "Race refers to the concept of dividing people into groups on the basis of various sets of physical characteristics and the process of ascribing social meaning to those groups."

In other words, race is not biological, it is invented by people to categorize people based on their looks. (Definition courtesy of Washington University in St. Louis)

Ethnicity: "Ethnicity is a characterization of people based on having a shared culture (e.g., language, food, music, dress, values, and beliefs) related to common ancestry and shared history." (Definition courtesy of the American Psychological Association)

Nationality: This refers to a person's country of origin. On a technical level, it may be where you reside, where you are a citizen, or simply where your family history begins.

In a Child Trends report, Victor St. John, Ph.D., along with coauthors Dominique Parris and Jessica Dym Bartlett, Ph.D., shares insights for how parents can handle the emotional fallout of their children's experience with racism.

"It can be important for adult caregivers to share their own experiences and beliefs about racism with children, but it's equally important to encourage them to express their opinions and feelings and ask the questions that are on their mind. . . . Children of color, especially, are likely to show or talk about their distress after witnessing or experiencing racism. Caregivers can validate their emotions and reactions by letting them know that it's okay to feel the way they do and that others likely feel the same way. It's also essential to find out what children know already and to correct misinformation."

Expert Insight

What I've Learned About Parenting from Ethnic Studies Classrooms

Artnelson Concordia has been a public-school educator for more than two decades. He was a founding teacher of San Francisco Unified School District's ninth grade Ethnic Studies program and now coordinates Santa Barbara Unified School District's Ethnic Studies program. He is the father of four boys.

As coordinator for an Ethnic Studies program for high schoolers, it's part of my job to think about racism a lot. In our program, we think about racism—what it is, its origins, its impact on people, particularly Black, Indigenous/Native, Chicanx/Latinx, Asian and Pacific Islander people, *and* we teach ways we can collectively disrupt it. The elimination of racism—and all forms of inequity and injustice and dehumanization—is at the heart of Ethnic Studies.

At its most fundamental level, Ethnic Studies is a humanization project. We teach that each individual person, each one of us, has inherent and tremendous value as human beings. Unfortunately, many people are denied respect and dignity because of any number of the various parts of our identities that make us who we are—race, gender, sexuality, economic class, etc. And because of this, in Ethnic Studies, we build awareness about the structures and dominant systems that surround us, and the decisions within those structures and systems that sometimes work in opposition to human dignity.

As the parents of four beautiful Brown humans, my wife and I make sure that topics of unfairness and inequity, making things right when we hurt people, speaking up for what is right, and standing up for ourselves and others, and having a strong sense of self, are a big part of the conversations in our home with the entire family. We try our best to model and nurture kindness, respect, and curiosity.

Around our dinner table, when we need to be, my wife and I are direct in talking about race and racism, about doing the right thing, about the ugly and mean behavior we see in the world. It can be messy and uncomfortable. And there have been many times we are not so sure we are saying things the "right way." In the end, we stay grounded in our values, we do our best, and then we reflect on how it went. But for the most part, what we're trying to build are resilient, inquisitive, kind, curious, strong people.

We want them to develop deep knowledge and love of themselves as third-generation Filipino-American kids: Brown, beautiful young people who have every right to be who they are.

I think if we're successful in helping them truly love and appreciate who they are and where they come from, that's the best way to protect them from internalizing racism (and other harmful and dehumanizing messages) and equip them to extend that love and appreciation out into the world.

Growing up, while I knew I was Filipino, there always seemed to be a negative evaluation of that part of me in comparison to the white world. I knew I was different from everyone I watched on TV. I know that's changed a great deal. But I grew up with a lot of shame and embarrassment and a deep desire to be "American"—and to be American in my conditioning was to be white. So I developed a lot of self-hate. I had to unpack and address it as I came into adulthood, and it took some serious work to get there.

So much of parenting to our values has to do with addressing, confronting, and healing all of the ways in which we were raised that we now understand to be harmful. Colonialism has taught Filipinos to devalue ourselves, to hate our languages, culture, food, phenotype in comparison to whiteness. If we don't confront those things, we will act them out unconsciously.

What I want to be able to do with my children is to help them develop that really strong, resilient sense of who they are. It really is the basis of mutual recognition and respect for others. There's not a moment I don't think about all of this stuff, and I understand it's part of my responsibility to young people and our larger community.

How big a problem is racism today?

"Racism is at its peak, and the levels vary according to where you are in the world and what race you are. As an American, most racism that I've seen from the media is blatant microaggressions and people saying the dumbest things on camera. But in other places in the world people will stare and call you names and slurs and say the most vulgar things you can think of to your face. There are places in the world that I have crossed off my visit list because I don't want to end up hunted, hate-crimed, accused of committing crimes, or dead for being Black."

—Preston, age 16

"Extreme."

—Juan, age 18

"Quite large but it's mixed in subtly; people don't even notice that among the factors of their decisions, is race."

—Jeff, age 16

"It's better than it once was back in the nineteenth and twentieth centuries, but it could be better."

—ML, age 15

"It's not as big a problem as it was before. Before, people thought that people who are different are bad, but now people understand that being different is not bad."

—Octavian, age 11

Racism Is a Health and Justice Crisis

As we noted earlier, racism still profoundly affects public health in the United States and across the globe. Racism still results in deaths, wrongful convictions, limited potential, and many, many more horrible outcomes. The effects on kids are profound.

Benito Murguia, ASWB, a therapist who works with many adolescents, told us that "the effects of these negative experiences can be stigmatizing, cause deep-seated resentments, fear, and mistrust of people and societal systems and structures as a whole."

"In a place where children desire to be protected and cared for and are not," Murguia added, "these experiences can be traumatizing."

Murguia notes that it's important for kids of color to have someone to talk to who understands their experiences with racism. "Having someone who understands the experience provides credibility to the conversation and the support being offered. As a whole, we need to be sensitive to the emotions and allow the space for them to express and process their emotions.

"What works best for all children," he adds, "is consistency, predictability, and clear and affectionate structures."

Being a Good Ally

What does it mean to be a good ally against racism? First, it means accepting the reality of racism and how it affects people's lives. It might sound silly to think of someone denying the reality of racism, but it happens—not just on an individual level, but on a legislative one.

In *How to Raise an Antiracist*, Kendi shares a startling example of legislating racism in the USA:

"[I]n December 2021, Republican state representative Jim Olsen introduced a bill that would prohibit Oklahoma state agencies and public school districts from teaching 'that one race is the unique oppressor' during American slavery or 'another race is the unique victim in the institution of slavery.'"

Why would legislation like this need to exist? Why would history need to be erased in this way?

Guilt and shame appear to motivate a lot of the current attempts to stop people from awareness of racism and accurately teaching the racist aspects of history of the USA.

What we do need to feel is responsibility to make the world safer and more just.

Instead of feeling guilt and shame over slavery or any other institutionalized racism that we did not cause . . .

--- No Wrong Answers: Questions to Get You Talking ----------

What does it mean to be an ally?

→ In what ways do allies sometimes make situations worse?

→ What is the most effective way for you, at your age and in your situation, to draw attention to the issue without putting yourself in the spotlight?

→ Who should you look to in order to know how to be helpful?

→ How will you know when a situation is dangerous?

→ What are some phrases we can both use when someone is doing something racist or bigoted?

→ If you don't feel safe speaking up in a situation, what can you do instead? Who could you talk to in order to help prevent it from happening again?

Accept the reality of today by acknowledging the reality of how racism from the past affects communities and institutions today—and take action against it.

Instead of sitting by when something doesn't feel right, afraid of people turning against you . . .

Simply speak up. Speak to the people in charge or the individual being bigoted or discriminatory. You don't have to get in a fist fight, you can simply say, "Hey, that seems racist; let's talk about what happened."

Allyship Means Being Accountable

We all bring different talents and skills to our allyship. Some people may be most helpful in assisting organizers, others may be great at protest, others may be fantastic writers or influencers, while some are just great friends. Regardless of our skills, following the lead of those doing the work within the community is the best place to start.

Keep in mind that if you are white, that doesn't mean you will never be subjected to oppression or discrimination. You can be white and face discrimination due to gender, sexual orientation, religion, disability, class, and more.

Recommended Reading

Guides and nonfiction for young readers:

Me and White Supremacy: How YOU Can Fight Racism and Change the World Today! (Young Readers' Edition) by Layla F. Saad

How to Be a (Young) Antiracist by Ibram X. Kendi and Nic Stone

Stamped (For Kids): Racism, Antiracism, and You by Jason Reynolds and Ibram X. Kendi

Guides and nonfiction for adults:

Stamped from the Beginning: The Definitive History of Racist Ideas in America by Ibram X. Kendi

Breaking Hate: Confronting the New Culture of Extremism by Christian Picciolini

Do the Work! An Antiracist Activity Book by Kate Schatz and W. Kamau Bell

Our Hidden Conversations: What Americans Really Think About Race and Identity by Michele Norris

The Sum of Us: What Racism Costs Everyone and How We Can Prosper Together by Heather McGhee

Bring the War Home: The White Power Movement and Paramilitary America by Kathleen Belew

The Identity-Conscious Educator by Liza A. Talusan

REMEMBER THIS:

1 Talking about racism doesn't have to be—and shouldn't be—shrouded in shame. Shame shuts people down and prevents us from learning. It's up to those who benefit from white supremacy to stop shame from standing between ourselves and allyship.

2 Being mindful of our own biases, whether internalized or externalized, is a key part of being antiracist.

3 History matters when talking about racism because not everyone has had equal access to opportunities. When we understand history better, we open our eyes to the ways in which our society is still unjust and find more empathy for those experiencing oppression.

4 Kids (and even some adults) are being recruited into anti-democracy and hate-based groups and ideologies online, often starting with social media and video games. No child is immune to being harmed by extremists who want to tear society apart, but some kids are more vulnerable than others and need intervention early so they don't end up hurting others.

5 Racism can actively harm children's (and adults') mental health and physical health and compromises their civil rights and freedom.

6 Allyship isn't a badge people with privilege wear, it's a long-term commitment to living true to our ideals and values, in solidarity with leaders in the movement, and in service of others, not ourselves.

"My strongest belief is that everybody should be treated equitably and equally."

—Elie, age 11

Chapter 16

Talk to Your Boys About

ETHICS, VALUES, RULES, AND LAWS

lmost all parents say they want their boys to live by their values, behave ethically, and treat other people well. The specific values families emphasize vary, but often include honesty, hard work, kindness, helpfulness, acceptance, organization, assertiveness, and ambition. While we aren't here to tell you what values are most crucial for your kids or what rules you should set in your household, we do want to encourage you to examine your own beliefs.

One thing that might surprise you in this chapter is how almost all of the rules in your home are likely linked to one of two things: safety or values—or both. That's why consistent rules and boundaries paired with conversation, respect, and clear expectations are so crucial.

CHECK IN WITH YOURSELF — — — — — — — —

Before beginning a big conversation about values and rules with your teen, consider why you believe these values are important. Ask yourself the following questions:

› What are your own values based on? Where did you learn them?

› Did your parents and caregivers' values stick with you?

› If not, which ones have you diverted from, and why do you think that happened?

› Growing up, did you feel the rules in your home and/or school were fair?

› Did your own parents or caretakers model the values they taught you through their behavior? Did they follow the rules and the law themselves?

› What were the most impactful values your parents modeled—negative or positive? How did the rules in your home fit with these values?

We asked boys:

What are some values you feel strongly about?

"Kindness. Honesty. Compassion."

—Elie, age 11

"Openness, integrity, kindness, service."

—James, age 21

"Honesty, trustworthiness, compassion."

—True, age 16

"Courage and empathy."

—ML, age 15

"Pride and honesty."

—Jeff, age 16

The Brain Science of Raising Ethical Adults

Remember that the teenage brain is under construction and wired to explore. In his book *Brainstorm*, Dr. Daniel Siegel explains that, in adolescence, "there is an increase in the activity of the neural circuits utilizing dopamine, a neurotransmitter central in creating our drive for reward. Starting in early adolescence and peaking midway through, this enhanced dopamine release causes adolescents to gravitate toward thrilling experiences and exhilarating sensations." This can look like increased impulsiveness, increased susceptibility to addiction, and hyperrationality (i.e., examining just the immediate facts and not seeing the big picture).

The prefrontal cortex is the part of the brain that helps us weigh the risks and benefits of doing something—to "zoom out" on situations and see the bigger picture and long-term consequences of our actions. It also helps us integrate other people's possible feelings and reactions into our decision-making—and helps kids make decisions that keep them out of trouble.

During the teenage years, this part of the brain is still developing, and will be until kids are in their early to mid-twenties. That's why teens so often make impulsive, selfish, or irrational decisions. Understanding the limits of our teens' ability to navigate the world reminds us that they do need boundaries, rules, and consistent enforcement—regardless of how grown up they think they are. They need structure, clear communication, and guidance to improve their decision-making.

We want to help you talk to your child about developing his own moral compass that can override his (natural) instinct to act without thinking, one that stays steady, guiding him toward healthy, thoughtful choices throughout his life.

Establishing and Keeping Boundaries

While it is developmentally appropriate for teens to question rules, push boundaries, and break rules, it's never easy—for us or our kids—to figure out which lines are OK to cross, and how to repair things after a misstep. Also, just because testing boundaries is natural, that doesn't mean we need to tolerate hateful or harmful behavior, or even to allow our children free rein of our homes and use of our money to support causes we find to go against our most important values.

Knowing that teens are likely to rebel, parents typically tend to fall into some version of these two camps:

Be "Cool" and Let Misbehavior Happen
This group believes rebellion is normal and natural at this stage, and that it cannot be avoided. These parents often let their kids set the rules—or at least give up on trying to enforce the rules. Often, they do this so their kids will be honest and open with them about their activities and come to them for help when needed.

Lock It Down Tight and Fight for Control
This group tries its darndest to keep their teens from rebelling—enforcing rules around everything from curfews to how their teens dress and who they hang out with. They likely monitor their teens 24/7 with check-ins and apps and may even routinely test their teens for drug use, regardless of whether the teen shows signs of use.

Which One Is Right?
While every family is different and every kid has different needs that should be considered, data show that parenting that incorporates a combination of both extremes is likely the best way to keep kids close and help them explore their own limits in the safest ways possible.

The key to effectively setting boundaries and enforcing rules in teens is connection and collaboration, as well as very clearly connecting these rules to their safety or your values—or maybe to both.

Do you feel like you try to live according to what you believe is right? Can you share an example?

"Yes. At an overnight camp I went to there was this kid who was getting bullied. I made friends with him and pulled him up the social ladder in our cabin so the bullies couldn't (or wouldn't) bully him."
—Elie, age 11

"One thing I have found myself doing recently is being extra open and honest with people, especially my group of guys I know well. When I see or feel like they are struggling I ask them how they are doing. If I feel like they are acting differently with me than usual I ask them if they are good and make sure that the conversation is open enough for them to be able to bring up anything I might be doing or have said that I don't realize is bugging them. I find my friends being more open and honest with me with things that don't involve me that are hurting them and [they] want advice on."
—James, age 21

"Yes, I do, I've always lived by the same basic beliefs. They've changed as I've grown older, but the same basic morals have always been a constant. For example, I try to treat everyone with the same amount of respect and kindness regardless of what I've heard about the person. This will not change until they have proven to me that they are not deserving of my respect."
—True, age 16

"I do my best, but like most people, it's difficult to resist the power of spontaneous peer pressure. That said, I stick firmly to the idea of consent (and respect as a whole), which is perhaps one of the most important values to keep outside influences away from. I try to not let anyone force me into something I'm not comfortable with, and I certainly don't allow them to do it to someone else."
—Rory, age 16

Creating Rules That Reflect Your Values

In our experience, life offers many opportunities to talk to children about values in ways that can help make it easier to set and enforce rules—even if we're just playing around with imaginary moral quandaries. For example, you can ask, "Is it ever OK to steal?" Discussing real-life situations you encounter with your kids—from very small ones that happen daily, to the big ones that keep you up at night—can be even more valuable.

Talking about values provides boys with a chance to practice using those so-called "higher brain" skills. Just like anything else, the more they practice, the easier and more reflexive it becomes!

We also recommend joining kids using the media they love, like binging a TV show or gaming with them. Not only is it fun, it offers our kids opportunities to learn from the choices (and mistakes) of the characters. Older movies and shows offer opportunities to talk about the ways culture has changed, how that happened, and why. Talking about characters or other anonymous players on a screen can make the conversation feel less personal.

Restraint is key to this exercise: Choose a few moments, and unless your kids are joining in calling out outdated or harmful tropes, don't mention the rest (unless they are really too bad to be ignored!). Keep it simple. You can always bring them up later when appropriate.

One benefit of talking openly about values is in discussing and enforcing the rules of your home. As we noted a few pages ago, nearly all of the rules we set for teens are founded in values, safety, or both. Here's an example:

Imagine your family has a rule where everyone must rinse their dishes after using them and place them in the dishwasher. On the surface, this doesn't seem to be about ethics or values at all—but if we dig a little deeper, there's actually a strong connection, one you can outline with your kids so they understand the deeper reason the rule exists.

Instead of saying: "That rule exists so the house stays tidy and we don't attract pests in the house."

Try saying: "Keeping the house tidy and cleaning up our dishes is about more than just keeping bugs and rodents away, it's also about respect. For example, if everyone rinses their own dish after using it and puts it in the dishwasher, then nobody has to collect all the dirty dishes from around the house, rinse the dried-on food, and load the dishwasher by themselves, because that is a really big job for just one person."

Considering that this sort of "default clean-up" tends to fall on the adults of the home—most often on the moms—kitchen clean-up rules start to more clearly become a matter of values. We don't want one member of the family to feel unfairly burdened or to just assume that they will donate their time and physical labor to cleaning up after everyone else. That would be unkind and disrespectful—two words that speak very directly to our values!

With all of that in mind, here's a five-step process you can use to create clear rules:

1. Set rules in partnership with your kid.
2. Discuss what your goals are (safety, success, etc.) and come up with what seems reasonable to you both, without compromising what's most important to you.
3. Explain why the rules exist. They're not random, and they don't exist simply so you can have power over your kid.
4. Explain the ethical, empathetic, or safety-based reason for the rules.
5. Make the consequences clear. Talk about what will happen if the rules are broken, and establish these consequences along with your kid.

Example: If the rule is that phones must charge in the kitchen after 9 p.m., and your son is caught using his phone in his room after that, the phone will be inaccessible to him after 8 p.m. and charge in your room instead of the kitchen for the rest of the month.

Reward honesty. Let him know that he can always fess up to mistakes and poor choices, and that his honesty will always be considered when determining the consequences.

Allow one "appeal to the court." The appeal is a system Joanna developed for her sons when they were little, that they still use today. When discussing rules, boundaries, and consequences—even when they are in trouble—the kids can ask to "appeal to the court" where they make a reasonable counteroffer. This offer must be well thought out and respectful, and if it is, it will be thoughtfully considered.

Example: In the "no phones in your room after 9 p.m." example, a kid might want to talk with a friend who is having a problem, be working on homework together on the phone, waiting for concert tickets to go on sale, or some other totally legitimate reason to want to bend the rules.

Follow through on consequences consistently, and if a change needs to be made, do so clearly and thoughtfully.

Example: If your son is grounded from his phone for three days, then he's grounded from it for three days. Be specific about how long the consequence will last (i.e., "You'll get your phone back Wednesday before school"). If you need to make an exception, be clear about why and explain what happens after. For instance, he can have his phone back for his appointment Tuesday so he can call you if there's an issue, but then the phone goes back to lockdown until Wednesday morning.

Sample Script for Setting Rules Together:

You: Now that you're in high school, let's talk about your curfew. In middle school, we wanted you home at 7 p.m. on school nights and 9 p.m. on weekends and over breaks. You've been super respectful of those rules so I'm thinking we could make them a little later. What do you think?

Him: Yeah, everyone else stays out later than me.

You: OK, here are a few things I want you to consider from my end. Weekdays, I still think 7 p.m. is good because you'll have more homework in high school and we need to make sure you can get a solid nine hours of sleep like doctors recommend.

Him: What if all my homework is done?

You: Good question. I'll consider an extension on a case-by-case basis, and I promise I'll be open-minded about extending it to 8:30 or so.

What mistakes do you think parents make when talking to their kids about morality and values?

"I think that modern-day adults often don't understand their child's experiences very well, for they are far different from when the adults were kids. Humans' perspectives and values in life change as our technology and world progress."

—True, age 16

"Parents could try putting themselves in their kids' shoes by thinking about how they would experience life if they were exposed to the same things that modern-day kids are. That way parents can paint themselves a better picture of what their child might be going through."

—River, age 13

"I think parents make the mistake of making their kids feel bad about things they do that they might not understand or mean. The problem with this is that it can instill a fear and anxiety in them that can be hard to take away. Growing up as an extremely anxious kid with a religious background, I always felt like I needed to be perfect or else I wasn't good enough for heaven or as a person. I don't completely blame this on religion at all, but it is an anxiety I am still working through today."

—James, age 21

"It's not so black-and-white. You might have a view that is just as valid as your neighbor's. Your child has the freedom to test their views and settle on one they think is right; this diversity in belief is what makes our society strong."

—Jeff, age 16

"Some mistakes that they make is the fact that they compare their morals and values with how it was when they were young, and since then, a lot of changes have happened with, like, gender, sexuality, religion, and more. These changes can affect morality and values drastically."

—ML, age 15

Him: OK, but don't be, like, so strict and just say no automatically, OK?

You: OK, I promise. Now, for weekends, I am the one who has to pick you up if you need a ride, and I'd rather not be out too late. Also, it always seemed to me that a lot of bad decisions are made after 11 p.m., have you ever noticed that?

Him: I guess. So, how about 10?

You: Sure. Let's try it and see how it goes.

Him: What if there's a concert or late movie or something?

You: I will totally make an exception when it makes sense and works for my schedule. Like, in the summertime if I have to work the next day, going to bed at 11 p.m. isn't an option.

Him: That's fair.

What About Non-negotiable Rules?

We believe you should hear your son out when he raises his "appeal to the court," but some rules will not be negotiable. Letting your kid have his say, and replying with respect, will go a long way in helping him feel heard and respected even when an exception won't be made.

Joanna's cousin, Rev. Ann Kansfield, a pastor at Greenpoint Reformed Church in Brooklyn, New York, and a chaplain for the New York City Fire Department, has always maintained that her children (currently teenagers) must attend church services every Sunday. This is part of their family's values system, and core to their family traditions.

Here is an example of a dialogue she might have with one of her teens:

Son: What if I don't want to go to church this week? Do I really HAVE to go?

Ann: Well, we're not going to physically force you to go, but it's important to us that you and your sister come with us. That's why we have the rule in place.

Son: Why? What's the big deal?

Ann: Because we'd like you to have a foundation to develop your own relationship with God.

Son: I don't need to go to services to have my faith.

Ann: That's great to hear, because you're totally right that faith isn't built on going to church.

Son: Then what's the big deal?

Ann: Well, first, we like spending that time with you guys. Also, it's usually one of your moms up there delivering the sermon, so it's respectful to show up for us.

Son: So I'm doing it for you?

Ann: Sure, maybe. But also, we think it's good for you to be open to hearing a message that might change the way you think about something or having a moment that gives you hope when you weren't expecting it. You get to take from the services things that are meaningful to you.

Son: What if I don't go to church when I'm older?

Ann: That is totally up to you. We just want to make sure you know the hope and peace church can offer, so you always have that to come back to when you're out in the world on your own.

Son: OK, I guess that makes sense.

Key Takeaways:

→ Ann's son's question was heard as an inquiry rather than a rebellion.

→ She shares the profound "whys" behind their family's rule instead of saying "Because I said so" or "Because I know what's best for you." Answers like these don't build trust, and they cause us to miss opportunities to build mutual respect and understanding.

→ She doesn't expect total conformity, but rather mutual understanding.

→ She holds fast to the family rule while entertaining all of his concerns and questions.

How to Discipline Without Eroding Your Bonds

There are times in all parents' lives when our kids break rules and make poor choices. When they push back on us persistently, it's natural to just stop trying to enforce rules. Therapist Eli Harwood, author of the book *Raising Securely Attached Kids*, told us that this is natural—but not a reason to let go of our values or abandon rules:

"When we hold boundaries with our children it might evoke frustration for them as a result of delayed gratification, but it also communicates confidence in our decision-making as the parent who is guiding and protecting their journey.

"When we are consistent with our process and boundaries, it also helps them to predict the routine around new exposures, which decreases pushback and anxiety. They know what to expect from our process and that, in the end, we want them to get to do fun things, but that we will also protect their well-being if the 'fun' things come with too many negative side effects."

Building Up Your "Emotional Bank Account"

In *Parenting the New Teen in the Age of Anxiety*, Dr. John Duffy offers a great tool called the emotional bank account. The emotional bank account represents the balance between positive and negative emotional interactions with your child. Obviously, the goal is to stay "in the black," with the majority of interactions being positive in nature.

A teen's emotional bank account can easily fall into the red when they are navigating the tumultuous waters of adolescence. "The good news here . . ." writes Dr. Duffy, is that "the balance can be shifted with any deposit or withdrawal. Anything smacking of discontent will read as a withdrawal: an inopportune judgment, a lengthy lecture, or a misplaced punishment, for example.

"If we are parenting from an emotional bank account in the red, our voice is unheard and our parenting is frustratingly ineffective," he adds.

A few ways to shift your emotional bank account back into the black without compromising on your values:

→ Before scolding, think about whether the issue is in your top five most important issues or otherwise urgent. If not, save it for another time.

→ Give yourself an hour to think on the issue before bringing it up with your child—sometimes a crabby mood will pass (on either side!).

→ Instead of withdrawing positive attention with misbehavior, add more positivity (in addition to the consistent consequences you've discussed). For instance: take him to lunch, plan something fun, give him an extra hug, order his favorite pizza, look him in the eyes and smile warmly.

→ Talk to him honestly about what you're doing, saying something like "I know things have been challenging, but I love you so much and you do so many things right. Want to order pizza and play a game together and just relax?"

We asked boys:

What do you wish adults understood about morals and values today?

"A lot of people tend to believe that the world is black-and-white, that things are inherently 'good' or 'bad.' I disagree with this—though sweeping blanket statements can generally be accurate (respect is good, murder is bad), it's important for parents to teach the idea of nuance. A more nuanced individual is more likely to be accepting of other viewpoints; they're not debating to assert their opinion as irrefutable, but instead to listen to the other side."
—Rory, age 16

"I think that current-day adults could maybe be more open-minded to change and evolution."
—River, age 13

"I wish adults understood how scary it is growing up as a kid/teenager today and seeing every single day on our devices we use in our pockets for hours a day how scary this world is. Kids are reminded every single day of how unmoral and valueless this world can be, even in our own cities, states, and country, through social media and the news. With smartphones, it's unavoidable seeing these things."
—James, age 21

Dealing with the Law

Rule-breaking can get serious fast when it happens outside of our homes, which is why we need to talk seriously with our boys about crime, punishment, and the police. Adolescent boys and young men are not only the group most likely to commit violent crimes, they're also the group most likely to become victims of crime.

Boys should know that one of the biggest risk factors for becoming a victim of crime is proximity to people committing crimes. In other words, staying away from people who are committing crimes may actually help protect our boys from becoming victims of crimes themselves.

Interacting with Law Enforcement

In the United States, the Fourth, Fifth, and Sixth Amendments are designed to help protect people during interactions with the criminal justice system. (International readers should look for the specific rights of citizens in their region before teaching these lessons.)

We must also bear in mind (and share with our sons) that police have a difficult job, and while there are good and bad cops just like there are good and bad doctors, lawyers, and writers, most are concerned with doing their jobs well and coming home safely to their families and loved ones.

Because risk to life is something the police encounter every day—but rare for many of the rest of us—it's helpful to put yourself in the mind of a police officer before thinking about how to respond. This can help keep everyone safer.

Ten lessons to teach our kids about interacting with law enforcement:

1. If you are being pulled over, signal and pull over the first chance it is safe. If it isn't safe where you are, make sure to acknowledge that you are being pulled over. If you can't pull over immediately, put your hazards on and slow down a little.

2. Keep your hands on the steering wheel and be polite and respectful when the officer approaches your car. All passengers in the car should have their hands visible and avoid making any sudden movements. If you have friends in the car, tell them not to act up.

3. Do not "guess" why you're being pulled over or what speed you were going. If they ask if you know why they pulled you over, say "no, sir" or "no, ma'am" (or simply "no").

4. Follow instructions and show your license, insurance, and registration. Move very slowly and with your hands visible to the officer, and tell the police what you are doing before you do it, especially when you reach for the glove compartment or any locked/closed part of the car.

5. Once you have your ticket or formal warning, ask if you are free to go. If the police say you are not free to go after giving you a ticket, ask if you are under arrest. If they say no, ask why they are detaining you. After they tell you (or if they don't), respectfully say that you were told that you should not speak to the police without a lawyer being present. If you are arrested and read your Miranda rights, immediately repeat this request, and do not speak to anyone until you have had a chance to consult with a lawyer.

6. If you are under eighteen, explain that you are a minor and are going to call your parents. And then please call them the first chance you can safely do so.

7. If they ask to search your car, decline by saying, "I do not consent to any searches" even if you know you don't have anything in your car. If they ask you why you are declining, say that you respect their jobs and are grateful for what police do, but that you were told never to consent to a search if you don't have to. Politely decline, but do not physically interfere or get agitated if the police search your car anyway.

   Note: In a lot of states, the police can do a limited search (for officer safety or for other reasons) of the interior of a car if they have a reasonable suspicion (which is less than probable cause) that something is afoot. A "furtive movement," for example, might be enough. Things can get complicated when it comes to the trunk.

8. If you are being arrested, they will read you your Miranda rights, which remind you that you do not have to speak to them. At your first opportunity, call your parents (if you are under eighteen) and say that you will not speak further without lawyer. If over eighteen, say you will not speak without a lawyer present. Use the word "lawyer" specifically.

9. Do not say a word until you've spoken in private with your lawyer (if you cannot afford one, the court will appoint you one; request one right away).

10. What you tell your parents or caregivers (or anyone other than your lawyer) may not be private. If you make phone calls from a jail, assume that they are being recorded unless you are speaking with a lawyer.

Remember that the goal of an encounter with law enforcement is for it to end quickly and safely. Follow the above rules, but use common sense, too. Don't be aggressive or give the police a reason to detain you. Complying with what they say is very, very important.

Important note to share with kids: there is a difference between being adversarial and respectfully asserting your rights.

A Note on Police Brutality

We want to make clear to our kids that a person's attitude should never be an excuse for an officer of the law to use brutality against anyone. But we also need to make clear to our children that they may interact with biased or dishonest members of law enforcement who do not care if it's fair or just to use unnecessary force without justification.

Boys of Color and the Law

We cover this issue in more depth in our chapter on racism and prejudice, but it's true that rules and laws are often not applied equally to all children.

"For children and youth, negative interactions with police in their communities—including being stopped, searched, arrested, subjected to use of force, or incarcerated—are linked to negative outcomes, such as poor emotional well-being, physical health, and social outcomes," writes

Victor J. St. John, PhD, in a report for Child Trends, a research organization focused on improving the lives of children.

"Black people had the highest rate of police-related deaths," St. John writes. "Black people are roughly three times more likely than white people to die from police intervention."

These facts can feel overwhelming, and we may want to hide our heads or keep our children "innocent" by not talking to our kids about racism in the justice system. St. John insists that it's better to address the issues early and often. He and his coauthor offer specific instructions for how to talk about discrimination in these settings:

"Highlight that law enforcement officers' job is to keep all people safe, and that it's not acceptable to treat people differently because of their race. Explain to children what they can do if they experience or witness racism or racial trauma (e.g., young children can tell a trusted adult). Given that older children (12 years and greater) have more procedural interactions with law enforcement officers and are likely to be unaware of their legal rights, older children can be educated about their legal rights and informed about what to do if they are profiled by law enforcement officers. [. . . It] is important to reiterate to children that no matter how a person behaves, it is never right to discriminate against someone because of their race."

When to Reach Out for Help

If you've tried the tactics shared in this book and he's still:

→ Misbehaving consistently, especially if he or others are getting hurt or at risk of being hurt

→ Showing signs of drug use

→ At risk of being labeled as a deviant or becoming "the bad kid" at school

→ Known for being "creepy" with girls or others he may be attracted to and doesn't adapt his behavior so others aren't made uncomfortable

→ Known to be cruel toward others and reasonable interventions aren't helping

→ Sharing serious concerns about his mental health or makes even casual or "jokey" threats to harm others

→ Showing signs of being at risk of suicide

Visiting the school counselor can be a great first start, as there may be school issues at play, as well. School counselors are unsung heroes and can be a parent's best friend and a fierce advocate for a child! School counselors are great resources for everything from poor grades and behavior issues to mental health challenges. If the situation is above a school counselor's experience level, they will suggest next steps.

Insights from a Young Black Man

"I was taught about the racial disparities of the criminal justice system at a young age. My father steered me straight with stories about how he broke the law as a kid and young man due to being poor/homeless. That was the only acceptable reason to do so and if he had had any other options he would have done so instead.

"I wish parents better understood the disparities in rules and the law. Too many don't understand or see how corrupt the system is. One person can do the smallest thing and be condemned for life while another can do the same or something far worse and get off scot-free."

—Kamose, age 27

REMEMBER THIS:

① Pushing back against your family's established values can be a natural part of adolescence, and we can help direct this limit-testing in ways that are healthier than the dangerous behaviors and law-breaking many teenagers fall back upon.

② Nearly all rules are based on two things: safety and your family's values.

③ Bad choices are not the same as bad kids.

④ Talking about values can (and should) be done in short, casual conversations using hypothetical examples, examples from your own real lives, or things you see or read in the media rather than during big lectures aimed directly at your kid.

⑤ Rules work best when kids understand why the rule exists and, when possible, are empowered to help decide the specific details of the rule and the consequences for breaking it.

⑥ Some rules are non-negotiable, but our kids should still be encouraged to ask why the rule exists and to suggest workarounds without being shamed or silenced. This doesn't mean we have to change the rules, just that we are willing to hear their feelings and opinions.

⑦ Teens benefit from learning how to respectfully interact with law enforcement while standing up for their civil rights.

⑧ The criminal justice system does not treat all teenagers the same, and biases related to race, ethnicity, class, and other identities still exist in our system. Families with boys of color often prepare their boys for interactions with the law and even school disciplinarians differently from families with white sons in order to help keep them safe during interactions with law enforcement.

⑨ Some forms of misbehavior are serious enough to seek help from professionals, and early intervention from mental health and/or education professionals can be very helpful.

CONCLUSION

Dear Readers,

Thank you for joining us on this journey. This book was guided by our hearts as well as our professional and personal experiences. We hope you get something from this book—at the very least, the sense that you are not alone.

Please remember that these conversations were only meant as a catalyst for starting tough, important conversations. You know your kid better than anyone, and the more you talk and open up together, the better you will get to know him. We hope you will adapt and create beautiful dialogues that are unique to your family with the boys in your life.

We are profoundly thankful to our experts for sharing their knowledge with us. We are also so grateful to our boys' panel, who made us laugh, cry, and really think. We are amazed by their compassion, brilliance, and honesty.

Here's to a lifetime of conversations, deep discussions, casual chitchat, hearty laughs, and ongoing growth and connection with the boys in your life.

Sincerely,
Christopher and Joanna

INDEX

dog-piling behavior, 198
dopamine, 198, 279
dress, rapid changes in, 60
drugs/substance use
  boys on, 136, 138, 142
  brain development and,
    138–139, 141
  consent and, 124
  expectations regarding, 141–143
  finding help for, 146
  harm reduction and, 144–146
  importance of help for, 58
  main points regarding, 147
  parental use and, 144
  rates of, 137
  responding to son's use, 147
  self-assessment and, 139
  signs of use of, 61–62
  starting conversation about,
    140–141
  test strips for, 146
  values related to, 143–144
Duffy, John, 20, 45, 189, 231, 288

eating disorders, 62–63
eating/food, changes regarding,
  60
"edgy" humor or pranks, 200,
  261, 262–263
EducateUS, 112
education. *See* school
8BitDad, 199
Elgersma, Christine, 189
embarrassment, sex and sexuality
  and, 94–95
emotional bank account, 288–289
emotional conformity, 102–103

emotional downloads, 45
emotional safe zones, 66
emotional vulnerability, 79–81
emotions
  boys on, 51, 55, 59
  changes to watch for, 60–61
  coping skills and, 48–49
  expressing "unmanly," 46
  friendships and, 208
  hesitancy to discuss, 42
  ideas of masculinity and, 26, 44
  main points regarding, 66
  normalizing discussions on,
    44–47
  regulation of, 47–50
  spirally down and, 40
  validating, 52
  See also anger
empathy, 2–3, 11, 32, 47, 105–106,
  221, 228, 231–232
Equimundo, 1, 32, 206–207
equity/equality, 276
Erasing the Finish Line
  (Homayoun), 154
ethical sexuality, 114
ethics, brain science and, 279
ethnic studies classrooms, insight
  from, 269–270
ethnicity, understanding term,
  268
Ever Forward Club, 33–34, 239
executive functioning, 154–155
exercise disorders, 62–63
expectations, setting, 69
Explosive Child, The (Greene), 11
extracurriculars
  boys on, 171, 181

Kivel, Paul, 28
Koplewicz, Harold S., 180–181

Lahey, Jessica, 138–139, 140
law enforcement, 291–293, 295
learning differences/challenges,
    161–163
LGBTQ+ community
    history of discrimination
        against, 104–105
    support for, 103–104
    See also homophobia;
        homosexuality
limits, setting, 77–79
listening
    active, 224–225
    importance of, 8, 10–11, 264
    reflective, 13–14
locker room culture, 178–180
loneliness, 206–207, 209, 211, 219

Maguire, Caroline, 214, 216
Making Caring Common project,
    106
Making Caring Common Project,
    113
maladaptive behavior, meaning
    of, 200
"Man Box, The," 28, 43
Maruyama, Hannah, 164, 165
masculine norms, rigid, 1
masculinity
    continuing to talk about, 36–38
    discussion questions on, 36–37
    emotions and, 26
    how to talk to boys about,
        31–32

lack of positive messages
    regarding, 34–36
main points regarding, 39
restrictive ideas regarding, 44
school and, 157–159
self-assessment and, 30
signs help is needed, 38
stereotypes of, vi, 27, 28, 29
toxic, 34–36
violence and, 237, 239–242
mask-making activity, 33–34
Masterminds & Wingmen
    (Wiseman), 209
mature thinking, 2
McGhee, Heather, 255–256
Mechanick, Jason, 50, 53–54
media literacy, 133, 192
Meleney, William, 58
memes, radicalization and, 261
Mendez, Damian, 174
mental health
    boys on, 51
    crisis regarding, 41
    importance of help for, 58
    main points regarding, 66
    self-assessment and, 42
    stigma and, 42, 43
    trauma and, 241
Middle School Superpowers (Fagell),
    182
Million Mask Movement, 34
mindfulness, 257
Miranda rights, 291
Monitoring the Future survey,
    137
morality, boys on, 285, 289.
    See also values

ACKNOWLEDGMENTS

From Joanna:

Thank you to my husband, Ivan, who stepped up to make space for me to take on such a huge project. His support made all this possible. To my kids, who shared their feedback, social media, games, and even their friends so this book could better represent life for young people today. All of my children generously shared their mom with the computer while we wrote this, and I'll always be grateful.

A big thank-you to my parents, who raised me to ask questions. To my grandpa, who taught me to question the status quo, and my brilliant, inspiring extended family—including Petra, who served as my research helper. I'm especially grateful to Tom Burns and Annie Martin, Sabrina James, Daniel Stageman, and Jamie Utt-Schumacher, for talking me through this book when it was just an idea.

Thank you to Christopher for agreeing to write a book with a stranger who showed up in your DMs saying, "I'm trying to find a coauthor for a book." And to Maura Phelan, for showing up in my DMs asking if I'd consider letting a stranger with a new agency represent me.

Finally, thank you to Maisie Tivnan, our editor at Workman, who let us be who we are and write the book we knew needed to be written. Your expertise and talent made our book the best it could be. Thanks also to the rest of the Workman team: Beth Levy, Becky Terhune, Reagan Ruff, Elissa Santos, and Scott Trebing.

From Christopher:

To my parents, Jean and John, thank you for always encouraging me to read, write, and think, and for keeping *Free to Be . . . You and Me* in heavy rotation on our family stereo. To my sister Cary and her wonderful family, thank you for being so supportive and encouraging. To my grandparents, my aunts and uncles, and my extended family—thanks for being interested in my ideas and I hope I make you proud.

To my wife, Thea, thank you for encouraging me to say "yes" to this enormous project and letting me share my excitement and learning along the way. I appreciate the ways you invite me to reflect on my parenting, and how you challenge me to dig deeper and get more connected.

To my sons, Cole and Abel, thank you for everything you've taught me about being a father and being a man today. You are both unique, fascinating people, and I love you.

Thank you to the community of writers who have shared wisdom with me, including Ashanti Branch, Ruth Whippman, Virginia Sole-Smith, Scott Todnem, Andy Milne, Melinda Wenner Moyer, Shawn Taylor, Jeremy Adam Smith, Cara Natterson, Vanessa Kroll Bennett, Peggy Orenstein, Shafia Zaloom, Lisa Damour, Richard Reeves, Anya Kamenetz, Debby Herbenick, Phyllis Fagell, Niobe Way, Chelsea Goodan, Devorah Heitner, and many more.

Thank you to the many dynamic communities I have been part of and learned from, including SFUSD Wellness and Health Education, CAHPERD, SHAPE America, the Missouri School of Journalism, Next Gen Men, the Conspiracy of Beards, and Diane LaFontaine-Aschmann's life-changing middle school English classes.

To Joanna, thank you for taking such a bold leap and asking me to write this book with you. It has truly been an honor.

ABOUT THE AUTHORS

JOANNA SCHROEDER is a writer, editor, and media critic known for her bold perspectives on parenting issues. She has been published in *The New York Times, Redbook, Good Housekeeping, Esquire,* and *The Boston Globe,* and has appeared on *Red Table Talk with Jada Pinkett Smith, Anderson Cooper 360°, CBS News,* PBS, NPR, and the BBC. She served as executive editor of The Good Men Project and managing editor of the Experts Division of Your Tango. She is the mother of two sons and a daughter.

CHRISTOPHER PEPPER is an award-winning health teacher whose lesson plans are used in schools around the world. He coordinates the Young Men's Health Groups in San Francisco public middle and high schools, which bring boys together to talk about their lives, masculinity, emotions, and relationships. He's been published in *The New York Times, San Francisco Chronicle,* and ParentData, and has appeared in *USA Today, Mother Jones, Vox,* and on NPR. He's the father of two boys and has been a foster parent.